W9-BSD-092

Journey Toward the Heart

Discourses on the Sufi Way

Bhagwan Shree Rajneesh

HARPER & ROW, PUBLISHERS

SAN FRANCISCO

Cambridge
Hagerstown
Philadelphia
New York

London
Mexico City
Sao Paolo
Sydney

1817

Compilation: Swami Amrit Pathik
Editing: Ma Yoga Anurag
Design: Swami Anand Yatri

A hardcover edition of this book, with the title *Until You Die*, is available from the Rajneesh Foundation. It is here reprinted by arrangement.

Grateful acknowledgment is made to Idries Shah, whose books *The Way of the Sufi*, *The Sufis*, and *Tales of the Dervishes* provide the versions of traditional Sufi stories that have been freely adapted in this book.

The text of this book is printed on 100% recycled paper.

JOURNEY TOWARD THE HEART: Discourses on the Sufi Way. Copyright © 1976 by Rajneesh Foundation, Poona, India. All rights reserved. Printed in the United States of America. No part of this book may be used or reproduced in any manner whatsoever without written permission except in the case of brief quotations embodied in critical articles and reviews. For information address Harper & Row, Publishers, Inc., 10 East 53rd Street, New York, NY 10022.

LIBRARY OF CONGRESS CARD NUMBER: 79-1762
INTERNATIONAL STANDARD BOOK NUMBER: 0-06-066786-9

80 81 82 83 84 10 9 8 7 6 5 4 3 2

CONTENTS

THE AUTHOR

Bhagwan Shree Rajneesh was born in India and obtained a master's degree in philosophy. He held the post of Professor of Philosophy until 1966. Since then he has devoted himself to the spiritual awakening of others, founding an Ashram at Poona to which his followers travel from all over the world. He has published many books both in English and Hindi.

INTRODUCTION

Looking back, it seems as though since the very beginning
I was headed towards Bhagwan. Every situation or
experience into which I dropped—apparently through
my own direction, but now I see quite asleep and groping
in the dark—somehow pushed me another step nearer
this path or, rather, this abyss . . . this bottomless,
unfathomable mystery.

The currents of my life-river have pushed and pulled,
tumbled and thrown me through enough pain and
exasperation, confusion and bewilderment, just spiced
with enough of a taste of serenity and bliss, to have
awakened a yearning within me for some deeper source
of being beyond the fickle tides of moods and emotions,
of mind and body.

So, tired and hungry, battered and torn, I was
washed up on the shores of India, finding myself warmed
and welcomed, cared for and comforted, by this entity
we call Bhagwan Shree Rajneesh. When he gave me
sannyas, I felt for the first time accepted by existence.
I felt I was okay, as though it was alright to be alive and
me. Something in me knew unequivocally: 'This is it!'
Little did I know what I had let myself in for! . . .

When I first came here I thought I knew what ego
was. I don't know exactly what I went through during
those first eight months—maybe a preparation, a courtship,
a seduction—but it wasn't until the dawn of surrender
and the death of ego began, that I realized what it really
is. The simple fact of saying yes made me painfully,
gut-rendingly aware of this 'I'—this proud, stubborn,
fighting, knotted up, uptight ego. Simultaneously, though,
by saying yes I experienced a glimpse of the blissfulness
of 'let-go', of the fullness and expansion available beyond

the confines of 'what *I* want', 'what I think is right', 'how I think it should be'—beyond 'no'.

So although I imagined I had decided to come to Bhagwan for a solution to my problems, I gradually became aware that 'I' am the problem, and that Bhagwan is really my death. As he says: 'You come for a wrong reason to a Master. This is natural—you are wrong, how can you come for right reasons to a Master? You have come for wrong reasons, and the Master exists for absolutely different reasons. He attracts you, he takes you closer and closer, just to kill you—and to kill you so utterly that the very seed of ego is burnt.'

When first it hit me, this realization was like a thunderbolt. In fact, I felt quite indignant that all I had grown and nurtured, built up and protected, would have to be dropped like an old skin. But by that time I was already caught, and it was too late to escape from him. Says he: 'A Master is a great death. If you can pass through a Master and his love and his blessings, your body will die, your mind will die, your ego will die: *all that can die will die*—only that which cannot die, the deathless, will remain; only the deathless you, the immortal you, the Brahma.'

Little deaths, with his help, by his grace, by some unknown force—of love?—have bloomed small flowers in this being. And this is my understanding of the Sufi saying: 'Until you die, nothing can you have from me.'

Never has death been so sweet as here at Bhagwan's hands. Every situation he creates gives another opportunity to die and be reborn into fuller dimensions of life. But ego dies hard, and it is not without resistance and pain that the bitter-sweet fruit is tasted. The fear of dying is ever-present—the fear of letting go of the known and allowing life to carry one on into each unknown moment with an open heart.

'The whole of my effort is to help you not to be afraid,' Bhagwan says, because only through the heart

will you be reborn. But before you are reborn, you will
have to die. Nobody can be reborn before he dies.
So the whole message of Sufism, Zen, Hassidism—these
are all forms of Sufism—is how to die. The whole art of
dying is the base. I am teaching you here nothing except
that: How to die.

'And this is the message of this series of talks:
Until you die, nothing is possible. You must die—only
then can something be given to you. The gift is ready,
already packed, your name written on it—but you are
not ready. . . .Nothing can you have from me until
you die.'

ma yoga anurag

Poona, July 1976

I
Until You Die

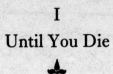

There was a rich and generous man of Bokhara. Because he had a high rank in the invisible hierarchy, he was known as the President of the World.

Every day he gave gold to one category of people—the sick, widows, and so on. But nothing was given to anyone who opened his mouth.

Not all could keep silent.

One day it was the turn of the lawyers to receive their share of the bounty. One of them could not restrain himself and he made the most complete appeal possible.

Nothing was given to him.

This, however, was not the end of his efforts. The following day invalids were being helped, so he pretended that his limbs had been broken.

But the President knew him, and he obtained nothing.

Again and again he tried, even disguising himself as a woman, but without result.

Finally the lawyer found an undertaker and told him to wrap him in a shroud. 'When the President passes by,' said the lawyer, 'he will perhaps assume that this a corpse, and he may throw some money towards my burial—and I will give you a share of it.'

This was done. A gold piece from the hand of the President fell upon the shroud. The lawyer seized it out of fear that the undertaker would get it first.

Then he spoke to the benefactor: 'You denied me your bounty—note how I have gained it!'

'Nothing can you have from me,' replied the generous man, 'until you die.'

This is the meaning of the cryptic phrase 'Man must die before he dies.' The gift comes after this 'death' and not before. And even this 'death' is not possible without help.

THERE ARE religions and religions, but Sufism is *the* religion—the very heart, the innermost core, the very soul.

Sufism is not part of Islam; rather, on the contrary, Islam is part of Sufism. Sufism existed before Mohammed ever was born, and Sufism will exist when Mohammed is completely forgotten. Islams come and go; religions take form and dissolve; Sufism abides, continues, because it is not a dogma. It is the very heart of being religious.

You may not ever have heard of Sufism and you may be a Sufi—if you are religious. Krishna is a Sufi, and Christ too; Mahavir is a Sufi, and Buddha too—and they never heard about the word, and they never knew that anything like Sufism exists.

Whenever a religion is alive, it is because Sufism is alive within it. Whenever a religion is dead, it shows only that the spirit, the Sufi spirit, has left it. Now there is only a corpse, howsoever decorated—in philosophy, metaphysics, in dogmas, doctrines—but whenever Sufism has left, religion stinks of death. This has happened many times. This is happening already almost all over the world. One has to be aware of it, otherwise one can go on clinging to a dead corpse.

Christianity has no Sufism now. It is a dead religion—the Church killed it. When 'church' becomes too much, Sufism has to leave that body. It cannot exist with dogmas. It can well exist with a dancing soul, but not with dogmas. It cannot exist with theology. They are not good companions. And with popes and priests it is impossible for Sufism to exist. It is just the opposite! Sufism needs no popes, no priests; it needs no dogmas. It is not of the head; it belongs to the heart. The heart is the Church, not an organized church, because every organization is of the mind. And once the mind takes possession, the heart has simply to leave that house completely. The house becomes too narrow for the heart. The heart needs the whole of the sky. Nothing less than that will do.

It cannot be confined in churches. The whole existence is the only church for it. It can throb under the sky. It can throb in freedom. But it dies when everything becomes a system, an organized pattern, a ritual—the state of Sufism simply disappears from there.

Christianity killed Jesus. Jews could not kill him. They crucified him, of course, but they failed. They could not kill him. He survived crucifixion. That is the meaning of resurrection—not that physically Jesus survived, but that the crucifixion proved futile. Jews could not kill him. They tried, but Jesus survived. Where Jews failed, Christians succeeded. They killed him without any crucifixion. They killed him through prayer. They killed him through dogma. They killed him through organization. Followers succeed where enemies fail. Apostles succeed where enemies fail.

Christianity is now a dead religion because it cannot allow Sufism to exist within its soul. It is afraid of Sufism. Every dogma is always afraid, because Sufism means infinite freedom, no confinement, no limitations. It is more like love and less like a logical syllogism. It is more of a poetry, less of a prose. It is irrational.

That's why every rational theology is afraid of it. Once you give an opening to the irrational, you don't know where you are. And remember: God is also irrational, and it is beautiful that He is irrational—otherwise He would have been a professor of philosophy in some university, or a pope, or a priest, but not existence.

Sufism has died many deaths in many religions. Jainism is a dead religion. It flourished once beautifully and gave birth to such a great mystic as Mahavir. Then suddenly the river disappeared; only the dry riverbed has remained. No river flows now, no greenery on the bank. It has become a desert land, completely deserted. What happened? Jainist followers became too intellectual, mathematical, logical. Out of the mystery of Mahavir they created doctrines and arguments. They became too calculative, too clever, and the spirit was killed. In Christianity, Sufism had to leave because of too much church ritual. In Jainism, Sufism had to leave because of too much intellectual, theological, philosophical effort.

Remember this: Sufism is not a church. It doesn't belong to any religion. All religions, when alive, belong to it. It is a vast sky of a particular quality of consciousness. How does it happen? How does one become a Sufi? Not by belonging to a particular order, but by dropping from the head to the heart, one becomes a Sufi.

You can exist in two ways. Either you can exist as a head-oriented person—you will succeed in the world. You will accumulate many riches, prestige, power. In politics you will be a successful man. In the eyes of the world you will become a pinnacle to be imitated. But in the inner you will fail completely, you will fail utterly—because into the inner the head-oriented person cannot enter at all. Head moves outwardly; it is an opening to the other. Heart opens inwardly; it is an opening to yourself. You can exist either as a head-oriented person, or you can exist as a heart-oriented person. When your energy, your life-energy, falls from the head towards the heart, you become a Sufi.

A Sufi means a man of the heart, a man of love; a man who doesn't bother from where this universe comes, who doesn't bother who created it, who doesn't bother where it is leading; in fact, who doesn't ask any questions—rather, on the contrary, he starts living. Existence is there: only fools bother about from where it comes. Only fools, I say. They may have shrouded themselves in very cunning philosophical words, but they are fools. A man who is wise lives the existence. It is here and now!

Why bother from where it comes? What does it *matter* from where it comes? Whether somebody creates it or not is irrelevant. You are here, throbbing, alive—dance with existence! live it! be it! and allow it to happen in its total mystery within you.

And this is the miracle: a person who doesn't bother from where it comes, a person who doesn't ask questions, receives the answers. A man who is not curious, but celebrating whatsoever is there—whatsoever is the case he is celebrating it—suddenly becomes aware of the very source, and suddenly becomes aware of the very culmination. End and beginning meet in him—because he himself becomes the mystery. Now the mystery is not something which is there as an object that you have to go around and around and see and look at and observe. No, because that is not the way to know it. That is the way to miss it. You may go around and around, about and about, but you will never penetrate into it. How can you know? You are beating around the bush. Your attack is on the periphery. Rather, penetrate into it, go to its center—become it.

And you *can* become, because you are part of it.

And you *can* become, because it is part of you.

And then suddenly all questioning dissolves. Suddenly the answer is there. It is not that you have come to a solution of your problems. No. There are no problems at all. When there are no problems at all, for the first time you become capable, capable of living the mystery that is life, capable of living God, capable of being gods.

A great Sufi—you must have heard his name, Al Hillaj Mansoor—was killed by Mohammedans, because he said, '*Anal Hak*, I am the God.' When you penetrate into the mystery of life, it is not that you are an observer, because an observer is always an outsider—you become one with it. It is not that you swim in the river, it is not that you float in the river, it is not that you struggle into the river. No—you become the river. Suddenly you realize the wave is part of the river. And the contrary is also true: that the river is part of the wave. It is not only that we are parts of God—God is also part of us.

When Al Hillaj Mansoor asserted, 'I am God,' Mohammedans killed him. Sufism is always killed by religious people, so-called religious people—because they cannot tolerate it; they cannot tolerate a man asserting that he is God! Their egos feel offended. How can a man be a God? But when Al Hillaj says, 'I am God,' he is not saying, 'I am God and you are not'; he is not saying, 'I am God and these trees are not'; he is not saying, 'I am God and these stones, rocks are not.' Asserting that 'I am God' he is asserting that the whole is divine, sacred. Everything is divine.

So these people, fanatics, believers in dogmas—they said that God created man, so man can only be a creature, not a creator; and this is profanity, the very apex of profanity to assert that 'I am God'—they killed him. And what was Mansoor saying when they killed him? He said loudly to the sky, 'You cannot deceive me! Even in these murderers I see you—you cannot deceive me. You are here in these murderers! And in whatsoever form you come, my God, I will know you, because I have known you.'

Sufism is not thinking about existence, it is being existence. It is not thinking, it is not doing something about existence. It is neither thought nor action. It is being.

And right now, without any effort, you can be a Sufi. If you stop thinking, and if you drop the idea of doing something, if you drop the idea of being a thinker and a doer, if you simply are content to be, suddenly you are a Sufi. And this will be my effort while I am talking about Sufism: not to indoctrinate you, not to make you more knowledgeable, but to make a Sufi out of you.

Sufis sing, they don't give sermons, because life is more like a song and less like a sermon. And they dance, and they don't talk about dogmas, because a dance is more alive, more like existence, more like the birds singing in the trees, and the wind passing through the pines; more like a waterfall, or clouds raining, or grass growing. The whole life is a dance, vibrating, throbbing, with infinite life.

Sufis like to dance; they are not interested in dogmas. And they tell beautiful stories. Life is more like a story, less like a history. And Sufis have created beautiful small stories. On the surface, you may miss. On the surface, it will look just like an ordinary anecdote. But if you penetrate deep, Sufi stories are very much pregnant—pregnant with significance, pregnant with the significance of the Ultimate. So I will tell you a few stories, discuss the stories, to help you penetrate into the deeper core. Just to make you understand a few things about the heart, to help you, your energy, your whole being, for a new journey toward the heart. To push you—because you will be afraid.

The heart is the most dangerous thing in the world.

Every culture, every civilization, every so-called religion, cuts every child off from his heart. It is a most dangerous thing. All that is dangerous comes out of the heart. Mind is more secure, and with the mind you know where you are. With the heart, no one ever knows where one is. With the mind, everything is calculated, mapped, measured. And you can feel the crowd always with you, in front of you, at the back of you. Many are moving on it; it is a highway—concrete, solid, gives you a feeling of security. With the heart you are alone. Nobody is with you. Fear grips, fear possesses you. Where are you going? Now you no longer know, because when you move with a crowd on a highway, you know where you are moving because you think the crowd knows.

And everybody is in the same position: everybody thinks, 'So many people are moving, we must be moving somewhere; otherwise, why so many people, millions of them, moving? They must be moving somewhere.' Everybody thinks like that. In fact, the crowd is not moving anywhere. No crowd has ever reached any goal. The crowd goes on moving and moving. You are born, you become part of the crowd. And the crowd was already moving before you were born. And then a day comes when you are finished, you die, and the crowd goes on moving, because new ones are always being born. The crowd never reaches anywhere!—but it gives a feeling of comfort. You feel cozy, surrounded by so many people wiser than you, older than you, more experienced than you; they must know where they are moving—you feel secure.

The moment you start falling towards the heart . . . and it *is* a falling: falling like falling in an abyss. That's why when somebody is in love, we say he has fallen in love. It is a fall—the head sees it as a fall—someone has gone astray, fallen. When you start falling towards the heart you become alone; now nobody can be with you there. You in your total loneliness. Afraid, scared you will be. Now you will not know where you are going, because nobody is there and there are no milestones. In fact, there is no concrete solid path. Heart is unmapped, unmeasured, uncharted. Tremendous fear will be there.

The whole of my effort is to help you not to be afraid, because only through the heart will you be reborn. But before you are reborn, you will have to die. Nobody can be reborn before he dies. So the whole message of Sufism, Zen, Hasidism —these are all forms of Sufism—is how to die. The whole art of dying is the base. I am teaching you here nothing except that: how to die.

If you die, you become available to infinite sources of life. You die, really, in your present form. It has become too narrow. You only survive in it—you don't live. The tremendous possibility of life is completely closed, and you feel confined, imprisoned. You feel everywhere a limitation, a boundary. A wall, a stone wall comes wherever you move—a wall.

My whole effort is how to break these stone walls. And they are not made of stone—they are made of thoughts. And nothing is more like rock than a thought. They are made of dogmas, scriptures. They surround you. And wherever you go, you carry them with you. Your imprisonment you carry with you. Your prison is always hanging around you. How to break them?

The breaking of the walls will appear to you like a death. It is in a way, because your present identity will be lost. Whosoever you are, that identity will be lost. You will be that no more. Suddenly something else.... It was always hidden within you, but you were not aware. Suddenly a discontinuity. The old is no more there, and something utterly new has entered. It is not continuous with your past. That's why we call it a death. It is not continuous: a gap exists.

And if you look backwards, you will not feel that whatsoever existed before this resurrection was real. No, it will appear as if you saw it in a dream; or it will appear as if you read it somewhere in a fiction; or, as if somebody else related his own story and it was never yours—somebody else's. The old completely disappears. That's why we call it a death. An absolutely new phenomenon comes into existence. And remember the word 'absolutely'. It is not a modified form of the old; it has *no* connection with the old. It is resurrection. But resurrection is possible only when you are capable of dying.

Sufism is a death and a resurrection. And I call it *the* religion. Let us now enter into this beautiful story.

> *There was a rich and generous man of Bokhara. Because he had a high rank in the invisible hierarchy, he was known as the President of the World.*
>
> *Every day he gave gold to one category of people—the sick, widows, and so on. But nothing was given to anyone who opened his mouth.*
>
> *Not all could keep silent.*

Go slowly with me:

> *There was a rich and generous man of Bokhara.*

It is a difficult combination: 'rich and generous'. The poor are always generous, the rich never. That's how they become rich. If a rich man is generous, a revolution has happened. A rich man becomes generous only when he has attained to a deep understanding that riches are useless. When he has come to know that all that this world can give is not worth taking, only then does generosity become possible—then he starts sharing. Otherwise, you go on accumulating more and more and more. The mind goes on asking for more. There is no end to it. If you are not alert, all the riches of all the worlds will not be enough—because the mind does not bother what you have. It simply goes on saying: 'More!'

It is said that when Alexander the Great was coming to India, he met a great mystic, Diogenes. Diogenes is one of the great Sufis. Diogenes used to live naked, just like animals. He was so beautiful in his nakedness—because it is ugliness that we try to hide, not beauty.

Why do you want to hide your body from others? What is

wrong with it? Society, civilization, culture, they have conditioned your minds to believe that something is wrong with the body. You feel guilty if you are caught naked. And laws exist and courts to force you not to be naked. And the whole of nature is naked. And it is so beautiful! Only man has gone ugly somewhere.

Some day, when man becomes more aware, man will be less and less attached to clothes. They may be used as utilities: the weather is cold—of course, you have to cover your body; but when the weather is pleasant and one can be like a simple, innocent animal, one has to be. Completely hidden under clothes, your bodies have left the sensitivity to feel. To feel the touch of the rays of the sun, and to enjoy it, you have completely forgotten the language. To feel the wind on your naked body, as trees feel, and dance, you have completely forgotten. Only your face has been left, only your head. Otherwise, your whole body has been numbed.

Diogenes lived naked, but his nakedness was very, very beautiful—because it was innocent. You can live naked as a perversion also. Then it will not be beautiful. Then you may be an exhibitionist—something has gone wrong in your psychological world. Diogenes lived naked like animals. And Alexander, it is said, felt jealous. He was robed in the costliest costumes possible and he felt jealous, it is said, seeing Diogenes naked. So beautiful!—envious. He asked, 'How can I also be like you?—so innocent, so beautiful.'

Diogenes said, 'There is no *how* to it.' And he was lying down on a bank of a river in the sand. It was morning and the sun was rising, and he must have been enjoying the poetry that comes through the sands to the naked body, the subtle messages, the warm sun falling on him.

Diogenes said, 'There is no need to ask for any how. This bank is big enough for both of us. You throw your clothes and lie down with me!'

There is no *how* to ask. Why ask how? How is a trick of the mind to postpone. If you ask how, then you are asking how to postpone—because you are saying there must be something to be practised. And practice will take time. And, of course, you cannot practise right now. Tomorrow comes in. And once the tomorrow comes in, then you are done.

Said Diogenes, 'There is no question of how! You just lie down and rest! And this bank is enough for both of us.'

Alexander said, 'Some day, I always dream that some day there will be a possibility—when I have conquered the whole world. I am waiting for that day, then I will also relax and rest.'

Diogenes laughed and said, 'Then you are foolish, because Diogenes can rest and relax without conquering the whole world. So why should you make it a condition that when you have conquered the whole world, then you will rest and relax? And I tell you: then it is not going to happen ever, because the mind will ask for more and more. And when you have conquered this world, then the mind will ask, "Is there any other world?"'

And it is reported that when Diogenes said this, that there is no other world but the mind will ask, 'Is there any other world?' suddenly Alexander felt sad. The sadness came immediately to him, knowing that there is no other world. Once you have conquered this world, then what will you do? There is no other world to conquer. The mind will feel very much frustrated.

The mind goes on for more and more and more. It doesn't bother what you have: you may be a beggar—it asks for more; you may be an emperor—it asks for more. The nature of the mind is to ask for more. It is not relevant what you have. It is the very nature of the mind just to go on asking for more. A rich man goes on asking for more, and remains poor. He goes on desiring for more, and remains poor. It is difficult to find a *really* rich man.

In my whole life I have come across only one man who was really rich. I have come across many, many rich men, but only one man who was really rich. And why was he really rich? He was rich because he understood the futility of it all. When I met him for the first time he brought thousands of rupees, poured them on my feet. I said to him, 'Right now I don't need them. If some day I need them I will send a message.'

That old man started weeping and crying. I couldn't understand what was the matter. He said, 'Don't say that—because I am so poor I have nothing else to give you except money.' He said, 'I am so poor! I have nothing *else* to give to you except money. And if you reject my money, it feels you have rejected me because I have nothing else. Money I can give. That only I have—nothing else.'

This is a man who has come to understand that riches are not real riches, and a man remains poor.

There was a rich and generous man of Bokhara.

'Generous' means he has really lived through riches, experienced the world, has come to a decision that this world is nothing more than a dream. And riches only give you an *illusion* of being rich, but they don't *make* you really rich. This man is disillusioned. That's why he has become generous. Now he can share. Now he can give all! Now there is no question. Now he is not asking for more. On the contrary, whatsoever he has, he is distributing and sharing with others.

Because he had a high rank in the invisible hierarchy...

And such a man immediately becomes very high in the world of consciousness. If you can share whatsoever you have, suddenly you rise in the hierarchy of the invisible. In this world you may look like a beggar; in the other world, for the first time, you have become the emperor.

Buddha renounced his palaces, his kingdom, his riches, and became a beggar. When he came back to his capital town, his father was very angry—as all fathers are. It is difficult to find a father who is not angry with the son, because whatsoever you do, it makes no difference. You may become a criminal, he will be angry; you may become a saint, he will be angry. Even if you become a Buddha... the father was angry. Because you can never fulfill anybody's expectations; that is impossible. How can *you* fulfill anybody else's expectations? He could not fulfill them himself, and he expects *you* to fulfill them. So whatsoever you do will be wrong.

The father was very angry. And Buddha had become Enlightened. He had come, a totally transformed being, resurrected. He was surrounded by infinite light, and a silence. It is said that

13

whenever Buddha would move, wherever he would move, even trees would feel his presence and flowers would come out of season. Wherever he would move, for twelve miles surrounding his body, suddenly a deep silence would happen. But a father is an exception.

The father was angry; he couldn't feel the silence; he couldn't feel the light—he could see only a vagabond, a beggar. And he said, 'It is enough! Now you have fooled around enough. Come back! And my doors are still open. Look at yourself: a son of an emperor—asking for your food in the same capital, begging. Look at your begging bowl, your torn clothes, almost rags! What are you doing to yourself? I feel ashamed of you! But I have a heart, the heart of a father, and my doors are not closed. You have hurt me deeply, but still I have the heart of a father. Come back! Don't move like a beggar—be an emperor!'

And it is said that Buddha said, 'I was a beggar. Now I have become an emperor—but how to convince you? I was a beggar when I lived in the palace. When you thought I was going to be the heir of your kingdom, I was a beggar and I was imprisoned. Now I am totally free. And for the first time I have understood what it means to be an emperor. But how to convince you?'

The moment you start sharing, you show that your consciousness has reached a point, a growth. A grown-up man always shares. If you cling to your things, you are not grown-up yet; you are juvenile. Why? Because you can possess a thing only if you share. There is no other possession. If you cling to a thing, it shows that the thing is bigger than you, bigger than your love, bigger than your being. That's why you cling to the thing. Your soul is in the possessions. You cannot share, you cannot be generous.

Because he had a high rank in the invisible hierarchy, he was known as the President of the World.

Sufis confer such titles on their beggars: 'President of the World.' Don't misunderstand! He is not a president in the sense Ford is, or Nixon was. They are the poorest men in the world, the very last, in a deep illusion that they are the first. This man must have removed himself to the very last. Only those who are disillusioned with the world can stand at the very end. They can become the very last. And Jesus says, 'Those who are last in this world will be the first in the Kingdom of my God.' Jesus must have been talking about such a man—rich, generous. And I tell you: if you are generous, you are rich; and if you are not generous, you may be in an illusion that you are rich, but you are poor.

Generosity is the real richness.

And to be generous, to share, you don't need many things. To be generous, you just have to *share* whatsoever you have. You may not have much—that is not the point. Who has much? Who can ever have enough? It is never much, it is never enough. You may not have anything at all, you may be just a beggar on the road, but still you can be generous.

Can't you smile when a stranger passes by? You can smile, you can share your being with a stranger, and then you are generous. Can't you sing when somebody is sad? You can be generous—smiles cost nothing. But you have become so miserly that even before smiling you think thrice: to smile or not to smile? to sing or not to sing? to dance or not to dance?—in fact, to be or not to be?

Share your being if you have nothing. And that is the greatest wealth—everybody is born with it. Share your being! Stretch your hand, move towards the other, with love in the heart. Don't think anybody is a stranger. Nobody is. Or, everybody is. If you share, nobody is. If you don't share, everybody is.

You may be a very rich man, but a miser, a non-sharing one. Then your own children are strangers, then your own wife is a stranger—because how can you meet a miserly man? He is closed. He is already dead in his grave. How can you move towards a miserly man? If you move, he escapes. He is always afraid, because whenever somebody comes close, sharing starts. Even shaking hands a miserly man feels is dangerous, because who knows?—friendship may grow out of it, and then there is danger.

A miserly man is always alert, on guard, not to allow anybody too close. He keeps everybody at a distance. A smile is dangerous because it breaks distances. If you smile at a beggar on the road, the distance is bridged. He is no more a beggar, he has become a friend. Now, if he is hungry, you will have to do something. It is better to go on without smiling. It is safe, more economical, less dangerous—no risk in it.

It is not a question of sharing something. It is a question of simple sharing—whatsoever you have! If you don't have anything else, you have a warm body—you can sit close with somebody and give your warmth. You can smile, you can dance, you can sing; you can laugh, and help the other to laugh. And when two persons laugh together, their beings are one in that moment. When two persons can smile together, suddenly all distance dissolves—you are bridged.

So don't think that to be generous you have to be rich. Just the contrary is the case: if you want to be rich, be generous. And so many riches are always available; so many gifts you bring with your life, and you take with your death with yourself. You could have shared, and through sharing you would have become aware how rich existence makes you, and how poor you live.

And the more you share, the more your being starts flowing. The more it flows, newer springs are always filling the river again and again. And you remain fresh.

Only a generous man is fresh. A non-generous man, a closed, miserly man, becomes dirty—bound to become so. It is just like a well. Nobody comes to it, and the well is not ready to give its water to anybody, then what will happen to the well? Fresh springs will not be supplying it because there is no need. The old water will become more and more dirty. The whole well will be dead. Fresh, living waters are not coming into it. This is how it has happened to many of you.

Invite people to share you.

Invite people to drink you.

That is the meaning when Jesus says: 'Drink me! Eat me!' The more you eat him, the more Jesus grows. The more you drink him, the more fresh waters are flowing in. The riches that life has endowed you with are not limited. But only a generous man can know about it. They are unlimited. You are not a company with limited sources—you are a company with unlimited sources. Behind you is hidden the Divine. Nobody can exhaust it. Sing as many songs as you can: you will not be exhausted; rather, on the contrary, better and better songs will be coming in.

It is said of one of the greatest poets of India, Rabindranath Tagore, that when he was dying, a friend came to him, a literary friend, a great critic. And he said, 'You can die in deep contentment, because you have sung so many songs. Nobody ever before has sung so many.' Rabindranath has written six thousand songs. The great English poet, Shelley, has written only two thousand. Rabindranath has written six thousand poems. And every poem is a marvel in itself, a beautiful diamond, unique. The friend was right. He said, 'You can die with deep contentment, fulfilled. You have sung so many songs. Not even a Kalidas, not even a Shelley, can compete with you.' And when he was saying this, tears were flowing in Rabindranath's eyes. He couldn't believe it. He said, 'You—and crying! Are you afraid of death? I could never believe that a man who has been singing his whole life that death is the great friend—afraid of death?'

Rabindranath said, 'No, not afraid of death. Death is beautiful, as beautiful as life. I am weeping and crying because better and better songs were coming lately. Up to now I was just a child. Now a maturity was happening, and God was giving me more and more. The more I sang, the more was flowing out of me. In fact, now the *veena* was ready and the time has come to leave. This is unjust. Now I was feeling ready to really sing!'

But I tell you: even if Rabindranath had lived one thousand years, the same would have been the case—because it is ever-flowing. You share and you know it is ever-flowing. You sing and you know it is ever-coming. There is no end to it. Even after a thousand years, Rabindranath would have died with tears in the eyes, because more was flowing. Nobody can exhaust it. God is inexhaustible. And you have God within you. Why are you so miserly?

Miserly, you become poor.

Generous, you become rich.

And generous you can become right now, as you are, because there is nothing else to it. You have simply to understand—and become! Nothing is lacking. All that you need to be generous is already the case.

Of course: he was known as the President of the World.

> *Every day he gave gold to one category of people—the sick, widows and so on. But nothing was given to anyone who opened his mouth.*
>
> *Not all could keep silent.*

Very, very deep, pregnant lines.

If you go to the temple and your prayer becomes a desire, it will never be heard. Because a prayer is possible only when desire is not there. A desire can never become a prayer. If you ask for something, you will miss. You are not praying. And God knows whatsoever your need is.

There was a Sufi saint, Bayazid, and he always used to say: 'God knows whatsoever my need is, so I have never prayed— because that is foolish! What to say to Him? He already knows. If I say something which He knows, it is foolish. If I try to find something which He does not know, that too is foolish. How can you find such a thing? So I have simply never bothered. Whatsoever my need is, He always gives.'

But at that time, he was very very poor, hungry, rejected by the town he was passing through. Nobody was ready to give him a shelter for the night. The night was dark and he was sitting under a tree; outside the town, it was dangerous. And one disciple said, 'But what about this situation? If He knows that His lover, Bayazid, is in such a trouble—that the town has rejected him, he is hungry and without food, sitting under a tree, wild animals all around, he cannot sleep even—what type of God are you talking about who knows everything that you need?'

Bayazid laughed and he said, 'He knows that this is what I need at this moment. This is my need! Otherwise, how?—why should it be there? God knows when you need poverty,' said Bayazid, 'and God knows when you need riches. And God knows when you have to go on a fast, and God knows when you have to participate in a feast. He knows! And this is my need right now.'

You cannot ask. If you ask, it will not be given to you. In the *very* asking, you prove yourself not yet capable of receiving it. Prayer should be silent. Silence is prayer. When words come in, desires follow suddenly—because words are the vehicles of desire. In silence, how can you desire? Have you tried it? In silence, can you desire something? How can you desire in silence? Language will be needed. All languages belong to the realm of desire. Hence the insistence of all those who know on becoming silent, because only when there is *no* word in your mind will desire cease completely; otherwise, with every word, desire is lurking behind.

Whatsoever you say, even if you go to the temple and the mosque and the church and you say, 'I don't desire anything,' it is a desire. Just look, watch—hidden somewhere is a desire. *And* you have heard that until you stop desiring, it will not be given. That's why you are saying, 'I don't desire'—to get it. But it is lurking in the back, in the shadow it is there. Otherwise what is the need to say, 'I don't desire anything'?

Be silent. Only silence is prayer.

So all the prayers that you have been doing are false. All the prayers that have been taught to you are not prayers at all—dead rituals. There is only one prayer, and that is to be silent. That is to be *so* silent that not a single word floats in the lake of your consciousness. No ripple. The lake is completely silent. It becomes a mirror. It mirrors existence. It mirrors God. In that moment of silence everything is achieved.

So, this story says:

> *Every day he gave gold to one category of people—the sick, widows, and so on. But nothing was given to anyone who opened his mouth.*

This Sufi story says, 'Keep your mouth completely shut'—not only outwardly, but inwardly also. Then much will be given to you. When you don't ask, much will be given to you. When you ask, nothing will be given to you. It looks like a paradox, but it is the very foundational law of existence. Don't ask—and suddenly you realize that much is coming.

It happened: A man came to Bayazid and he said, 'Because of your teachings my life is destroyed. Twenty years ago I came to you and you told me, "If you don't ask, riches will follow you. If you don't seek, everything will be given to you. If you don't hanker after beautiful women, the most beautiful woman will come." Twenty years wasted! Not a single, not even an ugly woman has come. And no riches—I have remained poor. You destroyed my life. What do you say now?'

Bayazid said, 'It would have happened, but you were looking backwards too much, looking again and again to see whether they were coming or not. The desire was there. You missed because of desire, not because of me. You were waiting always: "Now a beautiful woman is going to come and knock at the door. Now the goddess of riches will be coming." You were not silent. You were not in a state of desirelessness.'

Sufis say: 'When you don't ask, it is given.' And this teaching goes deeper than Jesus' teaching. Jesus says, 'Ask and it shall be given. Knock and the doors shall be opened unto you.' And Sufis say, 'Ask and it will never be given to you. Knock, you knock your head on the door, and it will be more closed than ever.'

But not all could keep silent. . .

even knowing this, that this man, this generous man of Bokhara, will give only if you keep silent. But it is so difficult, because the mind says, 'Make an appeal! Tell him the whole situation so that more can be fetched out of him.' And the story is beautiful, because now it comes to a lawyer. Anybody else may keep his mouth shut, but not a lawyer. He knows how to make the appeal in the court. He knows how to convince and seduce the judge. He knows if you keep silent you will lose the case.

In the world, words are very, very significant. A lawyer lives by words, because the court is the very temple of *this* world. Have you seen the buildings of high courts? They are the temples now. Much is wasted on them. Why? Even temples have become tiny, but high court buildings go on getting higher and higher and bigger and bigger. In fact, the power is there—the power of violence and murder, the power of law and language and logic. A lawyer is a logician.

He knew well that this man had a condition: if you remain

silent, he will give; if you ask, he will not give—'But even then not all could keep silent.' It is so difficult to keep silent. You know, I tell you again and again: Be silent!—but is it so? I tell you again and again, a thousand and one times, that God is ready to give to you, but show your readiness to receive by your silence. And you have not shown it. You would like to say to God that you are really in very, very much misery, in anguish, anxiety, so that something more can be fetched out of Him.

> *One day it was the turn of the lawyers to receive their share of the bounty. One of them could not restrain himself and he made the most complete appeal possible.*
>
> *Nothing was given to him.*
>
> *This, however, was not the end of his efforts.*

It is difficult to get rid of a lawyer; he will find other ways. Because if it was not possible, then he would find other ways, he would find other loopholes. From somewhere else he would try to enter into the house—maybe it is the back door. . . .

I have a great friend. He is a very famous lawyer. He was telling me that once it happened that he was fighting a case in the court of a very saintly man—and I know that judge also: he was really a saintly man. And he would not receive any bribery. On the contrary, if somebody tried to bribe him, it was certain he would lose the case. So what did this laywer do? He tried to bribe him from the opposite party. He found a way. Of course, the opposite party lost the case.

He sent a man, his agent, in the name of the other party, and tried to bribe the judge. And the judge was very angry—of course, the other party lost the case. And the other party was right. Nobody ever came to know how they lost the case. The other party was also puzzled. With such a saintly man it was absolutely certain that they were going to win. It was so simple! There was nothing involved in it. How did they lose the case?

The lawyer always finds a way. If he can enter from the front door, okay; otherwise from the back door. If in the day, okay, otherwise in the night.

This, however, was not the end of his efforts. The following day invalids were being helped, so he pretended that his limbs had been broken.
But the President knew him, and he obtained nothing.

The President is symbolic here. 'The President' means the higher consciousness which always knows the lower consciousness. You cannot deceive it. Unless the higher consciousness itself wants to be deceived, for certain reasons; otherwise you cannot deceive it. How can you deceive a higher consciousness?

But the President knew him and he obtained nothing.
Again and again he tried, even disguising himself as a woman . . .

In Mohammedan countries you can disguise yourself as a woman and nobody will be able to know whether you are a man or a woman.

. . . but without result.

You cannot deceive higher consciousness. Never try to deceive a Master. And you try, because your logical mind, the lawyer, tries in every way. It happens every day with me. It is rarely that you don't deceive me, or don't try to deceive me.

A person comes. He is happy; I see he is happy; for the first time, filled with an unknown joy. And I ask him, 'How are you?' and he shrugs his shoulders and says, 'So so.' Why is he trying to deceive? He would like more sympathy from me; this is what he is doing. If he says he is happy and joyful, then there is no need for any sympathy. And you are so foolish in your ways that you ask for sympathy and you could have got love—but you ask for sympathy.

Love can be given to one who is happy, sympathy to one who is unhappy. Love cannot be given to one who is unhappy. It is impossible. He is not in the right mood. You cannot give love to him; you can only sympathize. Love can be given only when somebody is happy and flowing; then he is in the right tuning and love is possible.

I was going to give love, but you tried to deceive me—and you got only sympathy. You cannot deceive. You are deceiving *yourself*. But you have become so trained in your deceptions, because in the whole of your life you have been doing that.

The woman in the house is singing, humming, and happy. The moment she hears the car coming in the driveway, the husband arriving, her face changes. Now she is getting ready to ask for sympathy. She becomes sad, tired. Just a moment before she was absolutely okay, nothing was wrong with her. Just the noise of the car and she has changed. The husband is coming—now she knows the trick: if she is unhappy, he will be sympathetic. If she is not unhappy, he will read his newspaper.

You have learnt deceptions. And they work! They work with the same level of people as you; they are also doing the same. The husband may have been humming a song while he was driving; the moment he reaches the house he makes a pose—tired, working the whole day for the wife and the children, dead tired, needs somebody to sympathize.

Remember: sympathy is a poor substitute for love. Never settle for sympathy. Sympathy is *nothing!* And nobody feels good when he gives sympathy to you. It looks like a burden: one has to do it; it is a duty. Somebody is ill and you have to talk to him. Somebody is ill in the hospital and you have to go and sympathize. It is a duty one has to do.

Never ask for sympathy. Be happy and love will be flowing towards you. Love is the right coin; sympathy is the wrong coin. It looks like love; it is not love.

So this is the trouble: you ask for sympathy, and when sympathy is given, you are not fulfilled—nobody can be fulfilled by sympathy. You were needing love and you asked for sympathy. You asked for the wrong food. If it is given, it will disturb your stomach. If it is not given, it will disturb your stomach all the same.

When you are asking for sympathy and it is not given, you will become more unhappy because nobody cares about you. If it is given it will not be a fulfillment because sympathy is very thin, it is nothing. You needed real, authentic love, a flowing of the heart. You needed your husband running towards you, but then you have to become a magnetic force, a happiness. Nobody runs towards unhappiness headlong. One tries to protect oneself, moves guardedly.

But these tricks you have learnt. And even when you come to me, you go on playing your tricks. You have learnt them too much.

> But the President knew him and he obtained nothing.
> Again and again he tried, even disguising himself as a woman, but without result.

You cannot disguise yourself, because a higher consciousness simply means a penetrating consciousness. Not only does it penetrate clothes—the *burka* of a Mohammedan woman: it penetrates your body; that too is a clothing, natural. It penetrates your mind; that too is a clothing, cultural. It penetrates to the very core of your being. It reaches directly to you.

Be true, natural, loose. Whenever you encounter a higher consciousness, be natural, loose. Whatsoever you are, put everything on the table. Don't save even a trump card. Put everything, all your cards, open on the table. You will receive much love, you will receive all—because when you put yourself completely naked you are ready to die. Unprotected, you open yourself—you become vulnerable.

And a Master is a death.

In fact, in the old Indian scriptures it is said that a Master *is* a death. When you come to a Master, you are coming to a very, very deep death. Even ordinary death is not so deep, because ordinary death will not destroy much. You will remain intact in your mind; only the body will be changed. The older body will be replaced by a newer body—but not the mind. The old mind will continue.

A Master is a great death. If you can pass through a Master and his love and his blessings, your body will die, your mind will die, your ego will die: *all that can die will die*—only that which cannot die, the deathless, will remain; only the deathless you, the immortal you, the *Brahma*.

Finally the lawyer found an undertaker and told him to wrap him in a shroud. 'When the President passes by,' said the lawyer, 'he will perhaps assume that this is a corpse, and he may throw some money towards my burial—and I will give you a share of it.'

Now it becomes a struggle. The lawyer is trying in every way to defeat the Master so he can say, 'Yes—even you were deceived.' He is trying to have the upper hand on the Master so he can say, 'You are not a higher consciousness than me.' This happens to every disciple. The disciple tries in every way with the Master to make in every way sure that 'is he really higher than me?' And the disciple tries in every way to prove that 'he is not higher than me, he is just like me.' Then your ego can grow more if you can come to a point and realize that 'the Master is not higher than me—he is just like me.' Then your ego is strengthened. Rather than dying through the Master, you have revived your dying ego, again you have supplied blood to it.

Every disciple when he comes to a Master is entering into a conflict. The Master will try to kill your ego completely, utterly. And you will try to save it; not only save it, but feed it, make it more vital, stronger. A disciple comes for certain reasons to a Master, and a Master exists for some other reasons. A disciple comes tattered, sad, because in life he couldn't fulfill his ego. Now he is moving towards the other world; maybe there he can fulfill his ego: he can become a great sannyasin; he can become the topmost Enlightened man in the world; he can become this and that. The world has failed; now he tries the other world: maybe he can find some anchor and save his ego.

You come for a wrong reason to a Master. This is natural—you are wrong, how can you come for right reasons to a Master? You have to come for wrong reasons. And the Master exists for absolutely different reasons. He attracts you, he takes you closer and closer, just to kill you—and to kill you so utterly that the very seed of the ego is burnt. That is what Patanjali calls *Nirbeej Samadhi*: when the seed is so absolutely burnt that whatsoever you do with the seed, now no sprout can come out of it.

The Master is a fire. The Master is a death.

Finally the lawyer found an undertaker—his last effort to deceive—and told him to wrap him in a shroud. 'When the President passes by,' said the lawyer, 'he will perhaps assume that this is a corpse, and he may throw some money towards my burial—and I will give you a share of it.'

This was done. A gold piece from the hand of the President fell upon the shroud. The lawyer seized it out of fear that the undertaker would get it first.

Then he spoke to the benefactor: 'You denied me your bounty—note how I have gained it!'

He's saying, 'I have deceived you. Where is your higher consciousness? Mister President of the World, where is your higher consciousness? Finally, I have won over you. I am victorious. You couldn't judge whether I was dead or alive!'

'Nothing can you have from me,' replied the generous man, 'until you die.'

The generous man used it—not that the lawyer deceived him—now he used the situation to give him a subtle message: 'Nothing can you have from me, until you die. Of course, this is not real death, so you have not received real gold—just a piece of the unreal gold of the world. False is your death, and the gold I have given is also false. But keep the message in your heart: Nothing can you have from me until you die.'

This is the whole message of the Sufi path: Die!

Die as you are so that you can become that which you really are. Die to the ego so that the Divine can be born in you. Die to the past so that you become open to the future. Die to the known so the unknown can penetrate in you. Die to the mind so the heart can start throbbing again, so that you can rediscover your own heart which you have lost completely.

You don't know what heart is! The throbbing that you hear is not the real heart; it is just the body part of the heart. There is a soul part to it, hidden behind it. These heartbeats are from the body part of the heart. In these beats, or *between* these beats, in the gaps, is the real beat of the real heart—the soul part. This is the matter part. You have completely lost contact with the divine part of your heart. You live a loveless life, a heartless life. You are like hard rocks. Even rocks are not so hard. They can be broken—and I say this with long and great experience. When I try to break your rock, it is very difficult, because your rock tries to protect itself in every way.

You try to protect your diseases, your illnesses. You try to protect your neurosis, your madness—because that's what you are identified with. You think you are that. You are not.

Until you die, you will never know who you are.

Right now you can sit in a yoga posture and repeat the mantra of Maharshi Raman, 'Who am I? Who am I? Who am I?'—you will not know. That mantra will be just in the mind. Raman knew through it—he passed through death. It happened when he was seventeen years of age. He was meditating continuously from his very childhood, must have carried the urge from the past lives. He was not like an ordinary child, not interested in this world from the very beginning. Whenever he had the opportunity he was waiting, and with closed eyes, moving into silence and deeper silence. Suddenly, when he was seventeen years of age, suddenly in meditation he felt that he was going to die. And when you are in a deep meditation and you feel that you are going to die, it is not just a feeling or a vagrant thought—it *grips* you in your totality, because there is no thought to fight with it. You cannot argue. It is so self-evident in a silent mind that you are going to die.

And it comes to every meditator—and blessed are those to whom it comes.

Suddenly he felt that he was going to die—and nothing can be done: death is absolutely certain. So what to do? He was sitting under a tree. He lay down, ready to die. Accepted. Relaxed his body. No struggle with death. And he found, by and by, that the body had become cold. It was a dead corpse. Even if he had wanted to move his hand he couldn't have. The contact with the body was lost. Then he felt the mind disappearing, like when water evaporates. And soon there was no mind. The contact with the mind was lost. Then he waited and waited and waited—when will death happen? And it never happened. He had come to the deathless. But this is a totally new man. The old man is there no more. The son to some father and to some mother is there no more. It is Raman no more. Suddenly Raman has disappeared. A Bhagwan is born: he has become divine.

When you reach to the bottom-most core of your being, the deathless, you are God. God means nothing else—God means the immortal, the deathless!

> 'Nothing can you have from me,' replied the generous man, 'until you die.'

And nothing can you have from me either, until you die.

And nothing can you have from God either, until you die.

In fact, until you die, you live a death, you live dead. Your life is nothing but a slow suicide—spread over seventy, eighty years, but a slow suicide, a slow death. From the very moment you are born, you are dying and dying and dying.

Until you die, you will live a dead life. And if you are courageous and you can take the jump into death, suddenly, for the first time, life dawns upon you. For the first time, the deathless dances within you. For the first time, what Jesus calls life abundant —you overflow with it! Now you are no more a tiny stream in the summer, just somehow pulling together, with vast sand all around, desert. You become a flooded Ganges in the rains: overflowing, broken all bonds, broken all limitations—life abundant.

But that never happens until you die.

So this is the paradox. Jesus says if you cling to life you will miss it; if you try to save the life, you will not have it. The only way to have it is to lose it. And this is what I call *sannyas*. It is an inner mutation. It is readiness to die, a readiness to die to the ego. One door closes, the door of the ego; another opens, the door of the deathless.

> This is the meaning of the cryptic phrase 'Man must die before he dies.'

You have died many times—but we are not talking about that death. That you have done many times. It has not done anything to you. You remain the same. You survive. You need a greater death.

There is a death which happens naturally, because anything that is born will die, anything that is combined together will fall apart. So your body is going to die, that is natural. It has happened millions of times, and it will go on happening if you don't become alert and aware.

There is another kind of death. The quality is totally different: a voluntary death, not a natural death. Not that the body dies, but that *you* take the jump—that *you* die. You don't wait for the death. This is sannyas. This is taking a voluntary jump into death itself.

Through death, the deathless is achieved.

This is the meaning of the cryptic phrase 'Man must die before he dies.' The gift comes after this 'death' and not before. And even this 'death' is not possible without help.

That's why I am here. Alone, you will not be able to even die. Such a simple thing you cannot do alone. It is so simple—it will be difficult for you to do it alone. A great help is needed of someone who has died before you. He can pull and push; he can create a situation in which, unknowingly, you are caught. A Master throws a net, catches hold of many fishes. Those who are ready to die will be chosen. Those who are not ready to die yet will be thrown back into the river.

You have come to me from many parts of the world. You can go on thinking that you have come to me—that is again a deception of the ego. I have caught hold of you, that's why you are here—not that you have come. You think you have come and you are wrong. I have been calling you in many subtle ways, pulling you towards me. And you have come. Now you are caught in the net. Still many of you are trying not to be caught.

Sannyas is just a surrender on your part, that you allow me to do whatsoever I want to do. Surrender is a trust: 'I leave—now you do whatsoever you want to do. Now I will not interfere.' It is just like when you go to a surgeon and leave yourself in his trust, because if you don't and you say, 'I have to watch what you are doing,' then surgery is not possible. You have to become completely unconscious—and in unconsciousness, there is total surrender. Even if the surgeon kills you, you will not be there to object.

Trust means that you leave yourself in the hands of someone —even if he is going to kill you, you are ready to pass through it. Sannyas means laying yourself down before me on the surgical table, and allowing me to cut whatsoever I want to cut. It is painful, It is very, very painful, because this surgery cannot be done in your unconsciousness—I have to do it while you are conscious. I cannot give you morphia, I cannot use chloroform; rather, on the contrary, I give you meditations to become more alert and more aware. This is a different type of surgery, a totally different type of surgery: your awareness is needed. You have to be completely a witness so that I can cut that part which is not in fact you but with which you have become identified—so I can show you a way where you can feel your innermost, your authentic being. It was before you were born. It is there before you die. It will be there after you are dead.

Existence goes on living in many, many forms. You need help so that you can feel the formless hidden behind the form. You are attached to the form, your eyes are closed with the form, and a great surgery is needed.

Says this Sufi saying:

The gift comes after this 'death' and not before. And even this 'death' is not possible without help.

And help is possible if you surrender.

In fact, if you surrender, the very death we are talking about becomes possible. Surrender is like death—that's why you are so afraid of surrendering. You try to protect yourself. You try to snatch something from me, remaining yourself—that is not possible.

You must die. Only then can something be given to you. The gift is ready, already packed, your name written on it—but you are not ready.

Nothing can you have from me until you die.

11 April 1975

II
Judge Ye Not

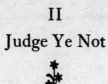

A young man came to Dhun-Nun and said that the Sufis were wrong, and many another thing besides.

The Egyptian removed a ring from his finger and handed it to him. 'Take this to the market stallholders over there and see whether you can get a gold piece for it,' he said.

Nobody among the market people offered more than a single silver piece for the ring.

The young man brought the ring back.

'Now,' said Dhun-Nun, 'take the ring to the real jeweller and see what he will pay.'

The jeweller offered a thousand gold pieces for the gem.

The youth was amazed.

'Now,' said Dhun-Nun, 'your knowledge of the Sufis is as great as the knowledge of the stallholders is of jewellery. If you wish to value gems, become a jeweller.'

JESUS SAYS: 'Judge ye not,' and this is one of the greatest sayings ever uttered by any man on the earth. It is one of the most impossible things for the mind. The mind judges immediately; without any grounds the mind makes a judgment. You have made many judgments without ever looking whether grounds existed for them or not. And if you look deep, you will find Jesus is right.

Every judgment is wrong because the whole world is so deeply interconnected that unless you know the whole you cannot know the part. One thing leads to another because it is interlinked. The present moment is interlinked with all the past; the present moment is interlinked with all the future. In this moment culminates all eternity. All that has happened is there; all that is happening is there; all that will ever happen is there. How can you judge? The world is not divided. If it was divided then a fragment could be known, but the world is a totality. All judgments are false because they will be partial—and they will claim as if they are the whole.

Yes, Jesus is absolutely right, 'Judge ye not,' because the very judgment will close you. It will be a deadness within. Your sensitivity will be lost, and with it your possibility for growth. The moment you judge, you shrink; the moment you judge, you stop; the moment you judge, you are no longer flowering. So the greatest thing is to be courageous enough not to judge. In fact, to suspend judgment is the greatest courage, because the mind is so eager to judge, to say good or bad, right or wrong. The mind is juvenile, it jumps from one judgment to another. If you ever want to get out of the mind—and without it there is no possibility of your inner growth—then, 'Judge ye not.'

I will tell you a small story. It happened in the days of Lao Tzu in China, and Lao Tzu loved it very much. For generations the followers of Lao Tzu have been repeating the story and always finding more and more meaning in it. The story has grown; it has become a live factor.

The story is simple: There was an old man in a village, very poor, but even kings were jealous of him because he had a beautiful white horse. Such a horse had never been seen before—the beauty, the very grandeur, the strength. Kings asked for the horse and they offered fabulous prices, but the old man would say, 'This horse is not a horse to me, he is a person, and how can you sell a person? He is a friend, he is not a possession. How can you sell a friend? No, it is not possible.' The man was poor, there was every temptation, but he never sold the horse.

One morning, he suddenly found that the horse was not in the stable. The whole village gathered and they said, 'You foolish old man. We knew it beforehand, that some day the horse would be stolen. And you are so poor—how can you protect such a precious thing? It would have been better to sell it. You could have fetched any price you asked, any fancy price was possible. Now the horse is gone. It is a curse, a misfortune.'

The old man said, 'Don't go too far—simply say that the horse is not in the stable. This is the fact; everything else is a judgment. Whether it is a misfortune or not, how do you know? How do you judge?'

The people said, 'Don't try to befool us. We may not be great philosophers, but no philosophy is needed. It is a simple fact that a treasure has been lost, and it is a misfortune.'

The old man said, 'I will stick to the fact that the stable is empty and the horse is gone. Anything else I don't know—whether it is a misfortune or a blessing—because this is just a fragment. Who knows what is going to follow it?'

People laughed. They thought the old man had gone mad. They always knew it, that he was a little crazy; otherwise he would have sold this horse and lived in riches. But he was living like a woodcutter, and he was very old and still cutting wood and bringing the wood from the forest and selling it. He was living hand to mouth, in misery and poverty. Now it was completely certain that this man was crazy.

After fifteen days, suddenly one night, the horse returned. He had not been stolen: he had escaped to the wilderness. And not only did he come back, he brought a dozen wild horses with him. Again the people gathered and they said, 'Old man, you were right and we were wrong. It was not a misfortune, it proved to be a blessing. We are sorry that we insisted.'

The old man said, 'Again you are going too far. Just say that the horse is back, and say that twelve horses have come with the horse—but don't judge. Who knows whether it is a blessing or not? It is only a fragment. Unless you know the whole story, how can you judge? You read one page of a book, how can you judge the whole book? You read a sentence in a page—how can you judge the whole page? You read a single word in a sentence—how can you judge the whole sentence? And even a single word is not in the hand—life is so vast—a fragment of a word and you have judged the whole! Don't say that this is a blessing, nobody knows. And I am happy in my no-judgment; don't disturb me.'

This time the people could not say much; maybe the old man was again right. So they kept silent, but inside they knew well that he was wrong. Twelve beautiful horses had come with the horse. A little training and they could all be sold and they would fetch much money.

The old man had a young son, only one son. The young son started to train the wild horses; just a week later he fell from a wild horse and his legs were broken. The people gathered again —and people are people everywhere, like you everywhere—again they judged. Judgment comes so soon! They said, 'You were right, again you proved right. It was not a blessing, it was again a misfortune. Your only son has lost his legs, and in your old age he was your only support. Now you are poorer than ever.'

The old man said, 'You are obsessed with judgment. Don't go that far. Say only that my son has broken his legs. Who knows whether this is a misfortune or a blessing?—nobody knows. Again a fragment, and more is never given to you. Life comes in fragments, and judgment is about the total.'

It happened that after a few weeks the country went to war with a neighbouring country, and all the young men of the town were forcibly taken for the military. Only the old man's son was left because he was crippled. The people gathered, crying and weeping, because from every house young people were forcibly taken away. And there was no possibility of their coming back, because the country that had attacked was a big country and the fight was a losing fight. They were not going to come back.

The whole town was crying and weeping, and they came to the old man and they said, 'You were right, old man! God knows, you were right—this proved a blessing. Maybe your son is crippled, but still he is with you. Our sons are gone for ever. At least he is alive and with you, and, by and by, he will start walking. Maybe a little limp will be left, but he will be okay.'

The old man again said, 'It is impossible to talk to you people, you go on and on and on—you go on judging. Nobody knows! Only say this: that your sons have been forced to enter into the military, into the army, and my son has not been forced. But nobody knows whether it is a blessing or a misfortune. Nobody will ever be able to know it. Only God knows.'

And when we say only God knows, it means only the Total knows. Judge ye not, otherwise you will never be able to become one with the Total. With fragments you will be obsessed, with small things you will jump to conclusions. And Sufis are very insistent on this: that you never bother that there are things which are completely beyond you, but even about them you make judgments. Your consciousness is on a very low rung of the ladder. You live in the dark valley of misery, anguish, and from your darkest valleys of miseries you judge even a Buddha. Even a Buddha is not left without your judgment. Even a Jesus is judged by you—not only judged but crucified; judged and found guilty; judged and punished.

38

You live in the valley, dark and damp; you have not seen the peaks even in your dreams. You cannot even imagine them, because even imagination needs a base in experience. You cannot dream about something which is absolutely unknown, because even dreaming comes out of your knowledge. You cannot dream about God, you cannot imagine God; you cannot imagine the peaks and the life that exists in a Buddha. But you judge. You say, 'Yes, this man is a Buddha, and this man is not a Buddha; this man is Enlightened and this man is not.' The Enlightened person is not harmed by you because he cannot be harmed in any way, but you are harmed by your judgment.

Once you judge you have stopped growing. Judgment means a stale state of mind. Now the movement has stopped, the effort to know more has stopped, the effort to grow has stopped. You have already made the judgment and it is finished. And the mind always wants to be in a judgment because movement is troublesome. To be in a process is always hazardous. To come to a conclusion means you have reached the goal; now there is no journey.

A man who wants to journey to the Ultimate should make it a basic point not to judge. Very difficult, almost impossible—because before you know it, the mind judges. Before you have even become aware of it, the mind has judged. But if you try, by and by, a subtle awareness arises. And then you can suspend judgment. If you suspend judgment you have become religious. Then you don't know what is right and what is wrong.

But, ordinarily, the people you call religious are the people who know everything—what is right and what is wrong, what to do and what not to do. They have all the commandments with them. That's why religious people become pig-headed, thick-skinned. Their journey has stopped. They are not growing at all. The river is not moving; it has become stale. If you want movement, growth—and infinite movement and growth are possible, because God is not a static point; God is the total movement of life, of existence—if you want to walk with God, then you have to move continuously. You have to be continuously on the journey.

In fact, the journey never ends. One path ends, another

opens; one door closes, another opens. A higher peak is always there. You reach to a peak, and you were just going to rest thinking everything is achieved—suddenly a higher peak is still there. From peak to peak, it never comes to an end; it is an endless journey. God is an endless journey. That's why only those who are very, very courageous—so courageous that they don't bother about the goal but are content with the journey, just to move with life, to float with the river, just to live the moment and grow into it—only those are able to walk with God.

Goal-oriented people are mediocre. All your achievers are mediocre. What can you achieve? Can you achieve the Supreme? If you can achieve the Supreme, just by your achievement it will not be Supreme. If *you* could achieve it, how can it be Supreme? Can you reach to the goal? You? Then the goal will be less than you. No, the goal cannot be reached. In fact there is no goal, and it is good that there is no goal. That's why life is deathless, because every goal will be a death. Then you are no longer needed.

A man who judges too much is stopping his growth from everywhere. And once judgments settle inside, you become incapable of seeing the new. The judgment won't allow it because the judgment will be disturbed by the new. Then you will live with closed eyes. You are not blind, nobody is blind, but everybody behaves like a blind man—has to: judgments are there. If you open your eyes the fear is that you may have to see something, something may be encountered, and you may have to change the judgment. And judgment is so cozy. You have settled in a house and forgotten the road, and the journey, and the effort, and the continuous movement, and the danger, and the hazards. You have forgotten the adventure. You have closed yourself in a small house, cozy, comfortable. Now you are afraid to look out of the window; you keep it shut. Now you are afraid to open the door. Who knows?—some strange fact may enter from there and disturb all your comfort and all your coziness and your security.

That's why you behave like a blind man. You are not blind —you are cunning. Through your cunningness you have become blind. And the mind immediately makes judgments. That is how to avoid the journey. It is an escape. People come to me, many sorts of people, but they can be divided basically into two types: those who are ready to open their eyes, and those who are not ready to open their eyes. For one who is ready to open his eyes, much is possible for him. For one who is not ready to open his eyes, nothing is possible. He is already in the grave, he is no more alive. He does not allow new winds to pass through his being, he does not allow new flowers to open into his being. He does not allow anything unknown. He is afraid, he moves on a settled path, and he moves in a circle, because nothing is more settled than a circle. He comes upon the same things again and again and again. He lives like a gramophone record: again and again and again the same. And then you say that you are bored! Nobody else is responsible. A bored person is a person who has remained with closed eyes. Boredom is a part of it. A man who lives with open eyes is never bored.

Life is so enchanting, life is so magical, life is such a miracle! Every moment millions of miracles are happening all around you —but you live with closed eyes, with your judgments. You pass a flower, and if somebody says, 'Beautiful!' you look, but you don't look. You say, 'Yes, a rose-flower, very beautiful,' but you are repeating something from the past—a gramophone record. You have said this same thing many times, too many times. To each flower you have said that. It has become a rubbish with no significance. You simply utter it because silence will be awkward. Somebody says, 'Beautiful flower,' and if you remain silent it may be awkward, embarrassing. So you utter something, 'Yes, the flower is beautiful,' but you neither see the flower nor the beauty. It is a cliché. And then you say you are bored?

You love a woman, and even hours have not passed, the honeymoon is not yet over, and already dust has started collecting around your woman. She is no more as beautiful as she used to be just a few hours before. She is no more as significant as she used to be. What has happened? You think that you have come to know her—you have judged her. You feel that now she is no more a stranger—you know her. How do you know a person? A person is an infinite process. You can never know a person.

In the morning the flower is different—because the morning

is different! And the sun is rising, and the birds are singing, and the flower is part of the whole. On the petals of the flower you can sing the song of the birds in the morning, you can see the new rays penetrating it, new life throbbing in it. In the afternoon it is a different flower. The whole climate has changed. The sun is no more the same, the birds are not singing. It is already dying. The sun has started setting already, the evening is reaching. The flower is becoming sadder and sadder—it is a new mood. It is not the same flower you saw in the morning. In the evening the flower is going to die; it is sad, to the very heart. Even if it sings a song, it is a sad song. You can see your own death in the flower if you are alert. You can see in the flower dying life and death meeting together, life transforming itself into death. It is totally a different mood.

You cannot know even a flower in its totality because of its millions of moods. How can you know a person? A person is a flowering consciousness, the greatest flower that has become possible through millennia of evolution. How can you know your wife? The moment you think you have known you are finished, you have made a judgment—you are already seeking another woman now. No, a wife remains a stranger if your eyes are clean. And you will come across many climates, many moods, many faces in the being of your wife, in the being of your husband, in the being of your child, in the being of your friend, and in the being of your enemy.

Nobody ever comes to know anything. But mind is cunning. Mind wants knowledge, because only with knowledge are you secure. With a stranger there is insecurity. With the unknown surrounding you everywhere you feel afraid, you don't know where you are. When you don't know the situation—the people, the flowers, the trees, that which surrounds you—when you don't know that, you don't know who you are, your own identity is lost. Feeling certain that you know your wife, your child, your friends, your society, this and that, and you know the history and the geography—with all this knowledge that is surrounding you, suddenly you feel who you are: the knower. The ego arises, strengthens.

Knowledge is food for the ego. Ignorance is death for the ego. And death of the ego is life for you. And life of the ego is death for you.

Don't settle. This is the meaning of the homeless sannyasin. In India we have tried it. One becomes a wanderer, homeless, uprooted, roots nowhere, so no identity. One lives with the unknown, moment to moment—everything surprises. To you nothing surprises. You know everything, how can anything surprise you? Nothing amazes. Everything surprises when you live in ignorance. When you live in not-knowing, everything is new—there is nothing to compare it with, there is nothing to relate it to the past, there is nothing to relate it to the future—everything is unique. It has never been before, it will never be again. If you miss it this moment, you will miss it for ever. There is no going back.

Every moment is a new mood in existence. Either you enjoy it, live it, or you miss it. Through knowledge you miss it, because you say, 'I know.' If I tell you, 'Come out of your house—the sun has arisen, it is beautiful,' you say, 'I know. Many times, many mornings, I have arisen earlier and I have seen it. I know—don't disturb me.' But this day's sun has never been there before, and this day's *you* has never been there before, and this day's me calling you to come out has never been before.

Everything is absolutely new, absolutely original. Just your mind is old. Through knowledge mind becomes old. When *you* are old everything looks dusty, used, secondhand. Then you get bored. Boredom shows that you don't know how to live in ignorance. A child is never bored. Everything surprises, amazes. He lives continuously in wonder, and this is the quality of a religious mind: to live continuously in wonder, constantly in wonder; to make wonder your very style of being. Then suddenly you see the whole world is totally different; it is not the world you used to know. Because you are not the same, the world cannot be the same.

Don't judge, and don't make an imprisonment out of your knowledge. Remain free, uprooted, homeless. These are symbols. A homeless sannyasin means uprooted from the past; he has no roots in the past. Not that he simply wanders like a vagabond; his vagabondry is deeper: spiritually he is a vagabond. Just going from one country to another won't help much; sooner or later you will settle somewhere, you will make a home. Even hippies sooner or later will settle. You don't see very old hippies—a phase. One moves from here and there, outwardly; then one gets fed up with it; then one settles. And remember, when a hippie settles, nobody settles like him.

An ordinary, straight person always feels the call to become a vagabond; an innermost call is always there. He may be settled with a wife and children and a good job, but the call goes on haunting him in dreams, in day-dreams, in imagination. It continuously calls him to become a vagabond. But when a hippie settles, he settles absolutely. He has known what it is to be a vagabond; he is finished with it. Again knowledge: he has known.

When we say, or when I say, become homeless, I don't mean it literally. I mean inside, live a homeless life—unsettled, uprooted, with no past; just this moment, this moment as the total, as if this moment is the all. Then suddenly you become aware: aware of the hidden, aware of the invisible, aware of the unknown surrounding you from everywhere. It is a vast ocean of absolutely new facts arising and disappearing. Life has never been old. Life has never been secondhand. It is original—it is the nature of it to be original and new. Only your mind grows old; then you miss it. And to live continuously in the new, you have to stop judging—then the highest consciousness will explode in you.

Judgment is a barrier. And it is not only ordinary things that you judge; judging becomes such a habit that you cannot help it. The moment something is there, you immediately judge—not a single moment is lost. And when you come to a person like Buddha, or Dhun-Nun the Sufi Master, you are near the original source of a consciousness constantly renewed. Nothing is old. Nothing comes out of the past. The mind comes out of the past; the consciousness is never out of the past—the consciousness comes out of this moment.

The mind is time, and consciousness is eternity.

The mind moves from one moment to another on a horizontal plane. It is like a railway train: many compartments joined together, past and future like a train; many compartments joined together on a horizontal plane. Consciousness is vertical; it doesn't come from the past, it doesn't go into the future. This moment it falls vertically in the depth, or it rises vertically into the height. This is the meaning of Christ on the cross—and Christians have missed the meaning completely. The cross is nothing but a representation, a symbol, of two lines meeting: the vertical and the horizontal. Christ's hands are spread on the horizontal. His whole being, except the hands, is on the vertical. What is the meaning? The meaning is: action is in time; being is beyond time. The hands symbolize action. Jesus is crucified with his hands on the horizontal, in time.

Action is in time. Thinking is an act: it is action of mind. That, too, is in time. It will be good to know that hands are the outermost part of the brain. They are one, the mind and the hand; the head is joined with the hands. Your head has two hemispheres: the right hemisphere is joined with the left hand, and the left hemisphere is joined with the right hand. Your hands are the reaches of the mind into the world, the reaches of the mind into matter—because mind is also a subtle matter.

All action, physical or mental, is in time.

Your being is vertical. It goes in depth; it goes in height—not sideways. When you judge you become more and more identified with the horizontal, because how will you judge? For judgment, past will be needed. Can you judge something without bringing the past in? How will you judge? From where will you get the criterion?

You say this face is beautiful. How do you judge? Do you know what beauty is? How do you judge this face to be beautiful? You have known many faces; you have heard many people talking about beautiful faces. You have read about it in novels, you have seen it in the movies—you have accumulated a notion, in the past, of what beauty is. It is a very vague notion, you cannot define it. If somebody insists, you will feel puzzled and confused. It is a very vague notion, like a cloud. Then you say, 'This face is beautiful.' How do you know? You are bringing your past experience in, comparing this face with that vague notion of beauty that you have accumulated through experience.

If you don't bring the past in, then a *totally* different quality of beauty will happen. It will *not* be your judgment, it will not come from your mind, it will not be imposed, it will not be an interpretation. It will simply be a participation with this face here and now, a deep participation with this mystery, with this person here and now. In that moment the person is neither beautiful nor ugly; all judgments have disappeared. An unknown mystery is there, unnamed, unjudged—and only in that unjudged moment does love flower.

Love is not possible with the mind. With the mind sex *is* possible; with the mind *action* is possible, and sexuality is an act. Love is not an act; it is a state of being—it is vertical.

When you look at a person and participate with no judgment—of either beautiful or ugly, or of good and bad, sinner or saint—when you don't judge, but simply look into the eyes with no judgment, suddenly a meeting is there, a merging of energies. And *this* merging is beautiful. And this beauty is totally different from all the beauties that you have known.

You have known the beauty of the form—this is the beauty of the formless. You have known the beauty of the body—this is the beauty of the soul. You have known the beauty of the periphery—this is the beauty of the center. This is everlasting.

And if this happens with a person, the same becomes more and more possible, by and by, with things also. You look at a flower, with no judgment, and suddenly the heart of the flower is open for you; there is an invitation. When you don't judge there is invitation. When you judge the flower also closes, because in the judgment is the enemy. In the judgment is the critic, not the lover. In the judgment there is logic, not love. In the judgment there is superficiality, not depth. The flower simply closes. And when I say it simply closes, it is not a metaphor—it happens exactly as I say it happens.

You go near a tree; you touch the tree. If you touch with judgment, the tree is not available there. If you touch it without any judgment, just feel it with no mind at all, embrace it and sit by the side of it—suddenly a very ordinary tree has become the Bodhi Tree; infinite compassion is flowing from the tree towards you. You will be enveloped. The tree will share many secrets with you.

This is how even rocks can be penetrated to their very heart. When a Buddha touches a rock, it is no more a rock—it is alive, it has a heart throbbing in it. When you touch a person, it is a rock, already dead. Your touch dulls everything, because in the touch is the judgment, the enemy, not the friend.

If this is so with ordinary things, how much more will it be so when you come across higher stages of being and consciousness?

Don't judge.

Millions have missed Buddha, millions have missed Jesus, millions have missed Zarathustra—just by judging. Don't repeat that stupid pattern. Whenever you go to a man of even a little higher consciousness than you, don't judge, remain open. Much help will be possible. If you go with a judgment, you don't go at all. If you go with a judgment, you have already missed. Put aside the mind!

Now, enter this story. Dhun-Nun was an Egyptian Sufi mystic, one of the greatest who has ever walked on the earth. He has a great insight, insight into human stupidity—and he can be helpful. But, as Sufis always do, they create a situation because they know that intellectually you may understand—but that understanding is not enough. Intellectually you may be convinced, but that conviction will not transform you. They create a situation and in the situation they reveal something. They don't say—they show.

How did it come to happen to Dhun-Nun? It is said that when he was a seeker himself, and not a Master, one day he was approaching a small village. He was coming from a long journey, from the desert—hungry, tired, thirsty, seeking a shelter—and he saw a woman on the roof of a house. She must have been working on the roof; the rains were soon to come and she must have been arranging the roof. He came nearer and nearer. When he reached near the woman, just near the house she was on top

47

of, the woman laughed. Dhun-Nun was puzzled, 'What is the matter? Why are you laughing? Why have you greeted me with such a mad laughter?'

The woman said, 'When I saw you just entering the village, I thought you seemed to be a Sufi mystic—because I couldn't see you, just your robe. Then as you came closer, I saw that you were not a mystic, not a Master, but still a disciple—because I could see a little of your face. But you were still far away and I couldn't peek into your eyes. Then you reached closer, and I could see your eyes, and I saw that you are not even a disciple, not even on the Path. And now that you have reached, and I can see you completely, I see that you are not even a seeker—you have never heard about the Path at all! That's why I laughed. Outwardly you look like a mystic, but your face doesn't cooperate with your dress, your Sufi robe.'

The very word 'Sufi' comes from a certain type of robe. 'Suf' means wool, and 'Sufi' means a man who is robed in a woollen shirt, a woollen robe. In a desert it is very difficult—hot, burning everywhere—and Sufis have chosen a woollen robe; and they have existed in deserts, the hottest parts of the world. Why? Because they say that when you are cool inside, nothing matters. When you are cool inside, *nothing* matters. On the periphery—heat; in the deepest center—coolness.

And this is a method, a device, to turn you from the periphery to the center. When the body is hot, and burning hot, you move to the center. You will have to move, because for the body, on the periphery, it is fire. What do you do when you pass on a road and it is burning hot and the sun is fiery? You seek the shade, a tree, and you sit there, relaxed. When the body is burning hot, Sufis have used it as a device. What will you do, continuously under a woollen rug, hidden under it, perspiring? What will you do in a desert? You will have to seek some inner point where no heat ever penetrates. You will have to seek shade.

The woman said, 'Outwardly you look like a Sufi, a Master, but when I saw your face, your face didn't cooperate with your robe; the face says something else. When I looked into your eyes, I saw that they say something else again; they don't even cooperate

48

with your face. And when I saw you in your totality, I saw that are not a seeker at all.'

It is said that Dhun-Nun threw his robe, entered into the desert, and for many years nothing was heard about him or what happened to him. For twenty years nobody knew where he was and what he was doing.

After twenty years...a sudden explosion. Dhun-Nun exploded over the whole of the Egyptian land. Thousands of seekers from every Sufi country started travelling. While Dhun-Nun was alive he became a Mecca; people were moving towards Dhun-Nun not towards Mecca. People used to ask him, 'What happened in these twenty years after the encounter with that woman? What did you do? What were you practising?' And he would say, 'Nothing, I simply sat in the desert—because whatsoever I do will be part of *me*, part of my ego. Whatsoever I do cannot be greater than me; it will always be less than me. And if I am wrong, how can I do anything right? So I simply stopped doing anything! For twenty years I practised nothing, or, only nothing I practised. I did nothing, or I only *did* nothing—I simply remained with my being. I was not a doer.'

What will happen if for twenty years you sit without being a doer? The horizontal will disappear, only the vertical will remain —not doing anything, just being. But that needs patience; otherwise no method is needed. Because you are impatient, I have to give you methods. Because you are in a hurry, I have to give you methods. If you were not in a hurry and you could say, 'I can wait, I can wait for eternity,' no method would be needed. Then you simply sit; even while you are doing things, inside you remain a non-doer. Of course, many things you will have to do. You will have to take a bath, and you will have to eat food, and you will have to go to sleep and prepare your bed. You will have to do certain things, but always remain a non-doer. This much is enough.

Remaining silently with yourself, without doing anything, the ego disappears. Not even trying to improve upon yourself, the ego disappears. Not trying to transform yourself, the ego disappears— just by accepting yourself as you are, whatsoever you are.

I see your only trouble is that you cannot accept yourself. You want to be somebody else—and that is the trouble. Otherwise, nothing is lacking; otherwise, everything is available. Non-doing for twenty years, Dhun-Nun became one of the most perfect Masters.

Now this story:

> A young man came to Dhun-Nun and said that the Sufis were wrong, and many another thing besides.

How can you know that Sufis are wrong without being a Sufi? And has anyone who has been a Sufi ever said that anything is wrong with the Sufis? It has never happened. Those who have been Sufis have never said that anything is wrong with it, and those who say that something is wrong have never been Sufis. How can you say?

Just the other day somebody was saying that all these meditative methods that I am teaching are wrong because Patanjali never mentions them in his *Yoga Sutras*. And the man said, 'We have never heard of such methods before. What is your authority? From where do you create these methods? They are neither Hatha nor Raja nor Bhakti.'

I asked the man, 'Have you ever meditated?' And he said, 'No.' I asked the man, 'Do you know what meditation is?' He said, 'No.'

When you don't know what meditation is, how can you say what is wrong with a meditative method? You don't know what meditation is, how can you know what is not meditation? You don't know what good is, and you go on condemning: 'This is bad.' You don't know what morality is, and you go on condemning: 'This is immoral.' Do you *know* what Sufism is? But you can condemn easily.

Condemnation comes easily to the mind. It is the easiest thing in the world to say that something is wrong. To say no is the easiest thing for the mind. Yes is the hardest thing.

Watch your mind, how many times it says no. Even sometimes if it has to say yes, it says it grudgingly. With no, it is very happy. The moment you say no to somebody you feel very powerful. You enjoy saying no because no helps the ego—yes dissolves it. And it'is easy to say no. It is very, very difficult to say yes, because with the yes a door opens—with the no a door closes. When you say no, watch what happens in your innermost being—suddenly all doors close. When you say no, you are closed. You become a monad of Leibnitz with no windows, no doors, no bridges. The no simply cuts all possibilities of bridging yourself to the other. All possibilities of love, prayer, surrender, all possibilities of meditation, are cut immediately, the moment you say—no!

No makes you an island, and *no* man is an island. And to feel that you are an island is the greatest illusion—you are part of the whole. When you say no, you are cut, you have broken all the bridges. And the ego always wants, enjoys, to say no, it relishes it.

Watch! Unless it is absolutely necessary, never say no! Even dropping the word will make you more and more alert. Even if you have to say no, say it in such a way that it becomes positive, takes the form of yes. Just by dropping the no you will feel many new things happening within you, because this is a very, very potential word. These two words are very potential: yes and no. They change your total being, because they are not ordinary words. They are not words, they are gestures—that's your way, your very style of life. A man who goes on saying no will become more and more sad, depressed; life will not knock on his door any more. If you continuously say no, how can life go on knocking at your door? Winds will not flow towards him; flowers will not be flowering on his path. He is sowing thorns by saying no.

The no-sayer is the only atheist. To say no to God is just the culmination of your total trend of saying no. To say yes to life is what theism means to me—to say yes to life, to open doors, to relate, to be available. Say yes and suddenly you feel windows opening inside. Just sit silently under a tree and say loudly, 'Yes!' and feel the change. Then say *no* and feel the change. You create a different climate; different vibrations come with the no. With yes you create an opening, as if you have thrown a pebble in a lake, and ripples arise, and they go on and on and on, spreading and spreading; they will reach to the very opposite bank. When you say yes you throw a stone of acceptance, of love, of prayer, of your being ready, of surrender—and then the ripples go on and on and on, and they reach to the very infinity. A yes-sayer is bound to become a theist some day, because yes ultimately culminates into the Divine.

Yes becomes the God. No becomes, finally, godlessness.

A young man came to Dhun-Nun and said that the Sufis were wrong, and many another thing besides.

How foolish!—but it happens. I know it; it happens with me every day. People, not knowing anything, even come to advise me that this should be done this way, that this should not be done this way. Man's stupidity has no bounds to it.

Only two things are infinite: man's stupidity and God's compassion. Otherwise, how does man exist? This is a miracle. . . so stupid, so adamant! But God's compassion is infinite. Existence goes on giving—it does not bother about your stupidity. Some day or other you will come back home and you will understand.

What foolishness to come to a man like Dhun-Nun and say that Sufis were wrong.

The Egyptian removed a ring from his finger and handed it to him.

This Egyptian, Dhun-Nun, was right. It was useless to talk to such a stupid person—he won't understand. And even if he understands intellectually, that won't be a real understanding. Dhun-Nun started creating a situation. He handed his ring to him and said:

'Take this to the market stallholders over there and see whether you can get a gold piece for it.'
Nobody among the market people offered more than a single silver piece for the ring.
The young man brought the ring back.
'Now,' said Dhun-Nun, 'take the ring to a real jeweller and see what he will pay.'
The jeweller offered a thousand gold coins for the gem.

The youth was amazed.

'*Now,*' *said Dhun-Nun, '*your knowledge of the Sufis is as great as the knowledge of the stallholders is of jewellery. If you wish to value gems, become a jeweller.*'

What exactly was he pointing out? That Sufism is not a system of knowledge. You cannot read about it. Scriptures won't be of any help, teachers won't be of any help—because they can explain, but explanation cannot become experience. And it is almost always that just the opposite is the case: that explanations become barriers to experience. Through explanations you start explaining things away. They don't lead you into experience; rather, they become substitutes. That's how pundits, scholars are born.

Sufism is not a knowledge: you cannot gather it from anywhere, from somebody; you cannot borrow it. It is not information. No teacher can teach it. Truth cannot be taught—it is an experience. It is not knowledge: it is being. It is not something that you learn: it is something that you become. Who can give it to you? Only you. Only you can give it to yourself. Only you can bring yourself to a point when you know what Sufism is—not by knowledge, but by knowing.

Always remember the difference between knowledge and knowing: knowledge is a dead, accumulated thing; knowing is a constant movement. Knowing is alive; knowledge is dead. Knowing is part of your being; knowledge is never part of your being. Knowledge is just part of your memory, and memory is nothing but a biological computer.

Sooner or later man will devise small computers which you can carry in your pockets. They will carry all the knowledge of all the libraries in the world. It will not be necessary to teach it to you: you can simply push a button and the computer can supply you the knowledge—so why waste twenty-five years of a man's life in universities with foolish teachers and foolish examinations, just training his memory? That can be done easily with a computer. And the computer is more efficient than any memory system can be, because a computer is completely dead—

and knowledge *is* dead. A computer carries it more efficiently than your mind. Your mind is not so reliable: it is somehow attached to an alive being, and the life also goes on flowing through it—that life disturbs it.

Knowledge is part of the memory system, not of your being. Knowing is part of your being. So knowing means to *be that* which you want to know. If you want to know God, God is not hiding somewhere so that you have to reach him. . . .

I have heard that when Soviet sputniks reached near the moon, they delivered a message to Soviet television: 'Up to now we have not found any God or gods.'

It is not somewhere up there! God is not a thing, God is not a person hidden somewhere. God is *your* innermost flowering. You come and ask, 'Show us God! Where is God?' It cannot be shown because it is hidden in you. It is your ultimate destiny.

Your God is still not there. Your God is still growing. Your God is still a potentiality, a possibility, not yet actual. And I cannot show my God to you—your eyes will not be capable of seeing it. And your God is still a potentiality; you have to work for it. It is still a seed: you have to water it, and find a soil for it, and help it to grow. I cannot show my God to you because you don't have the right equipment yet to see it. And the right equipment will be available only when you have fulfilled your godliness—but then there will be no need to see my God: you will be able to see yours; you will be able to see everyone else's. Even those who are still potentialities you will be able to see.

I can see your God—underneath the ground, still struggling like a seed trying to break the ground. The ground is hard. Sometimes there are stones and rocks also. Trying to break the hard ground, I can see your God, which will be some day, who is not yet. If *you* can see your own God, you can see God everywhere, because now you have the eyes to see. I don't see you as you are. Yes, that too I see, but that is just a passing phase. A cloud has arisen in the sky, but I see the sky. The cloud will go. I see you as you will be. I see you as you can be. I see you as, right now, if you are courageous enough, you can suddenly burst forth.

54

'Now,' said Dhun-Nun, 'your knowledge of the Sufis is as great as the knowledge of the stallholders is of jewellery.'

They cannot appreciate a diamond. They don't know what a diamond is. They may have thought that this beautiful stone will be good for the children to play with; or they can make measurements out of it—but the diamond is hidden for them. It is just a shiny stone, colourful, maybe good for the children to play with.

Have you ever heard the story of the greatest diamond, Kohinoor? I would like to tell you: It belonged to a villager in Golconda in India. He had found it on his farm. A river flowed on his farm, and there he had found it. It looked good, and he thought it would be good for the children—they could play with it. So he brought it home. The children played with it, and as children are, they got fed up with it. So they put it on the window-sill and everybody forgot all about it.

A visiting monk, a vagabond sannyasin, was passing through the town and he wanted a shelter for the night. So this villager invited him. The sannyasin took food, and then they gossiped, and the sannyasin was a vagabond so he had lots of news about the world and what was happening where. The villager listened, and just in talking about these things, the sannyasin said, 'What are you doing here? I know a place where diamonds are found on a river bank. With a little effort you can become the richest man, and here, working with this hard soil, you will always remain poor. Your whole life will be wasted.'

The next morning the sannyasin left—but he left a seed, a desire, an ambition in that poor villager's mind. He became obsessed. He didn't know where that river was, but he became so obsessed that he sold his farm and went in search. He told his wife and children, 'Five years at least you will have to wait; then I will return.'

He worked hard in many places, but after five years he still had not found any place where diamonds were so plentiful that they could be picked up easily. But in these five years he learnt one thing: what a diamond is. He came back home. When he approached his hut he couldn't believe his eyes: the greatest diamond that he had ever thought of, or seen in the market, was lying there on the window-sill. Then he remembered that the river flowed on his own farm and now he had sold it—and he had found the greatest diamond!

That part of the farm became the greatest source of all the diamonds in the world, Golconda. And all the greatest diamonds have come from Golconda, from that farmer's land. And this diamond which the children played with and got fed up with, and which was lying there uncared for and neglected, became the greatest diamond in the world.

And this is how it is on the inward journey also. Don't sell the farm! The greatest diamond is waiting there for you. But learn to become a jeweller—and the only learning is how to die, because if you die as you are you will be reborn as you should be.

Right is the Sufi saying: 'I cannot give you anything until you die.'

12 April 1975

III
Walking Without Crutches

A man once hurt his leg. He had to walk with a crutch.

This crutch was very useful to him, both for walking, and many other things.

He taught all his family to use crutches, and they became part of normal life. It was part of everyone's ambition to have a crutch. Some were made of ivory, others adorned with gold. Schools were opened to train people in their use, university chairs endowed to deal with the higher aspects of this science.

A few, a very few people, started to walk without crutches. This was considered scandalous, absurd. Besides, there were so many uses for crutches.

Some replied, and were punished. They tried to show that a crutch would be used sometimes, when needed; or that many of the other uses to which a crutch was put could be supplied in other ways.

Few listened.

In order to overcome the prejudices, some of the people who could walk without support began to behave in a totally different way from established society.

Still they remained few.

When it was found that, having used crutches for so many generations, few people could in fact walk without crutches, the majority 'proved' that they were necessary. 'Here,' they said, 'here is a man—try to make him walk without a crutch. See?—he cannot!'

'But we are walking without crutches,' the ordinary walkers reminded them.

'This is not true; merely a fancy of your own,' said the cripples, because by that time they were becoming blind as well—blind because they would not see.

LIFE IS a movement, a constant flux. Each moment it is new. But the mind?—the mind is never new. It is always lagging behind. The very nature of the mind is such that it cannot be one with the life. Life goes on: mind lags behind. There is always an inconsistency between life and mind—it has to be so.

You see a flower: the moment you realize that you have seen it, it is no more the same—life has moved. You see a river, but you don't see the same river again. You cannot. Says old Heraclitus: 'You cannot step in the same river twice.' And I say to you that you cannot step in the same river even once—because the river is constantly flowing.

The moment mind recognizes something, it is already no more the case. Mind goes on accumulating dead footprints. Life once existed there, but it is there no more.

And we are trained as minds; that is the misery. You go on missing life, and you will go on missing it—unless you drop the mind, unless you start living out of a state of no-mindness. Then you are one with the life. Then the inconsistency between you and your mind disappears. Then you no longer live according to some ideas, because ideas are of the mind. You don't live according to any ideology, religion, scripture, tradition—you simply live out of the emptiness of your being.

It is difficult in the beginning even to conceive how one can

live out of emptiness. But out of emptiness all the trees are growing, and out of emptiness stars are moving, and out of emptiness
the whole existence exists—and there is no trouble. Only man
has the absurd idea that without mind it will be difficult to exist.
In fact, with the mind it is difficult to exist—because existence
and mind are two separate, not only separate, but contrary
dimensions.

If you want to be consistent with the mind, you will be inconsistent with the life.

It happened: There was a case against Mulla Nasrudin in the
court, and the judge asked him, 'How old are you, Nasrudin?'

And he said, 'Of course, you know and everybody knows I
am forty years old.'

The judge was surprised and he said, 'But five years ago also
you were in the court and I asked you, and then too you said
that you were forty years old. How is it possible? After five years,
you are again forty years old?'

Nasrudin said, 'I am a consistent man, sir. Once I say I am
forty, I will remain forty for ever—you can rely on me.'

If you are consistent with the mind, you will become such a
reliable man. You will be consistent—and absolutely inconsistent
—because life goes on. It is never static. Not even for a single
moment does life stay anywhere. Life doesn't know any rest. Life
has no tradition to follow, no ideology to imitate, no pattern fixed
by the past. Life is always an opening into the unknown.

Life moves towards the future, mind moves towards the past.
Mind is always closed in the experience that has happened already, and life is always open for the experience that has never
happened before. How can they meet? How is there any possibility of their meeting? Then, by and by, mind becomes completely closed in itself. Not only that, the mind even becomes
afraid to see what life is.

The fear comes because the mind knows that if you look at
the life, you will be proved wrong. So better remain with closed
eyes, don't look at life. Interpret life always according to the
mind. Don't listen to it! That's how you have become deaf. That's
how you have become blind. That's how you cannot listen and

understand me—because here there is no person. I'm not talking to you as a mind. You can meet me only on the ground of life, not on the ground of mind.

That's why you will always feel I am inconsistent. I am. You cannot compare anything I will assert today with anything that I asserted yesterday. You will find me inconsistent. But what can I do? This morning everything is new. This morning has never been there before—and will not be there again. It doesn't belong to the past. It doesn't belong to the future. It belongs to itself—a unique phenomenon. The parrots chattering in the trees, they were not there yesterday. And who knows where they will be tomorrow? And the breeze—warm breeze passing through the trees, soft and warm like a woman—will not be there. Everything will be different! Everything was different yesterday. It is already different today.

And you are not the same. How can you be? If you are alive, you are a riverlike phenomenon. Twenty-four hours have passed. Twenty-four hours is like millennia; millions of seconds have passed. How can you be the same? I don't recognize you. I have never seen you before. You are absolutely new. How can I say the same thing to you that I said to you yesterday? And I am no more there, the man who was here yesterday.

Life is constantly a resurrection. Every moment it dies, every moment it is born anew. But you go on carrying the old mind. You will never fit anywhere. And you know it: you never fit any-where; you never fit with anybody. Wherever you are there is some trouble. Something is always missing, lacking. The harmony never comes out of your relationships—because the harmony is possible only if you are a flux-like phenomenon, changing, moving, merging into the new.

If you become a formless river of consciousness, then everything fits. Then you fit with life, and life fits with you— suddenly everything is absolutely okay. And that absolute feeling of harmony is what religious people have been calling God.

God is not a person. God is a state of being when everything fits. When you have no complaint, suddenly everything is beautiful. But the mind makes everything ugly, because mind lives as a tradition—and life is momentary.

This English word 'tradition' is very, very meaningful. You may not even be aware, but it comes from the same root as the word 'traitor'; 'tradition' comes from the same root as the word 'traitor'. Tradition is a betrayal of life, it is treachery.

Your mind betrays. If you can drop the mind, everything is attained. Dropping of the mind is the essence of all religion. Sufism is nothing but how to drop the mind, the tradition, the past. That's why religion always looks revolutionary—because it is always against tradition. It is always against the past. It is always against frozen words. It is always for life, flow.

No religion can be a tradition, but all religions have become traditions. That means they have gone false; they are religions no more. A religion remains religion only when it is true to existence and life—not true to any dogma, not true to any scripture, Veda, Koran, Bible. That's why Sufism was not understood by Mohammedans. They are one of the most fanatic peoples on this earth. How can they understand Sufism? Too book-oriented, too obsessed with the Koran—no other people are so obsessed with a book. Of course, when the Koran descended on Mohammed, it was a live moment, it was a fitting phenomenon—suddenly Mohammed was in the harmony of the universe, and the universe started unveiling its secrets to him. And the first word that came to Mohammed was: 'Recite! Recite in my name!' The word 'Koran' means recite, because it is the first word that came to Mohammed. It is a beautiful word—if you can understand *while* it is alive; otherwise it is ugly when it is dead.

It is just like a beautiful woman passing, moving. The very gesture, the curves of her body, the life that is flowing in her, the radiancy of her being, it is so beautiful. You can freeze her and make a statue out of her and put it in the garden—there will be no more beauty because beauty was in her very aliveness. A frozen woman, how can it be beautiful? It is a corpse. And those curves, when they were moving and alive, they had something of the Divine. Now nothing is left; it is only matter, a dead body.

When for the first time, on the Mount of Hira, Mohammed

heard this: 'Recite! Recite in the name of thy Lord!' he was as if awakened from a deep sleep. He looked around. Who has spoken? There was nobody. Life is not somebody—life is this All, the Whole. And Mohammed started reciting. He must have danced, he must have sung, in the name of the Lord.

In that moment there was music. In that moment there was dance. In that moment there was a heart, there was singing. In that moment there was celebration. Mohammed had been accepted. Mohammed had merged into the Whole, and the Whole had merged into Mohammed—the drop into the ocean, and the ocean into the drop.

It was the culmination of a being, the highest peak that one can rise to. But when others started writing it, it no longer had the same beauty; the words were now frozen. The Koran is a book just like the Vedas, Bible, Upanishads—very meaningful words are there, but dead. And unless *you* have come to feel that moment at the Mount of Hira, when the whole existence says to you, 'Recite in the name of thy Lord!' you will not be able to understand the Koran. You can carry it—it will become a burden; it will not give you life. On the contrary, it may take lives from many others. A burden is dangerous, and a burden ultimately becomes aggression; one feels irritated, destructive.

Mohammedans couldn't understand Sufis. And Mohammed is nothing but a Sufi. No tradition can understand Sufis. They are always the outcasts, thrown out of the society and the established pattern. Because they always bring the revolution with them. They come like a storm, and they shake the very foundations of the established society, the dead society, culture and civilization; the universities, the government, the church—all dead. But the majority of the people are also dead.

Because the majority of the people are also dead, a dead, established society fits. Once you become alive, once your life energy arises, you will suddenly feel that you fit with existence, but you don't fit with the society. And I tell you: if you don't fit with the society, don't bother about it, because ultimately it means nothing. The only thing that will be meaningful ultimately will be whether you fit with existence or not.

Try to be harmonious with life, howsoever arduous. Even if it sometimes seems impossible, but try to be in harmony with the Whole. Even at the cost of being thrown out of the society and forced to become an outsider, don't bother about it. This is what sannyas means to me.

Sannyas means an effort to seek ways and means to be in harmony with the Whole, *even* if it creates a rift between you and your society—because society is man-made. Even if you fit, nothing is achieved. One has to find his home into the Ultimate. And all societies are against God.

People think that there are societies which are not against God. No. Sometimes, very rarely, for a few moments in history, in the vast desert of societies, a few oases have existed—but they are exceptions. No society has really existed which was religious. For example, when Buddha was alive, then an oasis existed around him: a few thousand people—nothing compared to the whole world—a few thousand people converted, transformed, existed with Buddha. But the moment Buddha disappeared, that oasis disappeared, the very springs disappeared—how long can the trees exist without it?

A few oases here and there, rarely, have existed, but the society at large has remained anti-religious. But the people who manage the establishment are very cunning. They give society a ritualistic, formalistic, religious shape; churches exist, temples exist, and people go and pray; and holidays are there, religious holidays—but all formal. Don't be deceived by the formality of it; it *is* a deception. It is to give you a feeling that the society is religious and you need not go beyond society to seek religion. And religion is always beyond society, because religion is always alive, it is not of the mind. And society is always of the mind; it is an order maintained by the mind. Religion is not an order maintained by the mind—religion is a discipline, loose and natural. It is not that *you* maintain it and manipulate it; rather, on the contrary, you lose yourself into the riverlike phenomenon, and the river takes possession.

The mind is the corrupter—but it corrupts very diplomatically. It corrupts in such subtle ways: very difficult for you to even be conscious of what is going on.

For example: something in a certain moment is true, then the mind clings onto it and it says, 'When it was true in that moment it must be true for ever, because truth is eternal.' And I tell you: Nothing changes like truth—and that's why it is eternal. Because if it doesn't change, then it will die any day. It changes so continuously that it cannot die, because change means a renewal of life energy.

Truth is eternal, but not non-changing. Truth is eternal because of eternal change. It renews itself continuously. It never allows anything dead into itself; it simply throws it out. It never accumulates the dead parts, because through those dead parts descends death.

Mind will die, mind will have to die because it accumulates death. Life never dies because it goes on changing.

Remember this: Truth is not permanent, it is eternal. And it is eternal because it is not permanent. It is eternal because it is constantly changing. Through change it survives. Through change it becomes new. Through constantly changing, it becomes elusive to death. The death cannot take hold of it.

But mind has its own logical forms, which are absurd if you know what life is. But if you don't know life, then mind has its own logic. And the logic seems absolutely solid, absolutely error-proof. Look for this.

The mind says this has been true, so it must be true, now and for ever. Yes, the Koran was true; it was true in a particular situation. The situation was the merger of the soul, of the individuality of Mohammed into the Whole. In that moment a song was born. It was true. It was as true as the parrots chattering, the trees flowering, the sun moving—but that moment gone, Mohammed disappeared. That unity that existed in that moment is no more there. Now the Koran is a dead burden just like the Gita, Vedas, Bible.

Whatsoever I am saying to you is true this moment. Tomorrow it will become a dead burden. Don't carry it. Live it if you can live it right now. Enjoy, if you can enjoy it with me right now. Celebrate it! This very moment let your consciousness meet . . .

let it go deep in you. It can transform you. Be pregnant with it—but this very moment! Don't postpone it for tomorrow, because tomorrow it will not be valid any more. Nothing can be valid beyond its moment.

The mind says that if something is valid today, it will be valid tomorrow. That's how traditions are born. That's how very meaningful things become meaningless, absurd. That's how beauty is reduced to ugliness.

Krishna talking to Arjuna was one of the pinnacles of human consciousness. But the Gita? The Gita is just a memory. It won't help you. Krishna has to be encountered immediately, directly. You will have to become an Arjuna, and you will have to seek your own Krishna. And remember: you will not be the same Arjuna, because how can you be? You have a totally different being, a totally different quality of being—how can you be the old Arjuna again? No. You will never be. And you will never find the Krishna that Arjuna could find. You will have to find your own Krishna, one with whom you can meet and merge; one with whom you can have such a unity that the disciple doesn't feel any more that he is the disciple, and the Master has forgotten that he is the Master. Nobody knows who is who. In such a deep participation of being, again the song is born. 'Gita' means the song; 'Bhagavad Gita' means the divine song. Again, the Gita is born. But the same words will not be repeated, because this time Krishna is different and this time Arjuna is different—how can the same words be repeated again? And God is infinite; he need not repeat. He is not yet exhausted. He need not repeat himself again. That will be a very poor God if he again recites the Gita. That will not even be a God, not even worth listening to. Something new will again happen, and this new may not be consistent with the old.

There arises the problem of the real religious man and the false, pseudo-religious man.

The pseudo-religious man will always stick to the past, to the old, and the real religious man will always move with the new. And this is the paradox: moving with the new, you will attain to all that is hidden in the old; and clinging with the old, you will miss all that is hidden in the old and hidden in the new. The new is always the door of God. He goes on making new doors for you as you travel along; always new doors he goes on opening for you. Don't ask for the old doors.

Mind always asks for the old doors. If I say something to you, you immediately start comparing—whether it is written in the Gita, Koran, Bible. If it is written, your head nods; you say, 'Right.' If it is not written, suddenly you are closed; you are not nodding, you are not saying yes. And I tell you that whatsoever is written is already irrelevant, it is already passed, it is no more meaningful.

One has to seek the meaning constantly, because the very search for the meaning is a growth for your situation.

Now, this beautiful parable. Each word has to be understood. It is a parable with many meanings pregnant in it.

A man once hurt his leg. He had to walk with a crutch.

That's how religions are born. I know a man, a friend, a childhood friend; he was a very good doctor. And then he fell from a train in an accident. Accidentally, something changed in his head. The head was hurt; for three days he was unconscious, and when he became conscious he became a totally different personality. He had always been a very angry man; that anger disappeared. Something was broken in the brain; some energy pattern changed. He became very silent, very non-aggressive, very peace-loving. And then people started asking him how it happened. He said, 'It happened in a fast-moving train: you jump and hit your head on the earth. It has happened this way to me—why not to you?'

When I heard this, I went to see him and I said, 'What are you doing? What are you telling people?'

He said, 'But this is how it has happened to me—and I tried and tried *not* to be angry, and nothing happened. Suddenly, by accident,' he said to me, 'a key has been given to me.'

But I said, 'You keep this key secret and hidden; don't give it to anybody—because accidents cannot be repeated.'

And this is how many traditions are born. Buddha was sitting in a particular posture: it was accidental—because Enlightenment has no choice for a particular posture. It has happened when people were resting, lying down; it has happened when people were walking; it has happened . . . people were carrying water and it has happened. It has happened in all sorts of postures. The Enlightenment has no choice! It doesn't depend on the body posture. But Buddha was sitting in *siddhasana*, the Buddha posture, and now Buddhists have been following that for two thousand years: sitting in that posture, waiting for Enlightenment to happen. Foolish people, but they are in abundance everywhere.

This is how all yoga postures were born: something happened in a particular posture—that posture became very important. Then people go on trying gymnastics, forcing their bodies in this way and that, and think that in a certain posture a certain thing is going to happen. There is no relevance in it. Sitting on a chair Enlightenment is possible. There is no need to make a form too meaningful and significant; otherwise, you will be obsessed by it.

People go to the Himalayas because many people became Enlightened there—but it can happen anywhere. God is everywhere! There is no need to go to the Himalayas. Many teachers in the world go on prospering just because they did something and something happened to them. It may not happen to another, because individuals are different; they are as different as they can be.

My insistence is always that you will have to seek something, something which no tradition can supply to you. You will have to seek your own path, your own method. You can try with many methods, just to have a feel which method will be more suitable for you; and then, too, no method, no generalized form of any method, can be of much help. By and by, you will have to evolve your own individual method.

It is just like the print of your thumb—it is unique. Nobody else has that type of thumb all over the world. Not now, no, not even in the past—nobody ever had that thumb. And nobody will ever have it in the future.

You are a unique signature of the Divine.

No general method can help you. Generalized forms are good

to try to begin with, but one has to evolve his own style, one has to evolve his own method. Something has to be added, something has to be deleted, and, by and by, you have to create your own system around you. The path is not already there. You have to walk and create the path.

That's how a Master helps people. He will give them a generalized form to work with, just to feel their being, how it fits, how much it fits; whether it fits or doesn't fit at all. That's why I have created many methods, and I will go on creating many methods; it will depend on the people coming to me. Whenever a new person comes to me, I start thinking about something new for him. Many methods are needed so you can feel with every method and create an individual pattern of your own.

A man once hurt his leg. He had to walk with a crutch. This crutch was very useful to him, both for walking and many other things.

You can rest on it whenever you feel tired. You can scare stray dogs following you with your crutch. If it is necessary you can fight; the crutch can become a weapon. So many other uses also. And the man found that the pain disappeared, and he felt very restful. He had found a mantra, a TM, a transcendental meditation. He started teaching about it, he started helping people. People are in pain, hurt; they need crutches. And there are many other uses also.

He taught all his family to use crutches, and they became part of normal life. It was part of everyone's ambition to have a crutch. Some were made of ivory, others adorned with gold. Schools were opened to train people in their use, university chairs endowed to deal with the higher aspects of this science.

Fools abound—and they are always ready to be taught. And you cannot find a man, howsoever idiotic he may be, who cannot find a few disciples. People are ready, because people are in misery. They want something, some method, some path, some technique, to overcome their misery. That's why they become victims of many unnecessary things; not only unnecessary—irrelevant; not only irrelevant—positively harmful.

A few, a very few people, started to walk without crutches.

Because it is very difficult to go against the society. It is very, very difficult, because the society will create many, many hindrances, obstacles. It will punish you if you go against it. It will appreciate you, honour you, if you go with it. It will help your ego if you go with it. If you don't go with it, it will destroy your ego. Many people, knowingly, knowing well that this is foolish, simply go on, because why create unnecessary trouble? They make compromises.

This story seems to be an exaggeration; such an absurd thing, you think. It is not. This has already happened. You think, 'Why and how is it possible?—people who are walking normally already, how can they be seduced to use crutches?' They have been seduced. You are those people. Just try to forget this story.

Anger is natural, because you have not created it; you are born with it, endowed by nature. And nature *must* have some use for it, otherwise it cannot be given to you. But the society is against it; it says suppress it. And when you suppress anger, many more things are suppressed by it, because everything is interrelated in your inner being. You cannot suppress one thing; you cannot express one thing. You express one, millions are expressed; you suppress one, millions are suppressed.

A man who suppresses anger will *have* to suppress his love. Then he will become afraid of love, because whenever love is expressed, anger is also expressed. In fact, lovers are always angry towards each other—as angry as no enemies can be. They are intimate enemies: they love and they become angry also; and they know that love is so deep that anger will not be destructive to it—and it is never. It is destructive only if there is no love in the first place; otherwise, it is not. And if the love is not there, why call it destructive? It simply reveals the truth.

If love is there in the first place, nothing can destroy it, everything helps—even anger becomes a part of the harmony. And when you love a person and become angry, after the anger, when the storm has gone, the silence follows. You become more loving after the moment of anger; after the mood of anger, much love comes to the surface. You have to compensate: you were angry, love flows in—and this is a rhythm. Lovers fight, and then love. In fact, love is a very, very intimate fight.

I was once passing down a street and three urchin boys were looking through a key-hole. The first one looked in and said, 'They are fighting, the husband and wife.'

Another one looked and laughed and said, 'You fool! They are not fighting—they are making love.'

And the third one looked and said, 'Yes, they are making love—and very badly.'

Love is a fight, and it is a rhythm. In anger you go apart; the farther you go from your beloved or lover, the more the urge comes to come nearer. It is just like hunger: when you feel hungry, then you eat; and then there is a great satiety. Without hunger you can eat—all rich people do that—but then there is no satiety. Rather, on the contrary, when they have eaten, they feel burdened, heavy, dead. The same can happen with love: if you are never angry with your lover, you will be eating without hunger; sooner or later you will be fed up.

Nobody falls apart through anger. It is a rhythm: one goes away and comes back. Again and again you rediscover the beloved. Again and again a mini-honeymoon, every day. And love grows through it.

If you suppress anger, love will be suppressed. If you express love, anger will be expressed. But the society is against anger. That's why society is against love also. No society is for love. They are for marriage—marriage is not love. Marriage is an institution created by the mind. Love—love is a storm created by nature. And you cannot institutionalize a storm.

And people who live in marriage live in an institution just like prison—nothing of the heart; other considerations, but nothing of the heart. Money has been considered, the family has been considered; in fact, societies try that the lovers themselves should not be allowed to choose and decide, because youth is not reliable. Only old people are reliable, because when they are old they have a mind, an experienced mind—calculating, clever, cunning—so the father should decide. Or, if you have a grand-father, so far so good. Stars can decide, nothing wrong in it; you can go the astrologer and the stars can decide. That's okay—but you should not decide yourself, because if *you* decide, then by the very act of your falling in love, you are falling out of society.

Lovers are part of the society no more. Have you watched lovers? If somebody is in love with someone, they both move as a society in themselves. They don't bother about you; they want to be left alone. They don't want to go to the club, they don't want to go to the temple, to the church—no. They have found their church, they have found their temple, they have found the club—they are both satisfied with each other. They would like, really, that the whole world should disappear and they are left alone, on the whole naked earth.

Love is against society.

Society is against love.

And love is so natural—marriage is a crutch. Love is walking with your own legs; marriage is a crutch. Marriage makes you crippled; you are an independent being no more, your individuality is lost. You are a member of the society but no more an individual. An individual is not a member of anything. An individual exists as an individual.

You will be surprised why these Sufis have created this parable—they have created it meaningfully.

All nature has been crippled. Whatsoever is natural, the society is against it. Whatsoever is natural, they condemn it and they say this is animalistic. They make you cultured, conditioned, superficial. They give you a plastic being, a plastic flower; and the plastic flower has its own appeal—the appeal is because a real flower is always in danger, and the plastic flower is never in danger. Marriage has an appeal. If you insist for love, then there will be more and more divorces in the world. If there is marriage there is no divorce, because when you have never been in love, how can you fall out of it?

Marriage is secure. A real flower in the morning is alive, and by the evening is gone. A plastic flower stays, stays put; it seems permanent. Permanence should not rule your mind, it should not be a value; otherwise, you will never be able to move towards existence. Enjoy a thing while it is there. When it is there no more, forgive and forget and move. That's how one grows.

A few, a very few people started to walk without crutches. This was considered scandalous, absurd. Besides, there were so many uses for crutches.

And the people who insist for unnatural, artificial life patterns, always insist that they have uses. They always say that marriage is useful: useful for the family, for the children, for the society, useful for everybody—love is dangerous. And what is the use of love? What will you do out of it? It has no utility. For them it is just a romance, an emotionalism, sentimentalism. It has no use! It is not a commodity; you cannot sell it in the market; you cannot be profited by it. On the contrary, you will lose much because of it. That's why clever people say love is blind, cunning people say love is mad—it has no use!

But this has to be understood: Life has no use.

And always remember that wherever you start thinking about any utility, you are missing—because utility is needed, but it cannot be the goal. Utility can be sacrificed, but the non-utilitarian cannot be sacrificed. The non-utilitarian—love, meditation, prayer—they are the real goals. Through them you reach towards the Divine.

What is the use of meditation? What can you earn out of it? Nothing. What is the use of dance? Nothing. You cannot eat, you cannot drink, you cannot make a shelter out of dancing; it seems non-utilitarian. All that is beautiful and true is non-utilitarian.

A few tried to revolt—a few Buddhas, a few Christs, they revolt, and they want to bring you back to nature. But the people who are supporting the establishment, they always say, 'What is the use of it?' People come to me and they ask, 'What is the use of meditation? Even if we meditate, even if we attain to it, what profit? What does one gain out of it?' You will miss God, because God cannot become a utility. God is not a commodity. It is a celebration! And what is a life if you don't have any celebration in it? What is a life? It will be a desert.

In order to overcome the prejudices, some of the people who could walk without support began to behave in a totally different way from established society.

They started being natural. They started walking on their own feet. And when you start one revolution, millions start. If you can revolt in one way against society, you will suddenly become aware that many more things are there which have to be thrown out. The society has made you a junkyard. Once you know that one thing is wrong, you will be able to know many things are wrong. One starts a chain reaction.

Meditation is my way to create the chain reaction. Once you start meditating, many things will follow, because the more you become aware and silent, the more you will be able to see how the society has been killing you, poisoning you, how the society has been murderous. And they all say that they want to help you. In fact, they murder you just to save you. It is for your benefit that the society exists—and it has simply poisoned your whole being. The very source-spring of your being has been poisoned.

In order to overcome the prejudices, some of the people who could walk without support began to behave in a totally different way from established society.
Still they remained few.
When it was found that, having used crutches for so many generations, few people could in fact walk without crutches, the majority 'proved' that they were necessary.

This is how the vicious circle moves in the world. First you create a pattern, you force the pattern, and then in the end the victim cannot live without the pattern. Then you 'prove' it: 'Look!—nobody can walk without crutches.' You never allow anybody to walk without crutches. Every child is given many, many prejudices. And whenever he trys to live without prejudices he will find it very difficult, because they have become ingrained, inbuilt, they have moved into the very blueprint of his being. He will feel difficulties; he himself will say that it is impossible to walk. Try to walk on crutches for three years and then, then you will not be able to walk without them; then you will become a 'proof' that nobody can walk.

This is how the prejudices continue, because they have been implanted for thousands of years, and they have gone into your blood and your bones.

Whenever you feel a sexual urge, immediately a guilt feeling comes in; it has become inbuilt. If you look at a beautiful woman or a beautiful man and you feel an upsurge of energy, nothing is wrong in it. It is a response! It is natural: a beautiful person is there—it will be very insulting if no energy arises in you. If the society were natural it would accept the fact, and the woman would thank you that your face became red—such a beautiful compliment, and you were trembling. But no. You will hide the fact; you will not look at the woman. And the more you try not to look, the more nature rebels against it, and then a guilt feeling arises that you are immoral.

When you see a flower and say it is beautiful, you are not immoral. But when you see a human face and say it is beautiful, why do you become immoral suddenly? What is immoral in it? Why can't you appreciate it?

For centuries sex has been condemned—and sex is the source of all your energies. Because of condemned sex, all your energies have been condemned—because if you become active in one part of your energy, then other parts will also be rising with it. So you have been forced to live with low energy. Then you say life seems like a lethargy, no enjoyment out of it, no vitality. You seem to be continuously exploited, and you don't have any energy left to live. Life should be radiant, life should be overflowing— but the very source is sex.

Unless you accept your sexuality you will never be at ease with yourself, because your sexuality is such a deep force. You are born out of it, your every cell belongs to it; your very energy is sexual. And whenever you allow it, the same energy will transform into love. The same energy will go higher and higher and will transform into prayer. Once suppressed, then there is no possibility of meditation or prayer either—because what will be transformed? You will be always afraid.

It happens every day: people come to me—the moment they start meditations they feel an upsurge of sexual energy and they become very afraid and scared. They say, 'We have never been like that. What is happening? What has gone wrong? Are we doing something wrong in meditation?—because we feel so sexual!' This should be a beautiful, good indication—life is coming back, life is arising again, life is again flowing from the frozen sources!

Of course, sex will be the basic center which will be hit first, because there you have suppressed it. It is uncoiling: as if a spring has been suppressed under a weight—now the weight is removed and the spring jumps. This is beautiful! This shows that the meditation *is* functioning.

But you wanted otherwise: you wanted meditation to suppress sex. Then you have come to a wrong person. Then go to the old poisoners, the old life-negaters—they will give you meditations so that you can suppress more. But you will always remain divided, and you will always be in discord, and the ultimate harmony will never be possible.

I am trying to create a unity within you so the suppressed part is accepted back, the suppressed part is reabsorbed back into the total being, because without it you will not be able to move. Sex is your legs—the lowest part, yes, I know—but without your legs, your head cannot move. The lowest, I know, but the highest depends on the lowest. If the lowest is moving, the highest will move soon: with sex, soon love will arise. And when love arises, sex disappears—because the same energy becomes love. Then for the first time the real *brahmacharya*, the authentic virginity happens to you.

Sex simply disappears—it has become love. And then love rises higher, becomes prayer; then love also disappears, then it has become prayer. And prayer is the culmination. In prayer you are fulfilled. But it has to start from the very base, from the natural. From the natural to the supernatural, but *not* against the natural.

When it was found that, having used crutches for so many generations, few people could in fact walk without crutches, the majority 'proved' that they were necessary. 'Here,' they said, 'here is a man—try to make him walk without a crutch. See? —he cannot.'

'But we are walking without crutches,' the ordinary walkers reminded them.

'This is not true; merely a fancy of your own,' said the cripples, because by that time they were becoming blind as well—blind because they would not see.

I have been telling people: Accept your nature, and the very acceptance becomes a deep transformation, you will be transfigured. Sometimes, old sannyasins come to me, traditional sannyasins belonging to a Jain faith, or a Buddhist faith, or a Hindu faith; they listen to me and they say, 'It is not possible! We have been suppressing sex and it has not gone—and you say accept it and it will go?' Their logic is apparently clear. They say, 'We have been suppressing and fighting our whole life, and it has not gone. And here you are—you say, "Don't suppress it. Accept and it will go!" '

Their logic is clear. They say, 'How can it go without fighting when it has not gone with so much fight?' They say, 'No, it is not possible. We have tried and it won't move even an inch backward. And we have put our whole life at stake! And here you are teaching such a simple thing. Are we fools? It won't go.'

And I say to them, 'Look at me: it has gone!' And this is what—whether they say to me or not—they feel: they say, 'It must be your fancy. You must be imagining. ... This is not true; merely a fancy of your own.'

The ego dies hard.

And they cannot see. I tell them, 'Be with me, see me, observe me, watch me—all that you are seeking has happened!'

They say, 'It must be some fancy of your own. Realization is not possible in this age and time. It is written in the scriptures that no man can become Enlightened in Kali Yuga; in this age of technology, no one can become Enlightened. So how can you become Enlightened?'

I say, 'Look at me and watch and be close to me and be

intimate, and feel it.' They are not ready for it. Their scriptures say something else, so I must be deluding myself, I must be a dream, I must be fancying.

And this is not just that it is so with me—it has been always so. When Buddha became Enlightened, the same people came to Buddha and they said, 'No, it is not possible. It is *not* possible! How can you become Enlightened? Many millions of lives are needed. It is written in the scriptures. And what have you done? What austerities? What *tapascharya?* What yoga have you followed? Sitting under the Bodhi Tree, and suddenly you declare you have become Enlightened! What is the proof? You must be fancying.' They have not taken note of many Enlightened people. Mahavir: Hindu scriptures never mention him, because they never believed that he became Enlightened. Ego dies hard.

And when you live in a plastic, artificial world, forced, somehow disciplined, imposed upon, by and by, you become blind also—because when you don't use your eyes, they lose the capacity to see. And a man who is prejudiced avoids using his eyes, because who knows?—the fact may not prove his prejudice. So he avoids; he will not look. Or, if he looks, he will interpret it in such a way that the fact is there no more; he has created a fiction around it.

People who are too prejudiced . . . and all people are. Somebody is a Hindu, somebody is a Mohammedan, somebody is a Christian—they are prejudiced people. Without knowing, they have already decided what is true. Without experiencing, they have already come to conclusions. They avoid looking directly. And when you avoid continuously, of course, you lose the capacity to see, you become blind.

> 'This is not true; merely a fancy of your own,' said the cripples, because by that time they were becoming blind as well—blind because they would not see.

If you want to see you have to die to your ego—because that ego won't allow you to see, to be natural, to allow the fact to emerge.

Die to the ego.

Die to the past.

And the Sufi saying is right: 'You cannot have anything from me until you die.'

Die! It is hard, but it is the only way.

You cannot have anything from me until you die.

13 April 1975

IV
Straight to Freedom

A man came to the great teacher Bahaudin and asked for help in his problems, and guidance on the path of the Teaching.

Bahaudin told him to abandon spiritual studies and leave his court at once.

A kind-hearted visitor began to remonstrate with Bahaudin.

'You shall have a demonstration,' said the sage.

At that moment a bird flew into the room, darting hither and thither, not knowing where to go in order to escape.

The Sufi waited until the bird settled near the only open window of the chamber, and then suddenly clapped his hands.

Alarmed, the bird flew straight through the opening of the window, to freedom.

Then Bahaudin said:

'To him that sound must have been something of a shock, even an affront, do you not agree?'

THERE IS an old story: In Thailand there exists a very ancient temple. And the myth goes that in the beginning of Creation, God became angry with some angel. The angel had committed some disobedience, and it was so grave that the God threw him onto the earth and told him that he would have to live as an invisible snake in this ancient temple.

The temple has a tower with one hundred steps, and every pilgrim that comes to the temple has to go to the tower—that is part of the pilgrimage. And God said to this angel, 'You will have to live on the first step of the tower, and every pilgrim who comes, you will have to move with him.' In Thailand, they divide human consciousness into one hundred steps, and the snake would be able to go with the pilgrim only up to the point where *his* consciousness existed. If he had attained to the twentieth step of consciousness, then the snake would be able to follow up to the twentieth; if to the fiftieth, then the fiftieth. And God said, 'If you can reach thrice to the last step, then you will be freed of your sin.'

The myth goes that, up to now, only once has the snake been able to reach to the hundredth.

At least ten thousand pilgrims come every day to the ancient temple. Millennia have passed—pilgrims and pilgrims. And the snake has to follow every pilgrim. Sometimes, rarely, it can reach up to the twenty-fifth; very, very rarely up to the fiftieth, and only once to the hundredth. It falls back again to the first step. And now even the snake has become very, very depressed—there seems to be no hope. Only once up to now...and thrice he has to reach to the hundredth, only then will he be freed of the sin.

The myth is beautiful. It says many things. One: amongst millions of people, only once does it happen that a man becomes Enlightened. To become Enlightened is difficult, but there is a greater difficulty that I would like to tell you about. Amongst millions, one person becomes Enlightened, and amongst thousands of Enlightened persons, one person becomes a Master. And to become a Master is almost impossible. To become Enlightened you have to work with yourself, your barriers, your hindrances—but your own. To become a Master you have to work with others' barriers, hindrances. To work with oneself it is so difficult. To work with somebody else is almost impossible.

Many Buddhas have existed, but once in a while a Buddha becomes a Master. The famous name of Gautam the Buddha is famous just because of his being a Master. Millions of Buddhas preceded him, but they were not Masters.

It happened: One day somebody asked Buddha, 'You have almost fifty thousand sannyasins around you—how many of them have become like you?' Buddha is reported to have said that many had. But the questioner was puzzled. He said, 'If many of them have become like you, why does nobody know about them?'

Buddha said, 'They have become Enlightened, but they are not Masters. They are just like me, they exist on the same plane of being—that is one thing. But to persuade another to bring his consciousness to the same plane is a difficult art.'

To persuade the other towards higher peaks of being is almost impossible because the other will create all sorts of resistances. And the more you try to bring him up, the more his ego will be there to resist. And the ego will enjoy falling down more and more. The ego will be the enemy. And the other is identified with his own ego, he thinks he is the ego. So when a Master tries to transform or help, you create all sorts of barriers in order not to be helped.

Teachers are many, Masters few.

Teachers are very cheap; you can get them a rupee a dozen—because to be a teacher is nothing. You need a little intellectual capacity to understand things, a little capacity to explain things—if you are a little articulate you can become a teacher. Scriptures are there: you can memorize them. With a little practice you can attain to a certain logical penetration into things. You can silence people, you can prove things. And many will be attracted because people live in their intellectual center—they live in their heads.

A teacher is a head-oriented person, more heady than you. He can impress you, but that impression will not lead you anywhere. You will remain in the same rut. He himself is nowhere. A teacher is a man who teaches without knowing what he is teaching. A teacher is a man who talks about things he has not known, who talks about worlds with no experience. He has not tasted anything of the Unknown. He may have tasted many things of the Vedas, Koran, Bible, Upanishads; knowledge he may have gathered much, but knowing he has none. But you can adjust to a teacher very easily because he is of the same type; he belongs to the same level of being as you, to the same plane. Teachers become very, very influential; they lead great movements; millions are attracted to them—because they talk the same language that *you* can understand.

Masters cannot lead big movements—almost impossible. In fact, by the time they become known they are here no more; by the time people come to hear about them, they are gone. Then they are worshipped for thousands of years, but that worship won't help much. To be impressed by a Master is difficult, because that means dying to your own ego. To allow a Master to work on you is very courageous: you open your heart, you become vulnerable; and nobody knows where he is leading—you have to trust. Logic is not of much help, only love. And love is rare. Everybody is logical: who is loving? Everybody has cunning intellect, but who has a trusting heart?

This is the first thing to be understood before we can enter into this story.

Sufis don't believe in teachings and teachers. This man, Bahaudin, is one of the greatest Masters. The Master does not teach: he demonstrates; his whole being is a demonstration. He opens new dimensions and he invites you to look through these new dimensions, new vistas, new windows. He demonstrates, he does not teach. And even if he teaches, it is just to persuade your intellect to come to *his* window from where things have a totally different look.

And a Master has to be skilled in the greatest art: the art of the human heart—because subtle are the problems, very complicated and complex.

For example: a person comes to me. He is ready to take the jump—*he* thinks he is ready to take the jump, but he is not ready. And I see that this is not the right moment for him: if he takes the jump he will miss. I have to persuade him to wait; I have to persuade him to wait for the right moment. I have to divert his mind; I have to give him some other occupation so he forgets, at least for the present, about the final jump. He will be ready one day—and everything comes in its own season.

You cannot force a phenomenon like Enlightenment, you cannot manipulate it. You have to wait for it: it comes when it comes, it comes on its own. In fact, there is no way to force it; you cannot control it. All that you can do is to learn how to wait lovingly—how to wait, how to trust. When the right moment comes, it will happen.

Somebody comes; he says he is ready. He *thinks* he is ready, but I see he is not ready. So I have to divert his mind: I have to give him something to play with so the time can be passed and he becomes ripe. He thinks he is ready. It is not really thinking: it is the ego. He says, 'Right now, help me.' Then there is somebody else who thinks he is not ready—thinking is not of much value in the world of the innermost. Somebody is there who is not ready, thinks he is ready. Somebody is there who is ready, thinks he is not ready. I have to persuade, in fact, seduce him to take the jump. He hesitates. He's afraid. He says he is not ready. 'What are you doing? Why are you forcing me? Why are you haunting me?' But I know that he is ready—and if this moment is lost, it may be many years before the next moment comes again, or it may be many lives.

At a certain point the whole existence is ready to accept you, but you hesitate. This moment may not be there again soon. Maybe a life passes, or many lives, then again a moment comes. I have to watch. I don't listen to you, I cannot. I have to go on doing my own things. I cannot listen to you, because you don't know what you are saying. You don't know what is happening to you; you are in confusion. If I listen to you, then I will not be of any help to you. I have to go on my own, and I have to create a feeling in you that I am listening to you; and I have to go on persuading you that it is according to you that everything is being done.

Sometimes I see it will be good for you to stop all meditations, because, with your mind, even meditation can become a strain and it can become the barrier. Sometimes I have to force you exactly against yourself into meditation, because unless there is a certain strain in you, a tension, the transformation will not be possible. The art is very subtle. You need a certain tension—just as when the arrow is put on the bow a certain tension is needed, otherwise the arrow will not be thrown. But too much tension can break the bow.

Meditation is needed, with vigorous effort, but you don't know where to start and where to stop—that I have to watch. So sometimes I will say to you, 'Stop meditations,' and you cannot understand because, continuously, I teach 'Meditate!' And sometimes I have to say, 'Go into meditations,' and then you cannot understand because continuously I teach that no effort is needed—it will come when it comes, it is a happening.

Try to understand my situation. And I have to work with many, so I will be making many contradictory statements. I will say something to one, and just the opposite to the other—because both are different. So whatsoever I say is personal. When I say it to you, I say it to you, not to anybody else. And when I say it to you, it is not only personal, it is also momentary—because tomorrow you will have changed and then something else will be said to you. It is a continuous response, an alive response.

A teacher is dead, he has a dead teaching. He doesn't bother about you, you don't matter. He has a teaching, he continues. He is more focused on the teaching, less focused on you—in fact, not focused at all. A teacher is a madman—the teaching is important: the teaching exists not for man; man exists for the teaching, the doctrine. But for a Master, teachings are toys. Doctrines are good if they help, bad if they don't help. And sometimes they help and sometimes they don't help. To some they become a bridge; to some they become a barrier. Man is important.

To a Master, man is the measure of all things—individual, personal; not men, but human beings; not mankind, but *you*, in your total personality, in your unique personality. Whatsoever a Master says is addressed to a person, it is a letter. You cannot make a criterion out of it. You cannot make a generalization out of it. All generalizations are false—even this generalization that all generalizations are false.

Very subtle is the art, it has to be—because it is an effort to transform the human heart, the greatest thing in evolution, the highest peak to which existence has reached.

A teacher goes on giving you information about God, about Truth, about heaven and hell. A Master simply opens his being to you, demonstrates to you what Truth is.

What am I doing here? I'm drunk with existence—a drunkard. And I allow you to come nearer to me to be drunk with me, to participate. And the closer you come, the more drunk you will become. And a moment comes when the disciple and the Master sit silently—nobody knows who the disciple is and who the Master is. They have come so close, like two flames coming closer and closer and closer, and a sudden jump—and the two flames have become one.

To understand a Master you need to come close. With a teacher you can remain as distant as possible. There is no problem: closeness is not needed, intimacy is not involved. With a teacher you remain uncommitted. With a Master, the final, the utterly final commitment is needed. That is the meaning: 'You can't have anything from me until you die.' That is the meaning of this Sufi saying, because when you die then you are totally committed. Now there is no going back. There is nobody else you can fall back upon.

A commitment is a point of no return. Where will you go

back to? You have burnt the house. A cunning mind would like to be distant; not a participant, but an observer. Keeping the distance he keeps his house intact, so if something goes wrong he can go back, he can fall back. But all that is beautiful in life comes through commitment.

In the West, particularly, 'commitment' has become a wrong word, a taboo word. The moment you hear 'commitment', you become afraid. That's why in the West all that is beautiful *and* the deepest, is disappearing. Love is not possible; only sex is possible. Sex is without involvement; love is a commitment. Sex is between two strangers; love is between two who are intimate, not strangers, who feel an affinity—who are not there just to exploit each other, but to grow with each other. A commitment is needed in love. And without love, sex will become futile. It has already become so in the West.

Meditation is not possible if you are not committed. You cannot remain a spectator. If you want to be a spectator, then you will remain on the periphery. Commitment leads you to the very center of things.

To be with a Master is a commitment. It is the highest form of love, the highest form of meditation, the highest form of prayer. In the West, only teachers have existed. In the West, 'teacher' and 'master' are not two totally different words; they are synonymous, they mean the same. That's why in this story 'master' is translated as 'teacher'. Bahaudin is not a teacher: he is a Master. But in English there is no difference between a Master and a teacher. In English there exists no word like *guru*. It is a deep involvement with a person, such a deep involvement that you are ready to die for it.

Love, meditation, prayer, all are deep commitments.

And who is afraid of commitment? The ego is afraid of commitment—because commitment means now no more going back. The bridge is broken. You feel afraid. Only the future, the unknown future is there; past is no more. You will feel dizzy. And if you look in the eyes of a Master, you will feel dizzy—because he is vacant. It is like an abyss with no bottom to it. You would like to cling to something because there is danger, you will be lost for ever.

And this is so! But you cannot find yourself unless you are lost. And you cannot be reborn unless you die. A Master is a death and a life. A Master is a death and a resurrection.

Now, let us move slowly into this story:

> *A man came to the great Master Bahaudin and asked for help in his problems, and guidance on the path of the Teaching.*
> *Bahaudin told him to abandon spiritual studies and leave his court at once.*

Looks too cruel, too crude. Doesn't fit with the ideal of a Master. The man has come as a seeker, he wants help; he has come as a beggar—and this is no behaviour on the part of Bahaudin to say, 'Abandon spiritual studies and leave this court immediately, right now!'

Why is Bahaudin throwing him back? A Master exists to help, a Master invites people, a Master welcomes; he exists for that purpose—then why is Bahaudin behaving in such a bad way? No one expects such behaviour from a Master. And the man has asked only for some help in his problems, and guidance on the path.

> *A kind-hearted visitor began to remonstrate with Bahaudin.*

A kind-hearted man must have been there, and he said, 'What is this? Explain to me why you behave this way. And that man has not done anything wrong. An innocent seeker, and you throw him out—then what is the purpose of your being here? He asks for help and you close the door. He begs and you are hard.'

> *'You shall have a demonstration,' said the sage.*

Said Bahaudin, 'Wait! There are things which cannot be explained. Wait—you will have a demonstration.' Only a situation can explain certain things, because they become apparent only in an alive situation—explanation won't be helpful. And how can you explain?—because Bahaudin sees something in the seeker which this kind-hearted man cannot see. How can you explain light to a blind man? No explanation will be explanation enough. And whatsoever you say will look like a rationalization, will look as though you are hard and cruel and now you are trying to rationalize your behaviour. Bahaudin said, 'Wait—you shall have a demonstration.'

> *At that moment a bird flew into the room, darting hither and thither, not knowing where to go in order to escape.*
>
> *The Sufi waited until the bird settled near the only open window of the chamber, and then suddenly Bahaudin clapped his hands.*
>
> *Alarmed, the bird flew straight through the opening of the window, to freedom.*
>
> *Then Bahaudin said: 'To him, to the bird, that sound must have been something of a shock, even an affront, do you not agree?'*

It is really a beautiful situation. Bahaudin is saying many things without saying them. He is saying: 'The man who has approached was just on the brink of total freedom. He does not need any help. Help will become a bondage to him; he will be burdened by it. He does not need any more teachings; that phase is passed. He is almost ready to fly into the sky. He does not need any training. He needed to be pushed and that's what I have done. If I had allowed him to be here, that would not have been compassion. Throwing him away from the door and closing the door is the compassion.' Bahaudin is saying, 'I know this man. His heart is absolutely ready. Any moment the bird will be on the wing—now no more clinging to words, no need for any teachings, no need to understand the path!'

It is a need: in a certain phase of spiritual growth you need teachings and all, and you need to be taught about the path; you have to be assured about it. You need many trainings, but a moment comes when one has to grow above them. First one has to learn many things, and then one has to unlearn. First one has to be taught meditation, and then one has to be taught to throw it into the dustbin. First one has to be brought out of concepts, words, and taught silence. And then a moment comes when you have to throw that silence also; otherwise, that too can become a clinging. You can cling to a thought, you can cling to silence—

because then silence is nothing but a thought of silence. How do you know you have become silent? It is again a thought. How do you know that now you are happy? It is again a thought. And if there is happiness, and the feeling of being happy, and the thought, then somewhere in the background there must be unhappiness lurking and waiting just like a shadow.

First one has to drop unhappiness and then happiness also, otherwise happiness itself will become a prison. And you are so skilled in creating prisons: you can create a prison out of anything —even out of God. You have created prisons: your churches, temples, mosques, *gurudwaras*—out of the Divine you have created imprisonments for yourself. Out of beautiful scriptures... the Upanishads are beautiful, their poetry is the purest, but nobody reads the Upanishads for poetry. You read the Upanishads for doctrine—they have become a prison. As poetry they are beautiful, they are wonderful; as poetry—incomparable, there is nothing you can compare them with.

Just now I was reading an interview with J. Krishnamurti by a journalist. I don't think that the journalist could follow him, what he was saying. Krishnamurti said: 'I have read the New Testament. It is beautiful poetry and I loved it, but as scripture I get bored.' He is absolutely right. One should read the Bible: it is really one of the greatest literary accomplishments of the ages. And the New Testament is simply superb. Nowhere else can you find words so pregnant with significance—but not with meaning, because the moment meaning comes in, poetry is lost: it has become a doctrine. Significance, but not meaning. Grandeur, beauty, but no dogma.

Out of the Upanishads, the New Testament, the Koran— such beauty! If you can sing—beautiful! If you think—you have lost the track. If you can sing the Koran, nothing is so beautiful. Have you seen somebody reciting the Koran? It is something to be recited, to be sung, enjoyed. You can dance, that's okay, but don't think about it. The moment you think, a Mohammedan is born, a fanatical Mohammedan. If you love, enjoy, dance, sing, a Sufi is born. And a Sufi is farthest from a Mohammedan, the farthest possible. If you sing the Upanishads, a Sufi is born. If you believe in the Upanishads, a Hindu is born, a dead Hindu, rotten to the roots.

You are so skilled in making imprisonments for yourself that everything that falls to your hands becomes a chain. Even a Buddha, a Jesus, they come to liberate you, they try to liberate you, and finally they become a bondage—because. . .because of you.

This man who reached Bahaudin was ready, ripe to fall from the tree. Not even the slightest help was needed. Bahaudin could have allowed this man to sit in his court, to become part of it, to become a disciple—that would not have been compassion, and *no* Bahaudin can allow that. But on the surface he looks unkind; he looks as if he is without any compassion: a seeker comes and you close the door in his face. Remember: that is the difference between kindness and compassion. Kindness is something understood on the surface. Even an ignorant man can be kind, even a foolish man can be kind, even a criminal can be kind, a sinner can be kind—kindness is just a value on the surface of the mind—but an ignorant man cannot be compassionate. That's not possible. It is a quality that happens when the center has been achieved. When you are centered, then compassion happens. And compassion may not always look like kindness, remember; compassion may sometimes look *very* unkind.

The kind man, the kind-hearted visitor, remonstrated with Bahaudin: 'What have you done?' Bahaudin sees something which the kind-hearted cannot see. He has seen the man just on the brink of the abyss. If he is thrown out, he will be liberated. If he is allowed. . .and he is ready, he has come to seek discipleship. If he had gone to a teacher, a teacher would have been very kind-hearted, he would have received him. A teacher would have initiated him, but not a Master, because a Master is to help you to be totally free. If he initiates, it is just as a step, it is not the end. Finally, eventually, he is going to throw you into the open sky.

Once you are ready, you will be thrown into the open sky. A Master's house is just a training place where you get ready, but it is not the final home. It is where you get ready, and then the Master throws you into the sky because there is the final home, in total freedom—in *moksha*. A Master is helpful just on the way.

Before the temple of the Divine, he will suddenly leave you. Before the temple of the Divine, he will push you in, and if you look back you will not find him any more, he will not be there—because with the Divine you have to be alone. The work of the Master is completed.

But this man was already on the brink. He could not know it. How can you know that you are on the brink? You have never been on the brink before, so how can the mind understand? This man who is on the brink does not know; he has never been in this state before, so how can he recognize? He is seeking support. Not knowing that now there is no need for support. And if he is allowed to sit, many more things will happen which can be dangerous. I know that if Bahaudin allows him to sit, this man may fall in love with Bahaudin—it is difficult not to fall in love with Bahaudin—that love will become a bondage. You are so skilled, you are so efficient. So it is better to be hard from the beginning. If even for a single moment the man is allowed, it will be difficult for him to leave Bahaudin. The man should not be given even a glimpse of Bahaudin's heart, his love, his compassion. Bahaudin must show him a very hard face so he never thinks about Bahaudin again.

This was what Gurdjieff was doing to many disciples and they couldn't understand, because in the West it is difficult to understand. The East has its own ways. Gurdjieff was a Sufi: he was taught by many Sufi Masters, he moved in many Sufi monasteries, he lived with many Sufis, and he had the attitude of a Sufi. But in the West the understanding is not there; Sufi symbols, Sufi demonstrations, are not meaningful.

I was reading one book written by a disciple of Gurdjieff—a woman, a very talented musician—and she writes that Gurdjieff was angry about something she was told not to do and she had done. He was very angry and he told her: 'This is the last—*never* come back again and *never* come to see me.' Of course, the woman left him, but she left as a Westerner and missed. She thought: 'This man is not yet Enlightened; otherwise, why is he so angry?' You judge according to your own criteria. 'Why is he so angry? For such an ordinary thing. If I have disobeyed in such a trivial thing, he could have forgiven me! Great Masters are forgiveness, embodied forgiveness. Buddha is compassion, and Jesus forgives even his enemies, the murderers who killed him—he forgives them! And I have not committed anything like that. Just a small thing he has said, and I have not followed it—there seems to be no reason to be so angry.' And she had lived almost for twenty years with Gurdjieff; a disciple of twenty years' standing simply thrown out and the door closed. And Gurdjieff said, 'Never see me again. If you want to see me, then only when I am dead.' The ego was hurt. And she never went to see Gurdjieff again; she went only when he was dead—but she missed.

What was Gurdjieff saying? If in the East this had happened, where through a long, long, inner disciplehood, an inner discipline of many people, it would have been totally different. What was Gurdjieff saying in fact? He was saying: 'Either you come to see me dead, or you come to see me when I am dead; otherwise there is no point.' But that was implied. So she waited for twenty years more, when Gurdjieff died, then she went to pay her homage. She could have been dead herself. That was a situation. Gurdjieff was not angry because she had disobeyed: that anger was creating a situation; that disobedience was just something to hang it upon. Gurdjieff would have been angry whether she had obeyed or disobeyed; that was irrelevant. He would have found something and would have been angry. That was needed: a hard face, very angry, because a person who has lived with him for twenty years should not be deceived by the surface, should be capable of penetrating deeper, looking into the heart. And in the heart, Gurdjieff was so compassionate, so loving, but he had a very hard shell around him.

This woman who was thrown out, if she had a Western attitude. . .we don't know, the story says nothing about her, what happened to her; but it will be good to know, in fact, what is possible. If she had a Western attitude—a Western attitude means an egoistic attitude—if she thought that she had been thrown out because she was not worthy, if her ego was hurt, she would miss. If she had an Eastern attitude: If the Master is angry there must be compassion in it, otherwise why should he get angry? If the Master has closed the door there must be meaning in it, because by closing this door some other door is opened. If the Master has said to abandon *all* spiritual studies and leave his court at once, not even a single moment is to be wasted, that means there is some urgency, urgency in leaving all spiritual studies, the spiritual path, the seeking, everything; there is some urgency. If the attitude had been Eastern, that of a disciple, that of a humble person, that of one who is ready to die, that woman would have become Enlightened—just at that door, just that moment. But it depends. It doesn't depend only on the Master, it depends on the disciple also. It is a subtle cooperation, the subtlest harmony there is.

> *A kind-hearted visitor began to remonstrate with Bahaudin.*
> *'You shall have a demonstration,' said the sage.*
> *At that moment a bird flew into the room . . .*

And every moment birds are flying into the room, because every moment situations are flying into the room. Situations are never lacking. If you have the Master touch, if you have the Master key, everything becomes a situation. You can turn anything into a situation—it becomes a demonstration. A bird flew in. And as it happens, not only with birds, but with you too, as it happens with all types of minds. . . . You may have sometimes observed: a bird enters into the room—he has entered by the window, so he must know where he has entered, but the moment he has entered he forgets about the window; then he darts hither and thither. He looks very foolish, because he has entered and he knows, so why not go back by the same window? Why go hither and thither? And the more hectic, afraid, the bird becomes, the more the source is lost. Then a miracle happens: that the bird will go to every wall and knock his head, but not to the window. Don't laugh at the bird. The bird is poor—poor bird! But the same is the case with you.

Every day I encounter people who know how to enter into a situation, but don't know how to get out. You enter into a marriage, then it is difficult—how to get out? You know the window—how did you enter in the first place?—then why not step back? Disillusioned, you want to get out. Why is it so complex? Why can't you understand the thing and get out? It is very easy to get into a marriage; it is very, very difficult to get out of it. Everybody knows how to get in and nobody knows how to get out. You become angry—you never go to ask anybody how to be angry—and then you come to me and ask, 'How to get out of anger?' But how did you get in? The same phenomenon happening: the bird knows how to get into the room, and forgets completely. . . .

It seems that somewhere in the mind there is a deceptive mechanism; otherwise, why the problem? It is so apparent. The window is open, the bird has come in—go *out* by the same window! But it seems there is an idea in the mind, somewhere in the unconscious, that for going in a different route is needed, and for going out a different route is needed. That is the trouble. You get into anxiety and then you ask how to get out. You are in anguish and then you enquire how to get out. But how did you get in?

It happened: Mulla Nasrudin was walking with his child, and the child saw an unfamiliar egg lying down by the side of the road. And as children ask, he asked his father, 'I always wonder how the birds enter into the egg?'

Mulla Nasrudin said, 'I also wonder—but I wonder how they get out of it. And I don't know the answer. I have been wondering my whole life and now you have created a new question. I have not come across the answer as to how they get out of it, and now you have created a new problem: how they get into it.'

Somewhere in the unconscious the mind has a deep-rooted mechanism. It feels that there must be two ways: how to get in and how to get out. No, there are not two ways. It is the same: by the same door you enter and by the same door you get out. And if you can understand how you get in, you can understand how you get out. So when you become angry, just watch how you are getting into it. Step by step, slowly, watch—and suddenly you will be illuminated! You will feel a sudden light, that this is the way how you have to move backwards.

The bird entered.

At that moment—when Bahaudin said, 'Soon I will demonstrate'—a bird flew into the room, darting hither and thither, not knowing where to go in order to escape.

This is the situation of everybody. You have entered into life. Now you are darting hither and thither, not knowing how to escape, where to escape.

All techniques of meditation are nothing but aids to make you aware how you have come in. It is going backwards. When your mind becomes silent, you will be able to go backwards. You can relive the whole film backwards. You move towards childhood, then you move into the womb. And then a moment comes when you see the first thing: how you entered the womb. Your mother and father created only a situation. In that situation you moved in. The window was open—you moved in. And the same is the way to move out. Deeper meditations will reveal to you your whole past, not only of this life but of other lives also. Buddha talks of his many lives: how he was an elephant and how he died, and how he became a hare and how he died, and how he became a lion and how he died, he relates, and how he became Siddhartha.

Just moving backwards you come to the very door by which you entered into existence, and that is the door from where you can fly out. But it will need a very, very silent mind, alert, watchful, intelligent.

The Sufi waited until the bird settled...

In stories like these every word is significant.

The Sufi waited until the bird settled...

You cannot help a bird out while the bird himself is trying to seek the way out. You cannot. Your help will be more of a disturbance to the bird. You will make him more hectic and crazy. He will lose all consciousness if you try to help in that moment. And this is how I have to watch. Many times you come to me and you are so unsettled, so confused, that if I start helping you right now, it will confuse you more. I have to wait—when you settle, the confusion settles a little, things drop back into the unconscious.

By coming to me, everybody becomes unsettled. It has to be so—mm?—because you are entering a totally new way of life. It is as if a house was closed for many years, and then you open the door. For years dust has settled in the house; you enter the door and the dust is stirred, and everything becomes cloudy and confused. When you come to me you open a door in your own house that you have closed for many years, or many lives; much dust has settled there. When you open the door and a new wind starts flowing, everything is stirred. Everybody who comes to me becomes confused, more confused than he was ever. But this is natural.

And in that confusion if you escape from me, you have escaped a very potential situation. Many escape. They think that because of me they have become unsettled. No. Because of me they have entered into their own unconscious. Of course, dust has arisen, the mind has become cloudy, one doesn't know where one is, what one is. The old identity is lost. A trembling, a feverish state—and you want me to help you immediately. Of course, you think you need help immediately; but if I do something immediately, that will stir more dust in you. I will have to postpone a little. I will console you, but I will not do anything. I will promise you, but I will not do anything. I have to be a liar many times—because of you—otherwise you won't be able to understand. I can help you only when the bird has settled, then something can be done. Now the bird is in a situation where something can be of help.

The Sufi waited until the bird settled near the only open window of the chamber, and then suddenly clapped his hands.

The bird has settled near the window. Now the bird is not so crazy about getting out. When you are too crazy about Enlightenment, it is not possible. When you are obsessed about meditation, it is not possible. When you set a little, everything becomes possible. When you are in a fever, the first thing is to help you to come out of the fever. Right now nothing else can be done. No other training, no other discipline, is possible right now.

So whenever people come to me, I tell them: 'Just rest for a few days, settle, feel yourself at home,' then—*then* I can clap my hands. The Sufi—what did he do?—then he suddenly clapped his hands. Afraid, scared, shocked, the bird flew out of the window.

Alarmed, the bird flew straight through the opening of the window, to freedom.

Then Bahaudin said: 'To him that sound must have been something of a shock, even an affront, do you not agree?'

He asked the kind-hearted man, 'What is the attitude of the bird? The clapping of my hands must have been a shock, but that is the only way to help him. It was hard, it must have been an affront, but only through it did the bird achieve freedom. Now he is high in the sky, flying. Now he will be feeling thankful towards me; but when I clapped my hands, then the bird must have felt angry, the bird must have felt that I am hard, an enemy. The bird was scared, but now, when the bird is on the wing and enjoying the sky again, totally free, now he can be thankful towards me, now he can feel grateful.'

Many times I will hurt you. Many times I have already hurt you. Many times you will be shocked. Many times you will see the enemy in me, not the friend. But this is how it is—natural. I don't expect anything else right now. It is not possible for you. But when you are on the wing, moving into the infinite sky, then you will understand those hurts, that I had to hurt you. They were not because I was hard: they were the only way to help you. Then only will you feel grateful.

It happened: In a Zen monastery in China, a Master was celebrating his Master's Enlightenment day; the Master was dead. In China, a disciple celebrates the Enlightenment day of his Master only if he is an initiated disciple, otherwise not. People of the nearby villages gathered and they asked this Master who was celebrating his Master's Enlightenment day, 'Why are you celebrating? Because we never heard that you were ever accepted by the Master or initiated. Rather, on the contrary, rumour goes that when you had asked to be initiated he rejected you, you were thrown out. So why are you celebrating?'

The Master laughed and he said, 'Because he rejected me—that's why. His rejecting was the initiation, but at that time I couldn't understand it. Had he accepted me, I would not have been Enlightened so soon. He rejected me out of deep compassion. And his very rejection was the initiation; in his very rejection he accepted me. He said, "You don't need it." He said, "Go away! as far away as possible from me, otherwise you will make a prison out of me." And when *he* rejected me, I felt very much hurt; I carried the wound for years. And the wound was so painful that I never tried with any other Master. I became so afraid! I simply moved into the forest and started sitting on my own, because if this compassionate man had rejected me, who would accept me? This was the last shelter and the doors had closed. Now there was no shelter for me.

'Feeling unworthy, wounded, hurt, I moved. I never tried, I never knocked on any other Master's door again. I became so scared. But sitting silently, not doing anything—because I didn't know what to do: the Master had rejected me, he had not given me any method, any technique, nothing—feeling lonely, remaining lonely, in the beginning it was sad, in the beginning it was negative. In the beginning, I was continuously feeling the rejection. But, by and by, sitting silently, the rejection disappeared, sadness disappeared, because how long can you be sad? It comes, it goes. By and by, loneliness disappeared: I became *alone*. And, by and by, I started to feel that maybe the Master had rejected me just to throw me into my aloneness there in that forest. Maybe he had said that no method was needed—you just sit silently—maybe he had rejected me so that I wouldn't start clinging to him. By and by, the wound was there no more. It healed. And I started feeling deep love for the Master. And, by and by, the love became trust. And one day, suddenly, I realized and laughed loudly, a belly laugh, because this Master was something strange: he had initiated me through his rejection! That's why I am celebrating his Enlightenment day. I am his disciple: he initiated me through rejection—I have been initiated. I am *his* disciple. I am Enlightened because of him. And it would have been cruel had he accepted me.'

Subtle are the ways. And you cannot judge with your crude criteria. Your criteria are just on the surface.

Alarmed, the bird flew straight through the opening of the window, to freedom.

Bahaudin said: 'To him that sound must have been something of a shock, even an affront, do you not agree?'

And I ask the same to you: Do you not agree?

If you feel that the agreement is difficult, that means the ego is strong. If you feel that agreement comes, flows into your being, then the ego is not strong. And you cannot have anything from me until you die—don't you agree?

14 April 1975

V
Truth is not Veiled

A man came to Bayazid and said that he had fasted and prayed for thirty years and yet had not come near to an understanding of God.

Bayazid told him that even a hundred years would not be enough.

The man asked why.

'Because your selfishness is working as a barrier between yourself and the truth,' said Bayazid.

TRUTH IS not veiled. It is not hidden. It is always just in front of your eyes. If you miss it, it is not because of it, but because your eyes are closed. The veil is not on the face of truth: the veil is on you. And not only one—many, millions of veils.

If truth were hidden, then one Buddha, one Mohammed, or one Zarathustra, would have been enough. Once uncovered, everybody would have known it. It would have been just like it is in a scientific discovery—you need not discover it again and again. Albert Einstein discovers something. It becomes a common property. Then every schoolchild knows about it. It need not be discovered again. Once discovered, it is discovered.

But what happens? A Buddha discovers, a Mohammed discovers again. You will have to discover it again. What is the matter? The matter is this: that the veil is not on the truth—otherwise, one man would have unveiled it and everybody would have realized it—the veil is on you. So everybody has to unveil himself, and truth has to be discovered again and again by each and every one of you. It can never become a common property. It can never become a collective truth. It will remain individual.

But why are your eyes closed? There must be some great investment in them, in the closed eyes. And there is. And that has to be understood. If it is just a matter of opening the eyes, then why don't you open them? Who is holding you back? Who is preventing you? Truth is naked, absolutely nude. That is the nature of truth—you can call it God—and it is just in front of you, and it has always been so. But why don't you open your eyes? There seems to be a great investment.

It happened once: A woman was brought to me. She was a very beautiful person. Her husband died, and they had been married for only three months. And they had loved each other tremendously, against the whole society, the whole world. They had left everything just for their love. And suddenly the husband died. It was too much for the woman, the poor woman. She remained with closed eyes for three days. She wouldn't open them —because deep down she knew that if she opened her eyes . . . the husband is dead, the corpse is there. People tried to persuade her, they did everything, but she would not open her eyes. And she would go on saying, 'My husband is not dead. Who says my husband is dead?' They couldn't wait any longer: the body had to be burnt.

The day they burnt the body, the woman opened her eyes. But by that time she had lost the capacity to see!—a very deep investment. Eyes were perfectly okay, no physiological trouble. The medical doctors were amazed. They said, 'There is no problem! Everything is perfectly normal.' But she couldn't see. It was as if somebody behind the eyes had stepped back; somebody who was standing behind the eyes and looking at the world had stepped back. Now the window was there, but nobody to look through it.

For four weeks she remained psychically blind. And in her blindness she was continuously saying, 'Who says that my husband is dead? If he is dead, then where is his corpse? If he is dead then *where* is his corpse?' Even in dreams, in the night, suddenly she would start saying, 'Who says my husband is dead?' And she knows! Deep down she knows that the husband is dead, but the mind would not like to believe it. The mind would like to live in an illusion. Even an illusion is beautiful if the husband is alive, and the reality will not be so beautiful if the husband is dead. They had really loved each other very deeply.

The woman was brought to me. I had known them before. When she came to me, she was behaving as if she was completely blind. Somebody had to help her. I said to her, 'Your husband is very much troubled. Just this morning he has been to see me and he is suffering very much. Why don't you see!—and the medical experts say there is nothing wrong with your eyes.' I talked as if the husband was alive—now this was too much. Suddenly she broke, fell down, started rolling on the ground, and said, 'My husband is dead. Why do you say he has been to you this morning? He is dead!' And the eyes came back. Suddenly the stony feeling in the eyes disappeared—she was able to see.

What to do? What happened? Suddenly she realized a fact which she had been denying. Through the denial a false blindness had happened. Once she accepted the fact that the husband was dead, she screamed. I have never seen anybody scream that way. That must be what Janov calls the primal scream. From the very guts she screamed. It was not a scream done by her. It was a scream that possessed her whole being, every pore of it. The whole body-mind went into a volcanic state. The whole being trembled. It took almost half an hour for her to come back to normal. But the storm had gone and she was silent, and she looked at me and she thanked me.

This is the problem with every man. You know many things, but still you want to pretend against them. And there is no possibility of your ever being victorious against the truth. Nobody can be victorious. You can try for many lives more, as you have tried for many lives up to now, but *against* the truth there is no victory. Victory is always *with* the truth. You can create illusions, you can live in a blindfolded world of your dreams, you can live with closed eyes, but that makes no difference—your fictitious world is fictitious, and the truth is waiting there. And the more you live in the fictions, the more you will be afraid of their being shattered. This is the investment.

For example: you believe that you are somebody. Everybody believes that he is somebody special. And you know that it is not true, that it cannot be true. Deep down you realize the fact that nobody *is* somebody. Nobody is nobody! That somebodiness, the ego, is a false entity, a fiction. You cling to it knowing well it is not there. Still you hope against hope. You go on pretending. You go on trying to support a false entity—by money, prestige, power, knowledge, austerities. You go on trying to prove that you are somebody. You go on proving that you are the center of the whole world. And you know well that this is not true. How can you be the center of the world? The world was there when you were not, and the world will be there when you will not be there.

You are just a wave, and waves come and go. Only ocean exists.

You don't have any center. You can't have because the center belongs to the Whole. A part cannot have a center. Can my hand have a center of its own? If my hand has a center of its own, then it is no more a part of me—it exists independently. Can my leg have a center of its own? Then it is no more a part of me. Then when I say I would like to go for a walk, he may not like to—he has a center of his own—and he will say, 'No, I am not willing. At least not at this time. You will have to wait.' And I am hungry and I would like to eat, but my hand says, 'No, I am feeling sleepy and I won't move.' No—when you feel hunger, the hand moves. Even without any order, without any specific order being given to it, the hand moves. When you want to go for a walk, the legs simply move. You don't *order* them. They simply follow! They are parts, they don't exist separately. They exist in an organic unity.

Man exists as a part of the Whole, an organic part. You cannot have a center of your own. If you think you can, you are misguided. Only God has the center. Only the center of the Whole can say 'I'. When *you* say 'I', and if you believe in it also, then you are deluded. If you use it only as a linguistic device, then it is okay. But if you feel that you have an 'I' within you, then you are living in an illusion—knowing it well, because how can you avoid knowing the truth? There are many moments when you suddenly become aware that you are just a part of the Whole, a wave, but you go on postponing this realization, you go on postponing the recognition of the fact, and you go on pretending.

This pretension is the barrier.

You know well that you have not loved anybody, neither your father nor your mother, nor your wife nor your husband, children, friends—no, you have not loved anybody. You know it

112

well, but still you avoid it. And you go on thinking that you love. And you go on thinking that you are a great lover. If you were a great lover, you would have already attained. Even if you had loved a single person totally, the God would have been unveiled already, the Truth in its total nakedness would have been realized —because love is death of all pretensions.

When you love a person, you cannot pretend anything which is not true. When you love a person, you become completely naked, you reveal yourself. All pretensions drop in the moment of love. And suddenly you realize that whatsoever you have been thinking you are, you are not. Something else arises—an organic unity with the Whole. The self disappears and the no-self appears. You are, but now not separate; not a stranger, but a part of the Whole. And not simply a part because a part can be a mechanical part—an organic part of the Whole.

What do I mean when I say 'an organic part'? It means that you cannot exist without the Whole, and the Whole cannot exist without you either. This is the beauty of the realization of no-self.

For the first time, when you are not, your absolute significance is realized.

Up to now you were trying to prove that you were very significant, and nobody believed you, not even you yourself. Now you know that you are not. And suddenly, in this empty house, a harmony comes in, a music is heard. Suddenly, the Whole starts celebrating your no-selfhood. Buddha has called this *anatta*, the realization of no-self. And this is freedom.

Freedom is not of the self. Freedom is from the self. You are no more there, that's why you are free. If *you* are there, you can never be free. You are the bondage.

Listen to this cuckoo-bird. . . . The bird is not singing. The song is happening. There is no ego inside manipulating the song. There is nobody who is trying to do anything. It is simply happening. In a state of no-self, you will sing a song without the singer being there; you will dance a dance, but the dancer will not be there. You will move and live, you will be ecstatic, but there will be nobody inside the house, the house will be totally empty.

And this is the reality. And you know right now that you are an empty house, but you go on pretending that you are somebody. And you go on posing false postures.

You have not loved, but you go on pretending that you love —because if you love, then how can pain exist? If you love, then how can suffering exist? If you love, then why so much agony? It is not consistent. If you have loved then you will be ecstatic, but you are not and you go on pretending. In the name of love you have done many other things but not love—because unless you die, you cannot love. Unless the ego disappears, the love cannot come to flower.

Then how can you pray if you have not loved? But you pretend. You go to the mosque, to the temple and to the church, and you pretend prayer. Whom do you think you are deceiving? You may be deceiving yourself—so your prayers are just like deserts; nothing grows out of them. Even in deserts something grows, but your prayers are absolute deserts. Nothing grows out of them. You continue, nothing comes out of it. You remain the same. And life is moving out of your fingers every moment. Every moment you are dying and you go on pretending.

Your whole life becomes a long pretension of things that are not. These things which are not have become the veils on you. God is not hidden. Truth is there—just in front of you, in its total nakedness. But you are hidden. You are covered in many veils. And you go on acquiring more veils—of knowledge, learning, of this and that.

Drop the veils. Don't pretend.

It will be difficult. That's why I say you have an investment in your blindness. It is very loaded. It will be difficult, it will be painful to drop the pretensions. You will pass through a suffering, but one has to pass through it. It is part of growth. Nobody can avoid it. If you avoid, you are avoiding your growth. If you avoid, then do whatsoever you want to do—nothing real can come out of it.

You will have to pass through the suffering of disillusionment —remember this word. You can live in illusions, and you can create beautiful illusions also, but if they are false—they may be beautiful—they are not going to help. You can dream beautiful dreams, you can become an emperor in the dream, but you remain the beggar. Soon the morning is coming, and soon you will have to open your eyes. And soon the sleep will have gone and dreams disappeared. And then you will come to know that you are a beggar. Beggars always dream that they have become emperors.

All your pretensions are dreams—to falsify, to deceive, to deceive the fact that is always there, to deceive the truth that is always around you. But how long will you do this? And what can you achieve out of it?

Pass through the suffering of disillusionment—that's the only austerity I know of. You need not go and stand in the hot sun. You need not prepare a bed of thorns and lie down on it. You need not go for self-torture. You need not become a masochist. You need not torture your body. Those are all foolish things, stupid. The only austerity is to see things as they are, to see that your illusions *are* illusions. The only austerity is to be disillusioned, to drop all hopes. And in those hopes, the hope for God is included, the hope for *moksha*, liberation, is included. In those hopes, the hope that you will attain to the Eternal is included. Your heaven, paradises, all are included. They are all illusions, extensions of the same ego.

Disillusionment is the gate—then you can be transformed.

Look at things in their reality, whatsoever the cost. If you feel that if you look at things as they are your ego will be shattered, let it be shattered—the sooner the better. If you feel that if you look at your being as it is, you will feel like an animal, feel—that's what you are. Your prestige in the society will be at stake, let it be—because the society consists of persons just like you: deluded. To be honoured by them is not an honour at all. To be honoured by sleepy men, dreamers, is not worth it.

It happened that Buddha was talking in a village. Many people had gathered—very few seekers; many more just curious people, inquisitive. A Buddha had come: they had gathered to see him and to listen to him—not sincere. Buddha said something and they all clapped, and Buddha became very sad and he stopped. Anand, Buddha's disciple, asked, 'Why have you stopped? and why have you become sad?'

115

Buddha said, 'I must have said something wrong, otherwise how could these people have clapped? I *must* have said something wrong! —because these wrong people cannot recognize the truth. Their clapping shows they have understood me. I must have been wrong; otherwise, how can they understand?'

Buddha is reported to have said that to seek respect from persons who are almost unaware, unconscious, is just like seeking honour from the rocks—even that is better. Your social identity may be lost; you were known to be a saintly man, and if you come to reveal your reality, people will know that you are just like them —even worse. Suffer it! This is the price which has to be paid.

And remember: only disillusionment can prepare you for the next step. In fact, if you are absolutely disillusioned with the life that you have been leading, the way that you have been, almost half the journey is complete. If a man can know a false thing as false, he has already attained to insight—now he is ready to know the true as true. The first step is to know the false as false. Then the second step automatically becomes possible: to know the true as the true. Truth cannot be known directly. First you have to know what untruth is, because that is *where* you are. And you can start the journey only from where you are.

Seek, watch your pretensions, and drop them. This is what an honest, sincere, authentic man should be—true to himself. And whatsoever the price is, pay it; it has to be paid. If you have not loved, know well that you have not loved. And say to your lover or beloved that you have never loved, that your love was a subtle process of exploitation, that your love was nothing but a trick, a diplomatic trick to dominate; that your love was nothing but a facade for your sexual desire, that your love was nothing but an ambition of the ego. Find out what it is and let it be known to you and to others also.

This is what a sannyasin should be: dropping all illusions, remaining true to his being, whatsoever it is. Then suddenly many things become possible to you. Once you are unveiled, truth is unveiled—because truth was never veiled.

Look at this small incident:

A *man came to Bayazid. . .*

Bayazid of Bistam is one of the great Sufi Masters.

> *A man came to him and said that he had fasted and prayed*
> *for thirty years and yet had not come near to an understand-*
> *ing of God.*

From the very beginning the man had a wrong attitude. He
must have been a very calculating and cunning man; otherwise,
how can you count moments of love and prayer? How can you
say, 'For thirty years I have been praying'? This calculation shows
a businesslike mind. Thirty years!—he's counting. He must have
been a man of this world: greedy, calculating. He has moved into
the other world, but his attitude remains the same: 'I have fasted
so many days, I have prayed so many prayers—and yet nothing
has happened?' In fact, if you know what prayer is, the result
doesn't matter. Prayer is its own result. The value is intrinsic. You
pray and it is enough! because prayer is happiness, prayer is
ecstasy. Unto itself it is enough. Nothing else is needed. But when
you don't pray, then you wait for the result. Then prayer becomes
a means to some end—understanding of God, realization of God,
or something else. But prayer can never become the means to any
ends. Prayer is an end in itself. All that is beautiful—love, prayer,
meditation—they are all ends in themselves, they are not means to
anything else. And if you convert them into means, you miss the
point. Enjoy them!

It is just like in the morning when you go for a walk, and the
sun is rising, and the new day is born, and again life resurrects.
Out of the death in the night, everything revives: the trees are
coming back, the birds becoming alive, and a fresh breeze is
blowing. You go for a morning walk and you enjoy it. Do you
keep a diary saying: 'I have been walking for thirty years in the
morning, and nothing has happened yet'? A morning walk is a
morning walk—end in itself, intrinsic. You enjoyed it! Every
morning walk enriched you. It does not enrich you somewhere
in the future; it enriches you right now.

Life is always cash—it is not a promissory note; it does not
promise you. Life is cash money: *immediately*, here and now, it
gives you whatsoever it can give.

117

You feel happy, you start singing, or you start dancing—do you count it? Do you keep a diary saying: 'For thirty years I have been dancing and singing and yet no understanding of God has happened to me'? You have not danced at all. You are not a dancer at all. You may be technically equipped to dance, but you are not a dancer. You may be a technician, but you are not a singer. And that is the difference between a technician and a dancer.

A dancer dances!—and in that very moment everything is achieved, because in that moment he is lost. The ego dies. There is no dancer. The dance exists, but no center to it. It is a wave in the infinite ocean, moving, being, dissolving—nobody there inside to manipulate the steps of the dance.

Then there is a technician, a trained dancer: he manipulates. Howsoever perfect his dance may be, it is dead—because the manipulator is there. Then he will calculate: how much. . . .

There is a beautiful story I would like to tell you. It happened in the life of a great Indian musician, Tansen. He was in the court of the great Emperor Akbar—and he is incomparable. Once Akbar asked him, 'I cannot imagine that anybody can surpass you. It seems almost impossible—you seem to be the last word. But whenever I think this, a thought arises in my mind that you must have been a disciple to a Master from whom you learnt, and—who knows?—maybe he surpasses you. Who is your Master? Is he still alive? If he is alive then invite him to the court.'

Tansen said, 'He is alive, but he cannot be invited to the court because he is like a wild animal. You cannot invite him to the court. Wheresoever it happens, he moves. He is not a man of the society. He is like the winds, or like the clouds. He has no roots in the society—a homeless wanderer. And then, moreover, you cannot *ask* him to sing or to play. That's not possible. Whenever *he* feels, he sings. Whenever he feels, he dances. We will have to go to him and wait and watch.'

Akbar was so enchanted, he was mad after Tansen: 'And his Master is alive—it is worth taking the trouble.'

'Wherever he is,' Akbar said, 'I will go.'

He was a wandering fakir. His name was Haridas. Tansen sent messengers to enquire as to his whereabouts. He was found near the river Jamuna in a hut. Akbar and Tansen went to listen to him. The villagers said, 'Near about three in the night, just in the middle of the night, sometimes, he sings and dances. But otherwise, the whole day he sits silently.' So in the middle of the night, Akbar and Tansen, hidden like thieves behind the cottage, were waiting—because if he comes to know, he may not sing.

But Haridas started singing, and then he started dancing. Akbar was hypnotized. He could not utter a single word because no appreciation would have been enough. He continuously cried. And when they were coming back, after the song stopped, he remained silent. Tears continued rolling down. When he came to the palace, just on the steps he said to Tansen, 'I used to think that nobody could surpass you; I used to think that you were unique, but now, now I have to say to you that you are nothing compared to your Master. Why so much difference?'

Tansen said, 'The difference is simple. I sing, I play, to gain something else: power, prestige, money, appreciation. My music is still a means to some other end. I sing to get something, and my Master sings because he has got something. That's the difference. He sings only when he has something inside—then the singing flows, then he dances. It is a by-product. When he is filled with the Divine and cannot contain it, when it overflows, then only does he sing. His singing is an end in itself. He celebrates!'

And that is the difference between a real love and a false love. A real love simply celebrates. For real love there is no future. A real prayer is a celebration. It is not an effort, not a means to something else. It arises and it dissolves into itself. A moment of prayer is an eternity in itself. And a man of prayer never counts. It is simply foolish! Even a single moment is *so* much, even a single moment becomes such a deep contentment—one is fulfilled. One doesn't ask for more. Really, it is too much. A single moment of prayer is so much—you are there no more. It fills you completely and it overflows.

If you can attain to a single moment of prayer, love or meditation, you will feel grateful for ever and ever. You will not complain.

The man was not a man of prayer. The man was greedy; he

must have been greedy in this world, in the market. He has left the market, but the mind of the market still is there. He has left the riches of this world, but the attitude is still the same. He is counting his prayer days like coins. He says that he has fasted and prayed for thirty years and yet has not come near to an understanding of God. He will never come to an understanding of God, because he has not changed at all. He has carried all his worldly attitudes into the other world.

And remember: Your attitude is your world. You cannot take it to the other world. You will make the other world just like the world you have left.

A man came to see me—he is a very rich man and he has been donating money to many institutions, social welfare schemes, temples, this and that. He came to see me and he talked about his donations. He started introducing himself, talking about his donations and how much he had given. And his wife supplied the missing information; she said, 'Almost one *lakh* rupees he has donated.'

The man looked a little angrily at his wife and said, 'Not one *lakh*—one *lakh* and ten thousand!'

Counting what you have given, keeping the account. When you keep the account, you have not given at all, you have not shared. It has not been a gift. When you count, it may have been a bargain—a bargain for the other world—and this man is bound to complain some day because he will say, 'I have given so much and I have not come any nearer to the understanding of God.'

Bayazid told him that even a hundred years would not be enough.

Even a hundred lives would not be enough. It is not a question of time. If you do a wrong thing you can do it for eternity—it is not a question of time. If you do a wrong thing, you can go on doing it, but just by repeating a wrong thing millions of times you will not become right. And if you do the right thing even only once, everything is settled.

So you can go on praying for millions of lives—nothing will happen. And I tell you: if you pray rightly even for a single moment, everything has already happened. It is not a question of time and quantity: it is a question of attitude and quality. How much you pray is not the question: how deep. How many times a day you pray is not the question. Mohammedans pray five times a day, and this man must have prayed five times a day for thirty years. It makes no difference how many times—five or fifty. The question is of the quality that you bring to it, of your consciousness, awareness, love—how you pray.

There is a story in Bengal: A man, a very, very logical man, a grammarian, was there near about five hundred years ago. His name was Bhattoji. He was a famous Sanskrit grammarian. He never went to the temple. He became old. He was sixty, then his father called him and said, 'Now it is too much.' His father must have been ninety, and the father said, 'I have been going to the temple, praying every day. I have not told you anything about it because I was hoping you might come to the understanding yourself. But it is getting late: now you are also old, sixty. It is time to go. It is time to prepare for the other world! When will you go to the temple and pray?'

Bhattoji said, 'Seeing you going to the temple every day and coming back the same, I have been wondering whether the question is not of how many times, how many years, you pray; the question seems to be of *how* you pray: the question is of quality. Because I have been watching you every day for so many years. Twice a day you go to the temple and you come back the same! The prayer doesn't seem to work. And how is it possible? There must be something wrong.

'I will go tomorrow. Tomorrow is my birthday and I will go tomorrow and do whatsoever I can do. I will put forth my whole being into it. Only once I will pray—but I will not leave anything inside me. I will move totally into it, but only once. If something happens, it happens. If nothing happens, I am finished. Then I will never go again, because what is the use? There is no point!

If I put myself totally at stake and nothing has been left behind, then more I cannot do the next day. More is not possible, if I have done whatsoever can be done with a total mind. Once

121

I will pray. If something happens, it happens. If not, I am finished. Then I am not going to pray again.'

The father laughed. He said, 'You are foolish. One has to do prayer for lives together, then only does something happen. But let us see; you go tomorrow and try.'

Bhattoji went to the temple—never came back again. He died. Standing before the deity of the temple, he prayed once and died. Really, he moved totally in it. Nothing was left.

A prayer, a love, needs you in your totality. Not even a part of you should be left behind watching and calculating, manipulating. You should be *in* it—not a fragment of you, but you in your wholeness. That's why prayer becomes holy, because you are wholly in it.

To be whole is to be holy and there is no other holiness.

Bhattoji died. This is the meaning of the saying: 'Until you die'—disappeared, attained. He became Enlightened. Only the body was there, the body fell down.

When Bhattoji was not coming back and it was getting late, the father sent a messenger to see what had happened. Bhattoji was not there, only the dead body was there. But you could see on the face a transformation, a divine beauty. Even the dead body was showing an aura of the Unknown. He was transfigured.

Remember this: that whatsoever you do should be true, not a pretension; should be done, not by a greedy mind, but by a loving mind; should be done without any calculations—because prayer, or love, or God, is not a question of arithmetic.

> Bayazid told him that even a hundred years would not be enough.
> The man asked why.
> 'Because your selfishness is working as a barrier between yourself and the truth,' said Bayazid.

The word 'selfishness' has to be understood. Ordinarily, you call a man selfish if he works everything for his own self, if he manipulates everything for his own self. That is superficial selfishness. You can become unselfish on that level; it is not difficult. There are unselfish people; people who are always working for others, serving, always helpful. Unselfish people you know, but they are as dangerous as the selfish people and sometimes even more. You can escape a selfish person, but you cannot escape an unselfish person. He is very dangerous—because he is out to help you, and he is working for you. He creates a burden. And deep down, very deep down, this unselfishness is again selfish, because through it he wants to achieve the Divine.

You go and see the Christian missionaries. They really work hard, they serve people, they are great servants, but deep down the whole service remains selfish because through it they are waiting to cross to the other shore. Through the service they are creating rungs in a ladder, and on that ladder they are moving towards heaven. Heaven is the goal, service is the means. They are in the same trouble as this man who came to Bayazid must have been.

I will tell you one story.

It happened: There was a great festival somewhere in China, and many people had gathered. There was a well without any walls around it and a man fell into it. He cried loudly but the festival was very big, and the crowd was very big, and it was so noisy that nobody could hear. Then a Buddhist monk, a *bhikku*, came to the well—he was feeling thirsty. He looked down. The man was crying and weeping and saying, 'Save me!'

The *bhikku*, the Buddhist monk, said, 'Nobody can save anybody else—this is what Buddha has said: Be a light unto yourself! Nobody can save anybody; that is impossible. Don't wait for it! And, moreover, Buddha has also said that everybody has to suffer his own karmas. You must have committed some sins in the past and you have to suffer, so suffer silently. Don't cry and make so much noise, because by crying and complaining you are again creating karmas.'

The man said, 'First save me and then I will listen to your sermon. At this time it is impossible for me to listen.'

But the Buddhist monk went on his own way because Buddha has said, 'Don't interfere in anybody else's karma.'

Then came a Confucian, another monk. He looked in the well; the man said, 'Save me! I am dying and nobody seems to listen.'

The man said, 'Confucius is right: he has said that every well should be made with a wall around it. And don't you worry—we will create such a great movement! and we will change the whole society, and we will force the government to make walls around every well. You don't worry!'

He said, 'But by that time I will be dead. And how is it going to help me because I have already fallen?'

The Confucian said, 'That is not the point; the individual is not the point. Individuals come and go—the question is the society. But you can die with the deep consolation in your mind that it will not happen again to anybody else.' Confucius is a social reformer.

Then came a Christian missionary. He looked in the well. Even before the man said anything, he opened his bag; a bucket was there with a rope—a Christian missionary, always ready to serve—even before the man said anything. Because he was feeling tired and he was thinking: 'Now there is no possibility. And these religious people are coming!' He threw the rope and the bucket and told the man, 'Catch it and I will pull you.'

The man was very, very thankful. When he came out he fell at the feet of the missionary and said, 'You are the only religious man!'

The Christian missionary said, 'Don't you be misguided—this is what Jesus says, that until you become a servant to the least and the last amongst you, you will not be able to attain to the Kingdom of God. Service is *sadhana*. It is through service that one reaches Heaven. So, remember well, fall again and again in the well, because I am not the only missionary. And teach your children also to fall in the well so we can come and save them, because how are we going to get to Heaven if you don't fall?'

Even unselfishness remains, deep down, selfish, part of greed, and very dangerous: because when a person feels he is good he becomes authoritative, dominating. And he tries to change you: he takes you in his hand like a piece of mud and tries to give you a shape, a shape according to *his* ideology.

Missionaries are murderers. All social reformers are danger- ous. And people who are seeking service can be very, very violent, aggressive. They are. If you are in the grip of a good man, it is very difficult to escape. You are imprisoned. And he is doing everything for your sake. And whatsoever he is doing, he is trying to find a way through you to his own heaven. You are just the means. And this is the *most* immoral act in the world, to treat a man as a means. I call it the most immoral act, the greatest sin, to treat a man as a means. Every man is an end in himself.

Share if you can share, but don't try to transform anybody. Who are you to transform? Who are you to change somebody? Who has given you the right? Help if you can, but don't make this help a means. Otherwise, in the name of religion also, you will remain the same calculating, cunning, clever person, exploiting people—because of your selfishness.

So this is one meaning of selfishness and unselfishness—on the surface. But *real* selfishness is when there is no self. Working for your own self is selfishness. Working for others' selves is unselfishness. But behind both the self is present, so they are both two branches of the same tree, not very different; the innermost core remains the same. Real selfishness means no-selfness; then whatsoever you do, whether the world calls it selfishness or the world calls it unselfishness, it doesn't matter—it comes out of a no-self, unmotivated. The distinction is subtle.

Selfishness is a motivated action: you want something for yourself. Unselfishness is again motivated: you want something for the other, and through the other, deep down, you want something for yourself; via the other the same motive moves. Real selfishness remains the same, the form differs.

To me selflessness is the real thing. You must come to understand the state of your being as no-self. Then prayer is there, but it comes from a no-self, unmotivated. Then you don't calculate and count. Then you enjoy it and celebrate it. Then love comes unmotivated. It flows spontaneously for no reason at all —you cannot help it. It is there. It is natural.

When the self is absent, then everything becomes unselfish. It cannot be otherwise. Otherwise, you can go on doing things: they will remain the same, the quality will not change; and you will always feel something missing. You can do prayer for years and you will feel something missing. You can love many people and you will feel something missing. You will remain like a wedding party where the guests have arrived, and the feast is ready, and the musicians are playing, and much singing and everybody is ready, but the bridegroom is missing. You will be like a wedding ceremony where the bridegroom is missing.

If the self remains, you will always miss something; whatsoever you do, you will miss something. Once the self is not there, the bridegroom has arrived. Now whatsoever you do will be a feast, whatsoever you do will be a celebration.

Die first as you are so that the Divine can be born in you.

Right are the Sufis when they say: 'You cannot achieve anything until you die.'

15 April 1975

VI
Man Carries the Seed

El Mahdi Abbassi *announced that it was verifiable that, whether people tried to help a man or not, something in the man could frustrate this aim.*

Certain people having objected to this theory, El Mahdi promised a demonstration.

When everyone had forgotten the incident, El Mahdi ordered one man to lay a sack of gold in the middle of a bridge. Another man was asked to bring some unfortunate debtor to one end of the bridge and tell him to cross it.

Abbassi and his witnesses stood at the other side of the bridge.

When the man got to the other side, Abbassi asked him: 'What did you see in the middle of the bridge?'

'Nothing,' *said the man.*

'How was that?' *asked Abbassi.*

The man replied: 'As soon as I started to cross the bridge, the thought occurred to me that it might be amusing to cross with my eyes shut. And I did so. . . .'

M AN CARRIES the seed of his misery or bliss, hell or heaven, within himself. Whatsoever happens to you, it happens because of you. Outside causes are secondary; inside causes are primary. And unless you understand this, there is no possibility of a transformation. Because the mind goes on deceiving you, the mind always points to the outside: the cause is somewhere else—of your misery, or of your happiness. If the cause is outside you, then there is no possibility of freedom, then there is no possibility of any *moksha*, any liberated state. Cause outside, then you are bound to be in bondage for ever and ever. Because how can you change the outside cause? And if you do change one, millions more follow.

This is the difference, the basic difference, between a religious mind and a non-religious mind.

Communists will think just the opposite. Marx will not be ready to approve what El Mahdi says in this story. Marx says the cause exists outside man. Man is in misery because there are causes outside which create misery. Man will be happy if the causes are changed, replaced. A revolution is needed, according to Marx, in the outside world. According to Mohammed, Jesus, Mahavir, Krishna, this whole diagnosis is wrong.

Causes are inside. Outside are only excuses.

You can change the outside, but nothing will change if the

inside remains the same. The inside will create, again and again, the same pattern whatsoever the situation outside, because man lives from the inner to the outer.

It happened: I used to know a man. He married thrice, and he suffered much. First time he married, he chose a woman who was a sadist, who enjoyed torturing him. He would come to see me and he would relate his misery. Sometimes the woman would beat him, and he would show me the marks. But I had the feeling that somehow, deep down, he relished it, he enjoyed it, because whenever he would be talking about his miseries, his face would become radiant, not sad; his eyes would sparkle, he would become more alive.

I continued to watch him minutely. Sometimes his wife would go to her parents' home; then he was never happy. When the wife was with him he was unhappy. When the wife was not with him he was unhappy. But both unhappinesses have a distinction and difference. When the wife was there he was unhappy, but *happy* in his unhappiness; he enjoyed it, talked about it. And I had the feeling he was exaggerating; he was very poetic about it.

Then the misery became too much and the man divorced the wife. The day he divorced, I told him, 'Now be very alert—because I think you will fall in love with the same type of woman again. Because *you* remain the same, you will find again the same type of woman. So now be alert.'

He said, 'Never again can I marry such a woman. I am finished for ever!'

But within three months he became a victim again of the same type of woman. And he got married. And again he started his sad stories: that the woman was torturing him. I told him, 'I told you that this was possible, because who will choose the woman? You will choose the woman. You chose the first, you will choose the second. And you remain the same!' And I told him, 'You will always choose a sadistic woman, because you are a masochist. You *want* to be tortured—somebody to dominate you, somebody to crush you. You are a self-condemner, you don't approve of yourself, and you don't love your-

132

self. You need somebody to hate you and to kick you around.'

The second marriage also finished soon. The wife left. The last time when I saw him he was again after a woman, and I told him, 'Now be alert! Something within you will again choose the same type of woman.'

He said, 'Now no more. What do you think I am? Am I so stupid? I cannot forget the lesson.'

And again he is married, and I have received a letter from him—again the same old tale of miseries.

This man can go on living for thousands of years, and this man can move all over the earth—he will always choose the same type of woman, because the chooser remains the same. The misery is not in the woman he chooses; the misery is in the very choice.

You carry your heaven within you. You carry your hell. And if you feel miserable, don't try to find excuses in the outside world. They won't help. In fact, they will become the deceptions. Whenever you are in misery, try to find something within you which frustrates. Be mindful of that. Otherwise, for many lives persons go on moving in the same rut, the same vicious circle.

Mulla Nasrudin dreamt one night that he was in Heaven. So beautiful all around—a silent valley, sun rising, and the birds singing, and he alone under a tree. But soon he started feeling hungry, and there was nobody, apparently nobody, around. But still he said, 'Hey! Is there somebody?' And a very handsome man appeared and he said, 'I am at your service, sir. Whatsoever you say I will do.' So he asked for food. And whatsoever he asked was immediately supplied. Not even a single moment was lost: the food was there. He ate to the full, slept well. And this continued. Whatsoever he needed . . . he needed a beautiful woman and the beautiful woman was there. Whatsoever he needed! He needed a bed in the night and the bed was there.

And it continued for a few days—but how long . . . ? He started getting fed up, bored. Everything was too good, really too much. He couldn't tolerate it. He started looking for some misery because everything was so beautiful. He started looking for tensions, because he had never lived without tensions, some anxiety, something to be sad about and depressed. And everything was so blissful, unbearably blissful.

So he called the man and he said, 'It is too much! I would like to have some work. Just sitting empty-handed, I am getting fed up.'

The man said, 'Everything I can do for you, but that is not possible. I cannot give you work. Here, that is not possible. Whatsoever else you need I am ready to give. And what is the need to seek for work? When everything is supplied immediately, you don't need to work!'

Mulla Nasrudin said, 'I am fed up! It is better to be in Hell then, if no work can be given.'

The man started laughing and said, 'Where do you think you are?'

By the laughter, Mulla awoke. His dream was shattered.

In the morning he came running to me and he said, 'This dream is very symbolic. What is the meaning of it?'

I told him, 'In the first place, you should not have waited so long. When you came to the point in the dream where you were in Heaven, immediately you should have opened your eyes. How can *you* be in Heaven? You, and in Heaven!—how could you believe it?'

Wherever you go, you will create your hell around you. In fact, heaven and hell are not geographical; they are not places, they don't exist in space. They are attitudes. They are psychological; they exist in the inner space, not in the outer space. You cannot go to heaven, because how can you go to heaven? Where is heaven? And you cannot go to hell.

You always carry your hell or your heaven around you.

It is just like a spider's web. In the Upanishads it is said— one of the most beautiful symbols—the Upanishads say that everybody is just like a spider carrying its own web inside. Wherever the spider goes, it spreads its web around; it brings it out of its own intestine. And whenever a spider wants to move, it swallows the web again, and moves!

You carry your heaven and hell just like a spider's web. And wherever you go you will create the pattern around you.

This has to be very deeply understood, as deeply as possible, because many things will depend on it. Your whole transformation will depend on it. And if you miss this point, then you will go on missing.

A man has been coming to me at least for ten years. He starts meditation: a few days, at the most a few weeks, and he feels very good. He feels simply wonderful. And when he is doing meditation he comes to me and says, 'Absolutely fine! Nothing else is needed. I am so happy—as I have never been.' And suddenly, one day, he stops. Then he disappears for a few months, forgets about me. Again he comes miserable, sad, in deep anguish, and I again tell him to start meditation. And I ask him, 'Why did you stop?—because you were feeling so great, you were feeling so beautiful.'

He says, 'When I am feeling beautiful and great, something within me always says, "Now there is no need to meditate!" And I stop. And then I again fall in the valley, in the darkness, and the misery comes in. And then I again come to you.'

And I asked him this time when he came, 'How many times has it happened? Can't you learn anything from experience? In ten years it must have happened at least thirty times.'

He said, 'This time I am going to stick.'

But I know it is not possible, because this promise he has given many times before. His promise is not reliable. Thirty times he has given me the same promise and broken it. And he is not aware at all of what he is doing. The moment he reaches near an explosion, the mind steps back and says, 'What is the need? Now you are so happy—why bother about getting up early in the morning? Why bother about doing meditation? Now everything is good. It is not needed. When the illness is not there one stops the medicine, so stop it!'

Again and again and again, and never coming to any understanding through it.

In *Mahabharata*, the greatest epic in the world, there is a story, a very beautiful story. The five *Pandavas*, the five brothers around whom the whole epic moves, have been thrown out of their kingdom, and they are moving as fugitives in a forest. One day they were feeling very thirsty, and one of the brothers, the youngest, goes to seek some water. He comes near a beautiful lake, but the moment he steps in the lake to fill his water-pot, he hears a voice. Some invisible voice says, 'Wait! Unless you answer my questions, you cannot take the water from this lake. That's the only condition: you have to answer my three questions. And if you can't answer, then you will fall dead here and now. The first question is: What is the most important thing about man?—the *most* important thing about man?' And the young *Pandava* couldn't answer—he fell dead.

Then another brother followed and the same happened. And then the eldest brother, Yudhisthira, went to the lake in search of water, and in search of his brothers to see what had happened to them.

Four brothers were lying there on the bank, and the moment he stepped in the water he heard the same voice: 'Answer these questions, otherwise you will also be dead. And if you can answer, not only will you be alive, you can also drink from the lake, and the same water will make your other brothers alive. Just sprinkle the water on their faces. But first answer my questions. And the first question is: What is the most significant factor about man?'

And Yudhisthira said, 'The most significant thing about man is that man never learns.'

He was allowed to drink the water, and he was allowed to revive his brothers.

In fact, this is one of the most important facts about man: that man never learns. You may become very knowledgeable, but you never learn. Knowledge and learning are different. Knowledge is borrowed: it is parrot-like; you cram it, it fills your memory; your brain becomes a computer. Learning is totally different. Learning means learning through experience, never repeating the same mistake again, becoming more and more mindful, alert, aware.

And this is the message of this Sufi story. Something in you continuously frustrates you, and unless you catch hold of it and destroy it, whatsoever you do will be futile. Whatsoever you do, *you* will do, and it will be futile. That factor within you which

136

continuously frustrates has to be dropped, has to be destroyed completely, burned.

You may have observed—the observation may not have been very keen and deep and penetrating, but you must have observed —observed in a mistlike state of mind, vague, shadowy, with a smoke-screen, but you must have observed that you continuously commit the same type of mistakes again and again. What a misfortune! You cannot even invent new mistakes. What an unoriginal, mediocre state of mind! Mm?—you cannot even think of new mistakes to commit. You go on committing the same mistake. You are like a broken gramophone record. It goes on repeating the same line again and again and again. It becomes a transcendental meditation: Ram, Ram, Ram. It goes on and on. Your life is a TM, a broken gramophone record. Have you observed that you go on committing the same mistake?—in your relationships, in your love, in your friendship, in your business, you go on committing the same mistake again and again. And you go on hoping that this time things will be different. They will never be—because you are the same. How can things be different? You are hoping against hope. But stupid is the mind. It goes on hoping, and knows well, deep down, that this is not possible because you will frustrate.

You fall in love with a woman, and everything is so romantic, so poetic. But this is not for the first time that it is happening. It has happened many times. Many times you have fallen in love and many times the world was poetic and romantic. And the world became a dream and everything was beautiful—and then everything turned ugly. The same beauty turns ugly. The same dream becomes a nightmare. The same heaven becomes a hell. And it has been so again and again. But you will fall in love again, and again you will forget—and the same will happen!

You are a repetition. And unless you stop this repetitiveness, there is no possibility of change.

How should one stop this repetitiveness? First, one has to realize that it is there. That is the basic step. One has to realize that this repetitiveness is there. You are working like an automaton, not like a man—just like a mechanism, repeating.

Man arises in you only when you are not a machine. Man arises in you when you start moving on fresh ways, when you start moving on new paths, when you start moving into the unknown.

You always move into the known: the same that you have done, you do again. And you become more and more skilled in doing it. You become perfectly skilled in committing the same mistakes again and again. You become predictable. No man, if he is really a man, can be predictable. Astrology exists—*jyotish* exists—because of your mechanical life; otherwise, nobody can predict the next moment. But it can be predicted. Out of ten thousand people, nine thousand nine hundred and ninety-nine people are predictable.

There is a beautiful story: Buddha became Enlightened. He was passing from one village to another, and it was hot, summer. He passed by a bank; the river-bank was wet, the sand was wet, and he left his footprints on the sand. By chance it happened that a great astrologer had completed his studies in Kashi, the citadel of Indian, Hindu learning, knowledge, and he was coming back to his home. He had completed his studies and he had become perfect in predictions. When he was coming back, he saw the footprints on the sand—and he couldn't believe it, because in *his* scriptures these were the footprints of a great emperor who rules the whole world. 'Why should an emperor, a *chakravartin,* who rules the whole earth, come on such a hot day to such a small poor village? And why should he walk with naked feet on the sand?' In the sand, all the symbols were there. So he thought: 'Either my whole science is false—this man seems to be a beggar, but my science says he is the emperor, the greatest emperor in the world, so either my science is false, or I will have to find this man. Maybe he is an emperor, and by some accident, by chance he has passed through here.'

So he followed the footprints. Buddha was sitting under a tree. He reached Buddha—he was more puzzled than ever, looking at him. He looked like an emperor, and he was a beggar. His whole being was like an emperor. No emperor has ever been like that. But he was a beggar, in rags!

So he asked, 'Please clarify my confusion—you have confused me. For fifteen years I have been in Kashi, I have wasted fifteen years of my life in learning the science of prediction. And now that I am complete and I have been examined, certified, you frustrate me completely. Just tell me: are you a beggar? Or are you a chakravartin, a great emperor who rules the whole earth? Because on your answer will depend my whole life. If you say you are a beggar, I throw these scriptures which I am carrying—they are worthless—into the river, and go to my home; I wasted my whole life unnecessarily. Or, if you are a chakravartin, then tell me.'

Buddha opened his eyes and he said, 'Your confusion is natural. But, by chance, you have come to the man who is one in ten thousand. About nine thousand nine hundred and ninety-nine your scriptures will always be right. Only about one your scriptures will be false. But you will not come across that one again, so don't bother and don't throw your scriptures in the river. It is almost impossible to come across this type of man again.'

The astrologer asked, 'What is the secret? How did you become unpredictable?'

Buddha said, 'By being mindful. I don't commit the same mistake again. I don't repeat the same pattern again. I have become a man: I am no more a machine. You cannot predict me. The next moment is unknown—not only to you, but to me also. It is absolutely unknown. It will grow. Nobody knows what will happen.'

A conscious being moves from the known to the unknown. An unconscious being moves from the known to the known—he moves in a circle.

So the first thing to realize is that you are a repetition. It will be very shattering to the ego, because you always thought you were very original. You are not. Mind is *never* original. It is always mediocre. Because the very structure of mind is accumulation of the known. The mind cannot know the unknown. The mind can move within the circle of the known; it can go on repeating the same that it knows, but *how* can the mind know the unknown? There is no possibility.

To know the unknown the mind has to be dropped—then

suddenly you are amidst the unknown. The Whole is unknown. Everything is unknown. Then the Whole becomes a beauty.

Known is dead. Unknown is alive. The Ultimate Unknown is what religious people call God. By 'Ultimate Unknown' is meant: whatsoever you know, it will remain unknown; howsoever you know, it will remain unknown—it is unknowable. You go on knowing.

So there are three movements. From the known to the known; that is mind. From the known to the unknown; that is consciousness. And from the unknown to the unknown; that is superconsciousness. Then a man becomes a sage. Then a man becomes a god himself, when he moves from unknown to un-unknown. Then he has dropped the mind completely. Then there is no past. And when the past is not there, there is no future.

Only this moment, *this* very moment, exists. Now and here everything culminates. In the herenow, the Whole exists, in its total beauty and nudity, in its total sacredness and wholeness.

Remember: mind is repetitive, mind is unoriginal, mind is a mechanical thing, a computer-like thing, a biocomputer. One has to go beyond it. If you don't go, the mind will continuously frustrate you. It will give you again and again the same pattern. That's why Hindus are fed up and they say, 'God, when will the moment come when we will be freed from the wheel of life and death?' Why do they call it 'wheel'? Because of the repetition: the wheel repeats. The same spoke comes again and again on the top, goes down, comes again on the top. A wheel moves, repeats itself. There is nothing more repetitive than a wheel. That's why Hindus call the world the wheel. Their word for world is *sansar*. *Sansar* means the wheel which goes on moving. And their only urge has been one: How to get rid of this wheel?

This is very symbolic. How to get out of this repetition? How to move into the everfresh? How to move into the everalive? How to move out of death and out of this life?—because this life is nothing but a prolonged death, a gradual death. A child is born and he starts dying at the same moment. He will be dead within seventy years. Slowly, slowly, he will die. He will take seventy years to die. This life is nothing but a gradual death.

The wheel of life and death is what mind is. The first step is to become aware of it.

Second step is to be alert when the mind goes again into the rut. If you can be alert, you have introduced a new phenomenon into it.

For example: you are again falling in love. Become alert. Nothing is wrong in falling in love. It is beautiful. Fall in love— but don't repeat. Be alert! Just by being alert you have introduced a new phenomenon which was not there before. And whatsoever you say to your woman or to your man, say it with full alertness.

It happened: Mulla Nasrudin fell in love with a woman. And I have been telling him continuously to be alert, so when he said to the woman, 'You are the most wonderful, the most beautiful woman in the world,' suddenly he remembered what I had said. So he said, 'Wait! Excuse me—this is what I have been saying to many women, and I am not certain that I will not say it again after you to others.'

A new thing has entered into it. Suddenly he became aware that he has been saying this continuously to many women: 'You are the most wonderful woman in the world.' And women are very, very faithful. They trust, they simply believe. And they know this is not true, but they believe. They are repeating their own frustrations, and man goes on repeating his mechanism. Otherwise a woman will say, 'Wait! No need to go too far. Love is good, but there is no need that a woman should be the most beautiful woman and that only then love can exist, otherwise the love will not exist for long. Wait! There is no need to go too far.'

Why not love an ordinary woman? What is wrong in being ordinary and simple and homely? Why create dreams? And then when you create dreams, they are bound to shatter some day, because dreams cannot become real. They will frustrate. And then just holding those dreams and false promises and words will become too much of a burden on you. Then the same woman will look like a stone in your neck. Don't do that! Why not be natural? Why not simply say, 'I love you'? What is the use of bringing superlatives into it which will have to be withdrawn sooner or later? And when you withdraw them, everything will come down, the whole palace will fall. You were making it on a false foundation.

Second thing to remember is: whenever you are going to repeat an old habit, give a jerk to yourself, become mindful, and suddenly you will feel a change. You are getting angry again—give a jerk, slap your face; go to the water-tap and throw cold water in your eyes. And be mindful. Just become a little alert. And just see that you are going again into the same pattern. The very alertness changes.

Now, physicists say a very surprising thing. They say that even matter, when you observe it, changes its behaviour—because in fact matter is also mind. For example, you are taking a bath in your bathroom, and then suddenly you become aware that a child is looking through the keyhole. Do you remain the same, or does suddenly a change happen? Suddenly everything has changed! Somebody is near the keyhole, and you are a different person. Just a minute before you were making faces in the mirror—now you are not making them. You were humming a song—now the song has stopped. Just a child, or anybody, looking, observing, a new thing has entered; you are not alone, an observer has entered into it—and observation is a transformation.

And this is not only with man; now they say it even happens with trees. If you observe a tree, it changes its behaviour immediately. When a friend passes nearby, the tree has a welcoming attitude, happy. It dances a little. It calls you, 'Come nearer!' And there are enemies also: children, animals, the gardener, and they are coming with their clippers—Mukta! The tree is suddenly shocked, shaken to the very foundation, afraid, closed. And now these are scientific findings, what I am saying. These are not poetic imaginations, or philosophers' doctrines—now scientists approve these things, that even trees have minds. And when you observe them with love, they are different. When you observe them indifferently, they are different. When you come to them to destroy, they are different.

Just by observation you change a tree, its behaviour. And physicists say that electrons change immediately when there is an observer. Electrons! We don't think they have life, we don't think they have minds—they have. Religion has been proved absolutely right within these twenty years of scientific research: that the Whole is alive—a vast ocean of life and consciousness. Nothing is dead! Even a rock is not dead. When an electron changes its orbit, behaviour, attitude, what does it show? What tremendous energy is possible through observation!

When you observe your own self, a new factor has entered, the greatest factor in life—the factor of observation. Suddenly things change, you cannot repeat the habit. A habit needs unconsciousness to be repeated. Consciousness enters, habit falls.

People come to me and they say, 'We cannot drop smoking cigarettes,' or, 'We cannot drop drinking alcohol. What should we do?'

I tell them, 'Don't try to drop it. Drink with awareness. Smoke with awareness. Don't try to drop it, because that you have been trying for years. And that effort has also become a habit. Now nothing can be done out of it. You smoke with full consciousness, with meditative awareness. You smoke and be there. You take, inhale the smoke inside, mindful that the smoke is going in. You exhale the smoke, mindful that the smoke is going out. And soon you will find, one day, the cigarette has fallen from your fingers—not that you have dropped it: it has fallen.'

With awareness habits drop. Without awareness, if you try to drop the habit it will be almost impossible. The only way to drop with unawareness is to create another habit, a substitute habit. That will do. You can drop cigarettes, then you start chewing gum. You can drop chewing gum, then you start chewing *pan*. You will do something stupid. It makes no difference whether you smoke or whether you chew gum; you have to do something stupid—because you cannot allow your mouth to be relaxed. Deep down in the mouth and in the lips there is a tension, and that tension is creating the habit. You can change one habit to another, but the same pattern will be there; chewing gum or smoking cigarettes makes no difference. The best way is to suck your thumb, which children do. But nobody will feel good, you will feel awkward, if you suddenly start chewing and sucking your thumb. Chewing-gum, cigarettes, are nothing but substitutes for grown-ups. Children enjoy their thumbs because they are not afraid of the society. When you are grown up, the same need is there somewhere in the mouth—something to be sucked. Maybe your mother didn't give you as much breast as you wanted; the breast was taken away earlier than it was needed. Or your mother was very reluctant to give you her breast. Even if she used to give it, she used to give it with deep reluctance. That has remained there, deep down; the lips have not been relaxed. They carry a tension. They create a habit.

You can change, but this won't help—unless you become aware. If you become aware, you will find a tension in the lips. If you become aware, you will find a constant activity in the mouth; the mouth wants to do something. Women smoke less—particularly in the East, because in the West, women are less women—women smoke less because they chatter much. That is their substitute. They go on talking—the same activity—they go on talking. Through their lips the tension is released.

I have heard that once there was a great competition in China: Who can say the most absurd and unbelievable thing? It was a great competition. And liars and deceivers and poets and gossip-makers and news-reporters—all sorts of people gathered. And the man who got the prize said a very simple thing. He said, 'Once I went into a park and I saw two women sitting silently on one bench—for five minutes.' And the judge said, 'This is the most unbelievable thing.' He got the prize, the first prize.

Something or other will have to be done, unless you become aware. You become aware, then you feel the tension. Don't do anything. Just be aware of the tension in the mouth, and the very awareness relaxes it. No need to relax even! Once you become aware that there is tension, it is already relaxing—because tension can exist only in an unconscious darkness. It cannot exist with the light of awareness.

So the second thing is to become more and more aware when you are repeating your old patterns.

And the third thing: whenever you find that there is some misery, always look within. The cause is there. Whenever you find you are feeling blissful, look within. The cause is there. If you look out you will find a false cause which is not really a cause but a projection.

It is just like in a film-house: you sit and on the screen there are pictures. They are projected. The pictures are really behind, at your back; they are in the projector. But the projector is at the back and your eyes are focused on the screen. On the screen there is nothing; the screen is empty—just light and shadow playing, making forms. You have got your projector inside, of bliss, of misery, of heaven and hell. You have got the Devil and the God within you. Whenever you feel that somewhere you see the Devil, look within. You will find him there. Others are only just like screens. They reveal your reality to yourself. They are not the real causes.

Now look at this beautiful anecdote.

El Mahdi Abbassi—one of the great Sufi Masters—*announced that it was verifiable that, whether people tried to help a man or not, something in the man could frustrate this aim.*

Certain people having objected to this theory, El Mahdi promised a demonstration.

It happened in a certain situation. A man had come, he was very poor, a beggar, in much debt, and El Mahdi could have helped him, because even the King used to come to this fakir, this Sufi Master. Just a hint from El Mahdi, and the King would have supplied everything that this man needed. That's why that man came to El Mahdi. And he was crying and weeping, and he was saying, 'Help me! You just give a hint to the King and my misery will be there no more. Otherwise, for the whole life, even if I go on working I will remain a slave, and then too I will not be able to pay my debts—they are impossible. And I have children, and a wife and relatives, and we are suffering very much. We don't even have enough to eat, no clothes.'

But El Mahdi said, 'It is not possible. I cannot say anything to the King.'

This was the situation.

Certain people having objected to this theory...

because El Mahdi said, 'Even if this man is helped, the help will not reach him. Something in him will frustrate it.' People like El Mahdi look deep. They don't look at your surface; they look deeper in you. He must have looked into, penetrated this man. He must have seen that something in him would make him again and again poorer, poorer and poorer; he would remain poor. 'He cannot be helped. The help will not be of any use because he carries something within him which will frustrate it.' So he said that whether people tried to help a man or not, something in the man could frustrate this aim. But certain people, kind-hearted, objected to this theory.

... El Mahdi promised a demonstration.

He said, 'I will give you a demonstration. Wait!'

> *When everyone had forgotten the incident, El Mahdi order-ed one man to lay a sack of gold in the middle of a bridge. Another man was asked to bring some unfortunate debtor to one end of the bridge and tell him to cross it.*
>
> *Abbassi and his witnesses stood at the other side of the bridge.*
>
> *When the man got to the other side, Abbassi asked him: 'What did you see in the middle of the bridge?'*

A sack of gold was put there. There was nobody else on the bridge, and the man crossed the bridge—he could have seen the sack of gold. He could have taken it, there was nobody to claim it—but he had not seen it even.

> *'What did you see in the middle of the bridge?' asked El Mahdi.*
>
> *'Nothing,' said the man.*
>
> *'How was that?' asked the Master.*
>
> *The man replied: 'As soon as I started to cross the bridge, the thought occurred to me that it might be amusing to cross with my eyes shut. And I did so....'*

Such thoughts occur to you also. And you also do so.

I have seen many people reaching to a point where something was immediately possible, and just then some thought occurs to them—sometimes so absurd you cannot believe why this thought should occur to them. And they immediately change their route, change their mind, and the happening that was going to happen is stopped.

Your mind is a very complex phenomenon. It continuously goes on projecting things. This man was poor, in debt; this gold sack would have been more than enough. But suddenly—and he had crossed this bridge many, many times; never had this thought occurred before—suddenly a thought came in the mind that it would be amusing to cross the bridge with closed eyes. You may have also sometimes walked on the path with closed eyes. Just some day in the morning, there is nobody and the thought occurs. When the thought occurs, look around!—some sack of gold may be waiting for you.

A man used to come to me, a very, very intelligent man, a Supreme Court advocate, and whenever he would promise that now, from tomorrow, he was going to come and start meditation, something or other would happen. The wife would be ill. Suddenly there would be a case and he would have to go to New Delhi. Or in the morning when he was to come, he would be feeling so lazy that he would postpone it for tomorrow. It happened many times when he promised: 'I am coming, definitely coming for meditation tomorrow,' and something would happen. It continued.

I asked him once, 'Have you ever looked back?—whenever you promise, something happens. Is there some inner relationship with the happening? Your child falling ill, your wife not feeling well, you yourself feeling lazy, low energy—is there something related to it? Because it has happened so many times that it cannot be just a coincidence!'

And the man said, 'How can it happen? Because I am coming to meditate, not my child, and he doesn't know. He is not even aware that I am going to meditate, so how can it happen?'

But now, if you ask psychologists they have come to many

discoveries. Mind is not individual: it is a collective phenomenon. Your mind and your child's mind are not two minds, they are one; they meet somewhere. Now psychologists say that children are very, very perceptive, because they are innocent. And they are so receptive that they can receive the thought of somebody who is near to them. If the father wants to go to the club and the mother doesn't want to go—of course, she has not said that; even she herself may not be aware that she doesn't want to go, but suddenly the child is ill, feeling nausea. And now psychologists have stumbled upon the fact that the child is simply showing the unconscious of the mother, because if the child is ill then the mother will be allowed not to go.

By and by, as psychoanalysis penetrates the human mind, they have come to feel that you cannot treat a single person unless you treat the whole family—because a single person is not ill; the whole family is ill. The person who is showing illness is just the weakest link, that's all. If the family has four children, father and mother, six people in all, then the weakest of the family will fall ill; he will become neurotic. The whole family is neurotic, but the others are a little stronger; he is the weakest. You can treat him; if you take him out of the family he will become okay. But if you send him back to the family, he will again become ill. Now it is very difficult. What to do? The family has to be treated. But then things become more and more complex, because the family exists in the society, in the community. And the whole community must be ill. This family is only the weakest family in the community. Then things become so vast: the community exists in a nation, and the nation exists on this earth. And consciousness exists as an ocean. You cannot treat a single person then, it becomes very difficult, because many others are helping him to be ill.

In India, every village has its own idiot, and that idiot helps the whole village to remain sane. In my childhood, I stayed in many villages. With my grandparents I was in one village, then with my parents in another village. And I moved from one village to another village, and I was surprised that every village has its own village idiot, has to—because he is the sanity of the whole village. He goes neurotic, he goes mad; he cries and weeps all over the village; he runs from here and there, and urchins follow him and throw stones at him. That helps the whole village to remain sane. If you remove that idiot, somebody else will immediately become the substitute. And in ancient India the villagers worshipped the idiots. They did well, because he was doing such a great service. Idiots were worshipped like saints. They were called *paramahansas*—great ones who have achieved. It was good in a way, because the idiot was serving the whole village. If you felt a little neurotic, you could go and play with the idiot, and you could do everything to him; nobody would prevent you.

In India we have a festival—Holi. This Holi festival is just a catharsis for the whole country to throw out all nonsense. It is good, it cleanses. More days are needed because more nonsense is there. One Holi is not enough. In fact, every month a Holi-day is needed so people can throw stones, rubbish at each other, throw colours, dirt, and can use four-letter words. It cleanses.

Remember always that consciousness is a *vast* oceanic phenomenon. It is in you and outside you. And consciousness is telepathic, it communicates. If you watch it well you will come to know that many times your consciousness throws barriers; even if you are not throwing them, then somebody else's unconsciousness throws barriers because you would like somebody else to throw them. The father wants to come to meditate, but deep down he doesn't want to come. The child telepathically understands it. He is ill in the morning and the father cannot go. Now he has an excuse.

It happened: A man came to Buddha when Buddha was dying. For thirty years Buddha passed through his village—almost eight times in thirty years—and he never came to Buddha. He always postponed and postponed, as people do—you can understand. There are many people in Poona: when I have left Poona, only then will they become aware that I was here. I was in Jabalpur for many years. When I left Jabalpur, people from Jabalpur started coming to Bombay to see me. And they would feel very, very miserable that they hadn't become aware that I was there. And they told me that people of Bombay were very, very fortunate. I said, 'Don't be worried. When I leave Bombay, then they will be in the same plight as you are.' And I left Bombay; now they come here from Bombay. In my audience, more people are from Bombay than from Poona. Only when I leave Poona, then I will be in Poona. Never before.

Buddha passed for thirty years eight times through the same village. He remained in the village—once he remained there for four months, the whole rainy season—and the man couldn't find time. Busy-bodies, busy without any business. He had a small shop to run, and a small family to maintain, and always there was something or other. A guest came; or by the time he was closing the shop, suddenly a customer came and he was so poor he could not afford to let the customer go to somebody else, so he had to open the shop again—and by that time the sermon was finished. This happened for thirty years, many times . . . something or other.

And then the day he heard that Buddha was dying, he ran, he closed the shop and he ran outside the town to where Buddha was. And there he started crying and weeping because Buddha had taken leave, he had said the last goodbye to his people. He asked his disciples thrice, 'Have you something to ask?' And they were crying and weeping, and there was nobody to ask. And there was no need—for forty years he had answered everything they asked. And they were filled with so much emotion and pain because Buddha was leaving. They said, 'No, we have nothing to ask. You have given everything to us.' Thrice he asked, then he retired behind a tree. He closed his eyes, and he started dying. Because a man like Buddha doesn't die like you—he dies voluntarily. He leaves the body. You are forced to leave the body. He started dying slowly; he left the body, shrank inside; he left the mind, shrank more inside.

At that moment the man came and he said, 'No! Don't prevent me. Let me go to Buddha.'

And Anand said, 'I know you. We have passed through your village for thirty years continuously, many many times, almost eight times. Buddha has talked in your town—where were you then?'

He said, 'What can I do? Sometimes my child was ill; sometimes my wife was pregnant; sometimes a customer came, and sometimes guests suddenly came. I couldn't come. But now that I have come, don't prevent me.'

Anand, Buddha's disciple, said, 'Now it is too late. We cannot ask him to come back—he is already moving in.'

But hearing this, Buddha came. He came back to the body and said, 'Anand, don't prevent him, because otherwise it will always remain as a black dot on my compassion that I was still alive and a man knocked at the door, and I was still alive and I couldn't help him.'

Buddha is right in his compassion, and El Mahdi is also right. You cannot help a man against himself. Something in him will frustrate it.

Buddha asked him, 'What do you need? What's your question, what's your search?'

And the man asked many questions and Buddha helped him. But nobody has ever heard about that man and what happened. He never became Enlightened. He went back to the shop, to the same customers and the child and the wife and the same town. He became a little more knowledgeable, that's all. Buddha's compassion was not of much help. Good that Buddha was compassionate, but you cannot help a man against himself— something in him will frustrate it. He was very happy that Buddha answered his questions, but that's all. He could have gathered that knowledge from the scriptures or the disciples. Even such a great compassion, such a great blessing, was frustrated. He remained the same.

You can bypass a Buddha. Something in you will frustrate. Remember this.

> The man replied: 'As soon as I started to cross the bridge, the thought occurred to me that it might be amusing to cross with my eyes shut. And I did so. . . . '

Remember it and never do so. You are here with me: much is possible. All that is possible, is possible. Just be watchful for something that can frustrate within you. And sometimes for such trivia that you yourself will laugh. And for small trivia you can miss the opportunity. And you know because you are in the same plight. Very small things.

You ask for an appointment today and it is not given today; it is given tomorrow—you feel so angry. You can leave me. But what are you doing? And for what? As if you were just finding an excuse to leave? And I know when you should see me better than you know. Whenever you are negative, you want to see me immediately. And that is not the right moment, because when you are negative you can get, at the most, my sympathy. When you are positive, only then can you get my love, because to a negative mind love cannot be given. A negative mind will not receive. And you always come when you are negative. When you are feeling sad and depressed and low, immediately you seek me. When you are feeling high, you forget me. When you are feeling good and happy, who needs me then? There is no question.

Remember this: if I delay appointments, that is just because I know the depression will not remain for ever. This is today. Tomorrow it will not be there. Nobody can be depressed for ever. Things come and go. Moods come and pass. And I would like you to come to me only when you are positive, because then something can be given to you.

This is the difference between religion and psychiatric treatment. You go to a psychiatrist when you are negative, ill, when you are not in the right shape. You go to the doctor when you are ill. He will bring you to health. You go to a religious man when you are healthy so that he can give you a greater health. You go to a religious man when you are absolutely positive, feeling happy and blissful. Now, he can lead you to the higher realms.

To me, come not just for health, but more health than ordinary health; not just happy but for being blissful; not just healthy but for being whole. And small things can frustrate.

A sannyasin came to me just a few days before, and she said she wants to leave. I asked, 'What has happened?'

She said, 'A beggar wanted to see you and he has been refused from the door. I cannot be here. Why has that beggar been refused?'

Now she is ready to leave. Is her leaving me going to help the beggar in any way? Or who is she to decide who should be allowed and who should not be allowed? It is for me to decide. A beggar comes to beg small things; those things he can get anywhere. I allow only great beggars to visit me—who have come to ask for God. Not less than that. And who are you to decide about these things? But you get angry, and in anger you can leave. The beggar will remain a beggar; he won't be helped by your leaving me. But something in you has tried to deceive you. And something will frustrate you continuously everywhere, wherever you will go. That something in you will always find excuses.

Always remember you are here for yourself, for nobody else. That is none of your concern. It is for me to decide who is to be allowed and when, and who is to be rejected and when. Because sometimes it is needed that a man should be rejected. Sometimes it is needed that a man should be rejected many times. But in your state of mind you cannot understand that. No need. But don't find excuses, because those excuses will be suicidal to you.

16 April 1975

VII
Knowledge is Dangerous

A man went to a doctor and told him that his wife was not bearing children.

The physician saw the woman, took her pulse and said: 'I cannot treat you for sterility because I have discovered that you will in any case die within forty days.'

When she heard this the woman was so worried that she could eat nothing during the ensuing forty days.

But she did not die at the time predicted, so the husband took the matter up with the doctor, who said:

'Yes, I knew that. Now she will be fertile.'

The husband asked how this came about.

The doctor told him:

'Your wife was too fat, and this was interfering with her fertility. I knew that the only thing that would put her off her food would be the fear of dying. She is now, therefore, cured.'

The question of knowledge is a very dangerous one.

Yes, the question of knowledge is a very dangerous one—for many reasons.

The first is that when a man knows, he also knows the complicatedness of life, the complexity of life. When a man knows, he also knows the mysterious ways of how life functions. So it is not a question of asserting a truth. The basic question is how to lead someone to the Truth. Sometimes lies are used because they help; and sometimes truths cannot be used because they hinder.

Every great Master—Buddha, Jesus, Mohammed—they are all great liars. This will be hard to believe; but when I say it, I say it with much consideration. And I know why it is so.

The basic question is not to tell the Truth to you. The basic question is how to lead you towards the Truth.

Somebody asked Buddha, 'What is Truth?' and Buddha said, 'That which can be utilized.'

This is not a definition of truth, because lies can be utilized —but Buddha is right. If something can help you, it may be a fiction, but if it helps you and leads towards the Truth, it is true. And sometimes just otherwise may be the case: you know the truth, but it becomes the hindrance, and it leads you more and more into confusion, into darkness. So the final outcome should be the criterion; the end result should be the criterion.

It happened once: A Sufi Master was feeling thirsty. He was

surrounded by his disciples, and he asked a small boy, who was also sitting there listening to him, to go to the well. He gave him an earthen pot and told him, 'Be careful! The pot is earthen, but very valuable. It is an antique piece. Don't drop it, don't break it.' Then he slapped the boy's face hard two or three times and said, 'Now go!'

The people who were sitting there couldn't believe it. One of the kind-hearted men asked, 'What are you doing? This is absurd! The boy has done nothing wrong. He has not dropped the pot, he has not broken it, he has not done anything—and you punished him?'

The Sufi Master said, 'Yes, I know it. But if he had dropped the pot, then what would be the use of punishment?'

The Sufi Master is saying that in life, it is not always so that the effect follows the cause. In life, sometimes the cause follows the effect; sometimes the effect precedes the cause. Life is complicated. Sometimes the future comes first and then the past. It is not always so that the past comes first, and then the future.

Life is not as easy as you think. It is difficult, complex; past and future all meet into it. That which has been is still there somehow. How can it disappear? All that has been is still there! In this very moment, the whole past—not of humanity only, but of the whole universe—is implied. Your mother, your father, your father's father, and grandfather, and grandfather's grandfather, and Adam and Eve, all are implied in you. Something of you was in the Adam, in the Eve, and they are totally in you. The whole past is there—and the whole future also. All that is going to happen in the world, in the universe, you already carry it as a potentiality.

You are the whole world. Causes and effects, past and future—everything is joined together in you. Every line of existence criss-crosses on the point where you are.

The question of knowledge is dangerous. When a man knows, he knows this complexity. And whenever he does something, he has to consider the whole complexity—otherwise he will miss, he will not be helpful.

That's why I say that many people become Enlightened, but

very few are Masters; because to become Enlightened, you have to solve only your problems. When you become Enlightened, the knowledge is such a vast ocean that to manage it and to be able to help others becomes very, very difficult. And sometimes people who don't know this dangerousness of knowledge may be thinking they are helping. They destroy. They may be thinking that they are kind, but they are cruel. They may be thinking that they are pulling you out of your confusion, but they are throwing you more and more into confusion. It has happened many times, even sometimes with Enlightened people. The vastness is such, the complexity is so deep, but whenever you say something to somebody, it becomes simple. You have to bring it down, reduce it to a simple phenomenon. Much of it is lost, and then it may not be a help.

For example: Krishnamurti. He *is* Enlightened. If anybody has ever been Enlightened, he is Enlightened. But the complexity is such, and he has reduced the whole thing to such a simple formula, that the mystery is missing. He looks like a logician, he talks like a rationalist—the mystery is lost. He has been repeating particular formulas, and they have not helped anybody. Many are deluded through them, but nobody is helped—because he has a very fixed attitude, and life is not fixed. It is true: sometimes a man achieves the Truth without the help of any Master. The opposite is also true: sometimes a man achieves the Truth through the help of many Masters, not only one. It is true that you can grow alone; the opposite is also true, that you can grow in a community, in a school, in a family of seekers. It is true that a man can reach to the Final without any method; the opposite is also true.

With people who have a very logical attitude about life, this becomes difficult. They divide life into yes and no. They say, 'Either say yes or say no.'

You may have heard the name of a Western thinker, de Bono. He has something very beautiful to say to everybody. He has coined a new word—that word is 'po'. You will not find it in any dictionary because it is a new word. He says that there are situations when if you say yes you will be wrong, and if you say no you will be wrong again. There are situations when you need to be just in the middle—then say po. It is a word which doesn't mean yes, doesn't mean no, or it means both. Either below yes or no, or above yes or no, but undivided—po, yes plus no.

There are situations: if somebody asks a certain question in which you are deeply involved, if somebody asks, 'Do you think that you love me?' it will be difficult, because you are never a hundred percent certain whether you love or not. If you say yes you are committed to a wrong statement, because who can say yes? Only one who is total can say *yes* with his total being behind it. How can you say yes? The moment when you are saying yes, a part of you is still saying no. Wait, don't decide. There is confusion; a part of your mind is saying, 'I don't know whether I love or not.' If you say no, that will also be wrong—because a part of you is saying yes. And you are always part, you are not total. De Bono's word 'po' is handy: when somebody asks you again, 'Do you love me?' say, 'Po.' It means yes and no both: 'A certain part of me loves you, and a certain part doesn't love.'

Mulla Nasrudin was in court. There was a case against him, because the wife had reported to the court that he had been beating her. If the judge had asked, 'Do you beat your wife?' he could have said yes, or he could have said no, whatsoever the case may have been. But the judge asked, 'Mulla Nasrudin, have you stopped beating your wife?' If he says yes, that means he was beating her before. If he says no, it means he is still beating her.

So he came running to me after telling the judge, 'Give me a little time; tomorrow I will answer.'

When he came to me I said, 'You say po.'

And he said, 'What is this po?'

I said, 'That is the judge's problem. Let him decide what po is. You simply say it.'

The whole human language is divided into yes and no, into black and white—but life is grey. This po means life is grey; at one extreme it becomes dark black, at the other extreme it becomes white—but exactly in between the two, the grey waves and exists.

Two calamities have fallen on the Western mind: one is

Aristotle, because he gave you a logical attitude towards life which is false. He gave you either yes or no, and he said, 'Both cannot be true together.' And they are *always* true together; they are always true together. One cannot be true without the other, because life is both: day and night, summer and winter, God and Devil. Life is together, undivided. When a man comes to realize this undividedness of life, it becomes very, very difficult—what to say and what not to say. Whatsoever he says will be false, because language only allows either yes or no.

The second calamity that has fallen on the Western mind is the crucifixion of Jesus. Because of that crucifixion, the whole Western mind became disturbed. First Aristotle divided life in two and then the crucifixion of Jesus divided the heart in two. Aristotle divided the mind, the intellect, in two; and the crucifixion of Jesus divided the heart into two. If you are a Christian, you go to Heaven; if you are not, you go to Hell. If you are a Christian, only then are you human; if you are not a Christian, then nobody bothers about you. You can be killed very easily. There is no need to have a second thought about it.

The crucifixion divided the heart, the emotional part of man. And Christianity has done so much violence—no religion has ever done so much—because of the crucifixion. Jews have been killed for these two thousand years continuously. And Christianity has become a crusade, a war against the non-Christians, the pagans.

Love divided, heart divided, mind divided—the whole West has become schizophrenic, a split personality. And the whole effort of Sufism is how to make you one, so that all your divisions disappear; so that your heart is one, a unitary whole; your mind is one, a unitary whole. And not only that: your mind and heart also become one, a unitary whole. Then you attain to what is real.

But right now, how to help you towards the real? Devices will be needed, because just talking about the truth will not help. It has never helped. Rather, it has hindered. If truth is told to you, it will become a dogma, and the dogma is a hindrance. It will become a scripture, a tradition, and a tradition is a betrayal.

Truth cannot be said directly to you. Something has to be done to you so that you proceed, by and by, towards the Truth. The knowledge has to be transferred in a very indirect way. It cannot be direct. It has to be grown, by and by, within you through situations. And, of course, because you are false, only false situations will be helpful. Real situations will not be helpful. You *are* false, you understand the language of the false, and a false situation is needed continuously around you, to force you towards a certain window from where you can see the sky.

For example: you live in a closed house. You have never been out of it, you have never seen the sun, you have never heard the birds, you have never touched the breeze passing through the trees. You have never been out, never seen the flowers, the rains. You have lived in the closed house, completely closed, not even a window open. Then I come to you, and I would like you to come out and sing with the birds, and dance with the breeze, and be like flowers opening and opening, opening towards the infinite. But how to tell you about the world which is outside? The language is not there. If I talk about flowers, you will not understand. 'Flowers?' you will say, 'What do you mean by flowers? First prove that they exist.' How can it be proved if you have not known? And whatsoever is done to prove it, you can disprove it, you can argue about it. And people who have lived in a closed world are always argumentative—always. The more closed a mind, the more argumentative it is—because it has not known anything which goes beyond argument and logic and reasoning. It is confined. You have lived in darkness—how to talk to you about light and the sunshine, and the sunrays?

And you are not alone in your darkness; many exist with you in the darkness. I am alone there talking about flowers and light, and the world outside, and the open sky. And not only you, but the whole majority will laugh—I have gone mad. 'What are you saying? You must have been dreaming,' you will say to me. 'Your fantasy,' you will say, 'there exists no outside world. This is the only world; there is no other world. What are you talking about?'

And some of you must think that I must have some design,

some conspiracy, to take you out and rob you of something—'because there is no outside world! And why is this man continuously trying to prove that there is an outside world? He must have some profit-motive behind it. Don't be deceived by this man!' That's how you have behaved with Jesus, Mohammed, Mahavir; that's how you have always been behaving with people who bring you good news from some other world, who have been messengers of something unknown to you. The majority is with you; you can take a vote, and you can decide what is true and what is not true.

The difficulty is: in what language to talk to you, what parables, what symbols to use? Whatsoever is said will be misunderstood—because anything can be understood only when the experience, the basic experience is there. Even if a slight glimpse has come to you of the outside world, even once, if even from the keyhole you have looked, then there is a possibility. A contact, a communication becomes possible. But you have not looked at all. You have not even dreamt. You have not even imagined. Not even in fantasy has the outside entered in you. You are completely closed. What to do?

I will have to use some device. The device is neither true nor false. It is a 'po' device—you cannot say yes, you cannot say no. I will have to use your language and your situation. And I will have to talk to you on your terms, in your terms. It is useless to talk about the flowers—you don't know. It is useless to talk about the sky—you don't know. You have completely forgotten that you have wings.

Some device. For example, I can create a fever in you: 'This house is going to fall. Get out of it as soon as you can! Time is running out. This house is going to fall!' That's what Jesus did. He said, 'This whole world is going to fall. Time is running out! The end is coming near—the day of judgment.' It has not come up to now. And Jesus told his disciples: 'Before you are dead, the day of judgment will have come. So transform yourself, change yourself—repent! Because the time is running short and the house is going to fall. It is already on fire! Can't you see?' What is he saying?

You cannot understand the language of freedom, but you can understand the language of fear. Freedom cannot be said to you, but fear—yes, you can understand that. Death you can understand. You cannot understand *life*. So he says the day of judgment is coming near. And Jesus says, 'There is only one life. Once lost, lost for ever.' That's why Jesus never used the Indian device of reincarnation.

All the three religions born in the West—Jews, Mohammedans, Christians—they have never used the Indian device. All the religions born in the East—Buddhism, Hinduism, Jainism, Sikhism —they have all used the device of reincarnation. The situations were different; I will tell you why they used the device. And when people come to me and ask me, 'Is reincarnation a true doctrine?' I say, 'Po.' It is neither true nor false. It is a device; it is a device to help people. Try to understand. And both the devices bring you to the same point; both the devices bring you to the same state of mind—so they both are true because they both help. True in the sense of Buddha. They are pragmatic; you can utilize them —they have been utilized.

Jesus says, 'This is the only life,' to create a fever, a fear. Because if he says there are many lives, you will relax; you will say, 'Then there is no hurry. This house is not going to fall in *my* life, and there will be other lives, so why be in a hurry?' You can postpone. 'And if there are many, many lives, that means many millions of opportunities, then why be in such a hurry? Why not enjoy this house and the darkness a little more? Any time we can go out. The house will be there, we will be here. The door will be there; the outside is not going to be lost.' You can postpone.

Jesus dropped postponing. He said, 'There is only one life, only *this* one. And this life is continuously running out of your hands, running out of your fingers. Every moment you are more and more dead. And soon, in *this* life, before you are dead, the day of judgment will be there. And all your sins will be judged and you will be punished. And those who are with me will be saved!' What is he saying?

He is saying, 'Come with me. Be with me.' He is trying to

bring you out of your house. He will be moving out, and if you trust him, and if you have become too much afraid ... and he created almost a neurosis, a fear, a trembling. In that fear people followed him.

Once you follow Jesus, you are out, you know that that was a trick. You have been tricked out. But then you are not angry: you are grateful because that was the only way. And you were so false that even a Jesus has to use a lie to bring you out. But once you are out, you forget about the judgment day and God and the Kingdom; and you forget about death and fear. Once you are out in the world, the open world, of sky and the breeze and the sunshine, you celebrate, you enjoy, you feel grateful for ever and ever towards Jesus, because he was so compassionate, because he even used a lie to bring you out.

In India we have used another device, for certain reasons.

India is very, very old; the most ancient country in the world. It has existed for thousands of years. The West is very young, the East is very old. And when you talk to an old man, you have to talk differently; when you talk to a young man, you have to talk differently—because their attitudes have changed completely. A young man always looks towards the future; an old man always looks towards the past, because for an old man there is no future. The death ... and then there is no future. An old man looks towards the past; only the past exists for an old man.

As you grow old, the past grows more and more, and the future becomes less and less. For a child there is no past, only the future. If you talk to the child, you have to be future-oriented. That's why Christ goes on talking of the coming Kingdom of God, the life abundant—the future. In India, that would not have been useful at all. People have become so old, the whole mind has become so old, that you cannot be fooled by words like 'Kingdom of God'. They have lived too much, and you cannot allure them towards more life. They are bored and finished with life. You cannot tell them that abundance of life will be there. They will say, 'This much has been too much! What will we do with an abundance of life?' No. The Eastern mind wants to be freed from life and death both. The East is bored, as every old man is bored. He lived, groped in every dimension, and everything was found to be futile, fruitless.

An old mind is bored. The East is bored with life. You cannot promise more life. That will not be a promise; on the contrary, that will look like a punishment. So in the East we have been using a totally different device, and that device is: the wheel of life and death.

We say that millions of times you have been born—we give more boredom to the mind—for millions of lives.... Hindus say that everybody has been in this world, at least before human birth, eighty-four *crore* times—that is, eight hundred and forty million times everybody has been in the world. And everybody had been repeating the same pattern—childhood, the fantasies of childhood; the youth, the foolishnesses of youth; the old age, the boredom; and death. And the wheel moves and moves and moves. Eight hundred and forty million times you have been just the same: always hankering, desiring the same things; always achieving them or not achieving them, but in the end frustration; whether you achieve or you don't achieve, in the end frustration. The whole story always comes to the same point: frustration—of those who are successful and of those who are not successful. Just think! Eight hundred and forty million times you loved, and became frustrated. Eight hundred and forty million times you tried, became ambitious, succeeded in getting a little prestige, money, and then became frustrated. Eight hundred and forty million times born, and then, by and by, life going out and dying again.

What is the message of this theory of reincarnation? The message is: Enough is enough! Now, be finished with it! Now come out! If you remain inside, this wheel will go on and on and on. Now drop out!—a real drop-out. Not dropping out of the society, or of the school, but dropping out of the wheel of life and death. Just drop out and run away!—out of the house.

This is the language a bored man can understand. But both are devices. Don't ask me which is true. They are neither true nor false. The truth you will know when you are out of the

house; truth you will never know inside the house. So whatsoever helps you towards the sky, the freedom, the openness, that
is true. That's why I say all religions are true, in the sense that
they all help. And a religion becomes untrue when it stops helping.

It happens: whenever a society becomes old . . . now Jesus'
idea won't help the West very much. Now the West itself is
becoming old. That's why the Western mind is turning towards
the East. Now the philosophy of boredom will be more helpful
—now you are also old. Christianity has less appeal; Hinduism,
Buddhism, more appeal. Now you are old! Now Jesus' idea won't
be of much help. Jesus can remain influential in America only
for a few years—the Jesus freaks and Jesus people—because
America is still young, with no history, with no past. Otherwise,
the West is turning more and more Eastern. Reincarnation appeals
more than one life. The day of judgment looks childish, and one
life does not look enough. How can you judge a man just giving
him one opportunity? At least a few more opportunities are
needed to judge a man, because he has to learn by trial and error.
If you give him only one opportunity, you don't give him any
opportunity really. If he errs, he errs. There is no time left to
raise oneself above error. More opportunities are needed.

These are devices. The word 'device' means neither true nor
false. It can help. If it helps, it is true. It can hinder; then it is
untrue. Every religion is true when it is born, and becomes, by
and by, untrue—because situations change, and the religion becomes untrue. It fits in a particular situation, then it doesn't fit.
Then it becomes a burden. Then it kills you, it becomes murderous. Then it suffocates you. Then it doesn't give you more lease
on life. It becomes poisonous.

Every religion has its own day. And when people become
more aware, they will see when the religion is born, they will see
when the religion is young; they will enjoy the religion when it is
young and helpful. And when the religion dies, they will do the
same as you will do with your father and mother when they die.
Of course, with great suffering and pain you take them to the
grave, or to the burning *ghat*. You burn them with tears in your
eyes, but you have to burn them! You know that she was your

mother and she gave you birth, and he was your father and he was everything—but he is dead! Then unnecessary dead burdens will not be on the mind of man.

Right now, there are three hundred religions in the world— and almost all of them dead. Just a few have a little life—that, too, like a small candle, not like a sun—somehow pulling themselves together. If you understand that religion is a device, then it will be clear to you that a device cannot be a device for ever.

I am creating many devices. They will be dead one day. Then they have to be dropped! If you follow a particular meditation I have given to you, even in your life you will find, sooner or later, that it is dead. The work is done. It is no longer needed. You have gone beyond it. Then don't carry it and don't get attached to it, because that attachment will be suicidal. Just as you go on changing your clothes—your body grows bigger, you go on changing your clothes—in the same way you go on changing your devices. And when you are really out, then there is no need for any device. All devices were there just to bring you out of your closedness, out of your grave, out of your insensitivity, out of your unconsciousness.

It is reported in a Sufi Master's life, that he was passing along a street near a mosque. The *muzzin* was on the tower, and by accident the *muzzin* fell from the tower. Accidentally he fell on the Sufi Master and broke his neck, the Sufi Master's neck, but he was not hurt at all; the man who fell was not hurt at all. He fell on the neck of the Sufi Master, the neck was broken, and the Sufi Master had to be hospitalized.

The disciples gathered there, because this Sufi Master used to use every situation; so they gathered and they asked, 'How will you use this situation?'

The Sufi Master opened his eyes and he said, 'The theory of karma is false, because they say: You reap, you sow; you sow, you reap—as you sow, so you reap. But that is false. Look! Somebody else falls, and somebody else's neck is broken. So somebody else can sow, and somebody else can reap.'

Remember this. Sufis say that life is so interrelated that the theory of karma cannot be right. And they are true, because that device is also true. If life is so related, then how can the theory of karma be meaningful? The theory of karma says that you are connected with your past life, only with your past life; you are a sequence of your *own* karmas, and you reap the results of your own karmas. But Sufis say life is interrelated: Everybody else's karma is my karma, and my karma is everybody else's karma. It is a net of interrelationships. You shake a flower, and Sufis say that the very foundations of the stars are shaken. You do something, but the whole is affected. You throw a small pebble in the lake, and the whole lake is affected.

Everybody is just like a small pebble in the lake. And whatsoever you do creates waves, vibrations. When you are here no more, those vibrations will still be continuing somewhere— somewhere near a star, very distant from the earth, but those vibrations will be there. You look at a man and you smile. Sometimes it happens . . . .

It happened to one of my friends. He was travelling on a train. Just at a midway station, a small station, the train stopped. It was not a regular stopping station for the train; for some reason the train stopped. Another train was standing at the platform, and this friend was in an air-conditioned compartment. Out of his window, out of the glass-covered window, he just looked outside. In the other train, a beautiful woman . . . just for a second; just for a second and the train left. And that woman changed his whole life. And the woman may not have even known that somebody had looked at her. He says that the woman was not looking at him, she was not even aware—but the form of the woman, the face, the proportionate body of the woman, has persisted in his dreams.

He has not married yet. He's searching for that woman. He does not know her name. He does not know where that woman has gone, from where she was coming, where she was going. Nothing is known. Just for a single moment the train stopped. He looked out of the window—and the window was not open, just glass-covered, in an air-conditioned room—he just had a glimpse, and then the train left! Just a small pebble in the lake.

He has remained unmarried and he says, 'Unless I find *that*

woman, or something of that woman, I am not going to marry.'
And I don't think there is any possibility of him finding her,
because almost nine years have passed. But the whole history of
the world will be different—because this man may have got
married to a woman, may have given birth to an Adolf Hitler.
Who knows? But he is not married. The Adolf Hitler will remain
unborn. The third world war will not be there. Who knows what
would have happened had he not seen this woman from the
window? Now the whole history will never be the same as it
would have been—just the stopping of a train for two or three
seconds, and the whole universe will never be the same again.

Can you think! If Hitler had not been born, the whole world
would have been totally different—*totally* different. If the mother
of Adolf Hitler had miscarried, then . . . ? Or if she had been on
the pill, then . . . ? Just a small pill!—and the whole history of the
world would have been *totally* different, totally! You might not
have been here. Hitler created such change. Everybody is creating
change. And I'm not talking only about great mischief-makers like
Hitler, or great mahatmas. No. Even a dog in your town is as
important to the total as any Adolf Hitler. You never know: if
the dog was not there, the world would have been different. Just
a vagabond dog that belongs to nobody—but it is part, it is part
of the whole. And every part is as important as any other part,
because in the whole every part is as significant as any other part.
There is no small, no big; no one more important, no one less
important.

The whole is whole because of all.

Sufis say that the theory of karma is basically an egoistic
attitude. And they are right! It says that you *are*, so whatsoever
you sow you will reap. It gives strength to you, the ego.

They have used another pattern to bring you out of the
whole thing. You are no more. The whole is. Just a wave you are.
What is the point of thinking that you are? Sufis say that when
you understand this interrelatedness, you simply drop your con-
cept of the ego, you are no more a self. Sufis say only God has the
right to say 'I'. Nobody else. Because only He has the center,
nobody else.

This is a device. Hindus have their own device when they say, 'You reap whatsoever you sow.' They are saying that if you are miserable, you are the cause—don't throw the responsibility on anybody else. If you are miserable, you are the cause; if you are in anguish, you have sown some poisonous seeds somewhere, in some life, and you are reaping it. Why do they insist on it?

For two reasons.

One: if you are responsible, if you feel you are responsible, only then can you drop them; otherwise, how will you drop them? If you think that everybody else is as responsible as you are, then you will continue as you are. What can be done? You cannot change it on your own. The dropping is impossible.

And second and more significant: the Hindu device says that this whole phenomenon of your past, of whatsoever you have done, or whatsoever you have thought, is *right* now present in you. People think the past cannot be undone. Hindus say no, it can be undone—because the past is part of the present. You carry it. Not only can you change the present and the future, you can change the past, you can drop it. The more responsible you feel, the more it becomes possible to drop it. And they say that because you are *solely* responsible for your life, freedom is also possible. If everything is connected, then when everybody becomes Enlightened, only then can you become Enlightened. And this can become a loophole. You can postpone: 'When everybody becomes Enlightened, then only ... otherwise how can I alone become Enlightened?'

To help you, many devices have been created. They all come from people who know, but they are all limited. No device can be unlimited. It is devised by a certain man, devised for certain other men. It is meaningful only in a certain context. That's why knowledge is dangerous. If you carry it out of context, it will cripple you. If you carry it out of context, it will suffocate, it will become a poison. It will not lead you out. On the contrary, just the reverse will be the case: it will become a hindrance, a closed door. That, too, has to be understood.

For example: Sufis say that you cannot drop ego if you believe in the theory of karma. Right—this is the right use, but you can use it wrongly. You can say, 'Everything is so interrelated, then how can I become Enlightened alone? That's impossible. Either the whole becomes Enlightened, or the whole remains ignorant.' Now, you are using the same device to remain in the same house, closing it.

The same passage can lead you out. The same passage can lead you in. By the same staircase you can go up, and you can come down. It depends on you.

Hindus say that you are reponsible for your karmas. This is good. If you are responsible, you can change; transformation is possible—you alone are involved. You can drop or you can carry as you wish. And who would like to carry anguish, misery, hell? You will drop it. But you can use it in just the opposite way. You can say, 'If I am responsible for my karmas . . .' then the I becomes very, very important. So you cannot find more egoistic people than Hindu sannyasins.

If you go and look at a Sufi, you will always find him absolutely humble. If you have ever come in contact with a Mohammedan Sufi, you will always feel him to be absolutely humble. No comparison exists anywhere. A Sufi is absolutely humble. His face, his eyes, his very being, will be humble, because he is a nonentity—the Whole exists.

If you come to a Hindu sannyasin, you will never find a more egoistic person. The way he walks, the way he looks—look at his eyes, and particularly at his nose—you will find ego written all over. He has wrongly used the whole thing. If you are responsible for your karmas, then the ego is strengthened, then you become more and more of the ego.

You can use a device wrongly. Every device is double-edged. Remember this. That's why the question of knowledge is said to be a dangerous one.

Now we will enter into this story.

A man went to a doctor and told him that his wife was not bearing children.

The physician saw the woman, took her pulse and said: 'I cannot treat you for sterility because I have discovered that you will in any case die within forty days.'

When she heard this the woman was so worried that she could eat nothing during the ensuing forty days.

But she did not die at the time predicted, so the husband took the matter up with the doctor, who said:

'Yes, I knew that. Now she will be fertile.'

The husband asked how this came about.

The doctor told him:

'Your wife was too fat, and this was interfering with her fertility. I knew that the only thing that would put her off her food would be the fear of dying. She is now, therefore, cured.'

The question of knowledge is a very dangerous one.

The doctor lied. The doctor said something that was not going to happen. But through it something else happened. He said, 'The woman is going to die.' She became so worried. Death became a haunting, a nightmare. She must have thought continuously of death. She couldn't eat. But she didn't die. And after forty days, the doctor said, 'She is cured. Now she will be fertile.'

What happened? He could have said in the very beginning 'You go on a diet, or you fast.' That would have been true—but that would not have been wise, because the woman was not going to diet, and for forty days she was not going to fast. In fact, many other doctors must have told her before, and she had never listened. So it would have been true to say, 'Diet or fast for forty days and you will be cured,' but it would not have been wise.

Truth is not always wise, and untruth is not always foolish. The question of knowledge is a very complicated one.

The doctor created a situation. He was really a wise doctor. He created a situation: he knew that only the fear of death would be of any help. He shocked the woman by the fear of death; he gave her such worry and anguish and anxiety that she completely forgot about food. Who eats, who enjoys eating, when death is knocking on the door? Every moment she must have been looking at the clock, at the calendar: One day is gone. Who bothers about food? and how can you enjoy food, when death is there? It was impossible. But she didn't die. Rather, her body was completely renewed. A new lease of life happened.

Untrue, but wise—and this is how every Master is.

Gurdjieff has been much criticized, because he was a liar. And the lying came from the Sufis; he was a Sufi. He was disciplined in Sufi monasteries and schools. And in the West, in fact, he introduced Sufism in this age in a totally new version. But then it was impossible for the ordinary Christian mind to understand him, because truth is a value, and nobody can think that a Master, an Enlightened Master, can lie.

Can you think of Jesus lying? And I know he lied—but Christians cannot think about it: 'Jesus lying? No, he is the truest man.' But then you don't know—the question of knowledge is very, very dangerous. He lied about many things. A Master has to—if he wants to help; otherwise, he can be a saint, but no help is possible from him. And a saint without help is already dead. If a saint cannot help, what is the use of his being here? There is no point in it. All that he can attain through life, he has attained. He is here to help.

Gurdjieff was very much criticized, because the West couldn't understand; the ordinary Christian mind could not understand. So there are two versions about Gurdjieff in the West. One thinks that he was very mischievous man, not a sage at all, just a devil incarnate. Another is that he was the greatest saint the West has come to know in these past few centuries. Both are true, because he was just in the middle. He was a 'po' personality. You cannot say yes, you cannot say no about him. You can say that he was a holy sinner, or, a sinning saint. But you cannot divide, you cannot be so simple about him. The knowledge that he had was very complex.

A man came once to Gurdjieff, and he talked about himself —that he was a vegetarian, and that he never touched alcohol, and that he never smoked, and this and that. Gurdjieff said, 'If you are to be with me, you have to leave everything in my hands.'

The man was not aware of what type of man Gurdjieff was. He said, 'Of course! I have come to you—I surrender.'

And Gurdjieff said, 'Then the first thing is: now eat meat.'

The man was really in difficulty. He couldn't believe it. He thought Gurdjieff was joking. He said, 'You, and saying that?'

Gurdjieff said, 'Yes, that's the only way I can break down your ego. This vegetarianism is not vegetarianism—it is just part of your ego. So here you will have to eat meat, drink as much alcohol as you can, smoke, move with women, and leave everything to me.'

You cannot believe a saint talking like this. But then your saints are not very wise. And Gurdjieff did help that man— because that was the trouble. You will always find people who are vegetarians, teetotallers, non-smokers, always you will find very subtle egos. And alcohol cannot harm as much as the subtle ego can harm. And the man followed. It was very difficult, nauseating for him. But once he said it, he followed.

Within three weeks the man was transformed. And Gurdjieff would give him so much to drink . . . Gurdjieff used to have a feast every night, and the feast continued for three, four, five hours. At nine, ten, it would start, and it would end in the middle of the night. And Gurdjieff himself was such a capable man that he could drink as much as possible and would never get drunk. And he would force the disciples to eat. Their bellies would be bursting, and they would be crying and tears would come into their eyes, and they would say, 'No, now no more!' And he would force.

He was trying to change your body chemistry. And he changed many people who followed with him, who were capable and courageous enough to move with him; not afraid people who ordinarily become religious, but brave people. This man I am talking about, he followed. He would fall down drunk, and then the next day there would be a hangover. Within three weeks Gurdjieff transformed his whole mind. And, by and by, he dropped the meat, dropped alcohol, dropped everything. And that man said then, 'For the first time I became vegetarian— because that old vegetarianism was not true. It was just a mask for the ego.' When he forced meat and alcohol on this disciple, he was breaking down the ego. He shattered the man completely.

And sometimes just the reverse would happen. A man would come who was a drunkard, and a meat-eater, and a smoker, and

Gurdjieff would stop everything. He would put him on a diet or on a fast.

A Master, if he is to help, has to be very very wise. Gurdjieff used to call his way 'The Way of the Sly Man'. All Masters are sly. If they are to help, they have to be. But your concepts think that Masters are just innocent virgins, just dream-stuff, no substance, marble statues. You can go and touch and feel the coldness, that's all. There have been such people, but they are worthless. They have helped nobody. They may have enjoyed a certain silence and peace, of course, but that silence does not have the quality of life in it. They are dead marble statues. The silence is cold. The silence is not warm enough to be alive. They have stilled themselves, they have become controlled, but they are not free. They have not attained to the freedom.

A man who is really free is beyond good and evil, sin and virtue. In fact, he is beyond all dichotomies, all dualities. He is both and he is neither. And only such a man, with so much enriched life—which comprehends opposites in it, which comprehends all contradictions in it—can be of any help and benefit to anybody. But to come to such a Master is difficult, because you come with your notions, you come with your ideologies, you come with your judgments.

So this is the trouble: You will be influenced by a man who cannot help you, and you will escape from the man who could have helped you. This is the misery of the human mind. Be aware about it so you don't commit the same mistake.

The question of knowledge is a very dangerous one.

17 April 1975

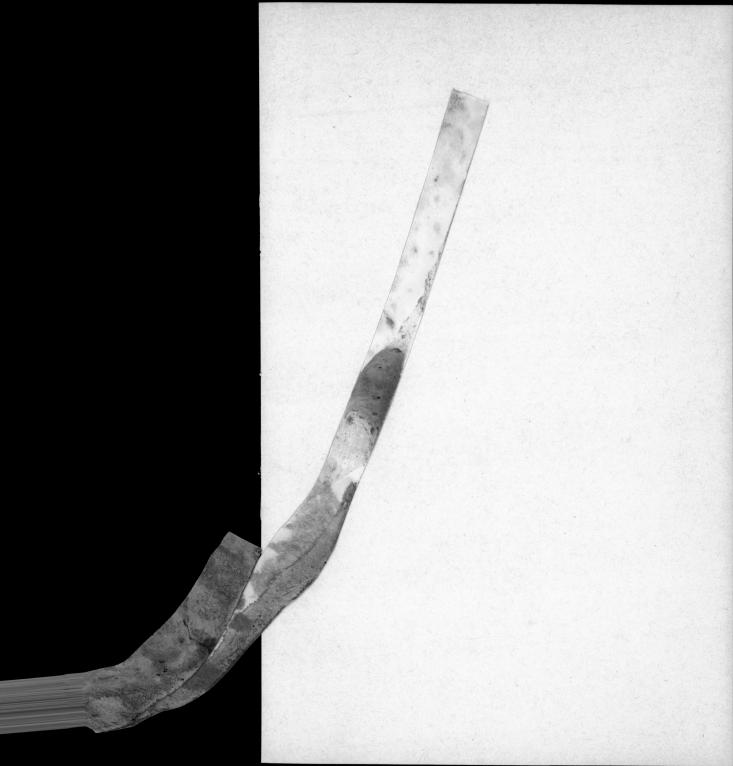

VIII
This Too Will Pass

A powerful king, ruler of many domains, was in a position of such magnificence that wise men were his mere employees. And yet one day he felt himself confused and called his sages to him.

He said:

'I do not know the cause, but something impels me to seek a certain ring, one that will enable me to stabilize my state. I must have such a ring, and this ring must be one which, when I am unhappy it will make me joyful, and at the same time, if I am happy and look upon it I must be made sad.'

The wise men consulted one another, and threw themselves into deep contemplation. Finally they came to a decision as to the character of this ring which would suit their king.

The ring which they devised was one upon which was inscribed the legend:

'THIS, TOO, WILL PASS'

THIS IS a great story. Great, because it has been used for centuries by Sufis. And this story has helped many people towards Enlightenment. It is no ordinary story. It is what I call the objective art. It is a device. It is not just for reading and entertainment. It is something which should become your very style of life, only then do you come to know the meaning of it.

On the surface it is so simple. Anybody can understand it; nothing of special intelligence is needed. But if you contemplate over it, deeply, then deeper and deeper layers are revealed to you. And the story becomes a weapon in your hand. You can cut by it the very knot of ignorance. It is a powerful device. Once understood, it becomes a master-key—to open the innermost door of your being. It is very potential, pregnant with deep meaning. But one has to contemplate over it, meditate over it, intensely. With consciousness, one has to make every effort to find the innermost meaning of it. And only that won't help much; that will help in the beginning. But if you really want to understand the story, you will have to live it. You will have to *live* it—only then will you come to understand what it means.

A few things before we enter into the story.

Religion is not ritual. It is not something that you do. It is something that you become. So there is always a possibility of a false religion existing somewhere in the society. False religion is when the inner transformation has been substituted by outer ritual. Then you go on doing things and those things will become a deep-rooted habit with you, but nothing is achieved. People go to the church and the temple, and they repeat the same prayers again and again. Nothing is happening to them. Somewhere on the way they have missed; somewhere on the way they have lost the real coin—and they have substituted it by a false coin.

Remember this, that the real, authentic religion is concerned with the being, not with the doing. It has nothing to do with your outer way of life. It has something to do with your center. Of course, when the center changes, the periphery follows; your outer life also changes. But the reverse is not true: you can change the periphery—the center will not change. And you will live the life of a hypocrite, a life of hypocrisy. You will have a different periphery from the center, not only different but just the opposite, the very contrary. And you will be split in two.

Religion is not ritual. Remember that. Religion is an inner consciousness, an inner awakening. Many things on the surface will change, but the change *must* occur within you first.

Think of yourself as a circle with a center. The circle is concerned with others. The circle touches others' boundaries, other circles. The circle lives, the periphery lives, in the society of other peripheries. A certain morality is needed. To live with the others, a certain regulation, rule, a system, is needed. That's okay. But that is not religion.

Morality is how to live with others, and religion is how to live with oneself. Morality is how not to go wrong with others, and religion is the method of how not to go wrong with yourself. Religion is that which you do in your total loneliness, in your innermost shrine.

Obviously, the periphery will be changed, because the light from the center will come, by and by, and infiltrate the whole periphery. You will become luminous. Even others will start feeling the luminosity, the light that comes from you. But that light will not be the light of your actions, good actions. The light will be something that is not concerned with good and bad.

The light will be just like when a flower opens, and the fragrance spreads—neither good nor bad. The sun rises, and the light spreads—neither good nor bad. And the clouds come and rain. They don't bother who is good and who is bad.

When the light comes from the center, it is beyond morality; good and bad, everything is dissolved. Simple light, superb in its own self, in its intrinsic value.

The word 'religion' is very beautiful. It comes from a root which means 'religere'. Religere means to rejoin, to reunite. With whom? With yourself, with the source of your being. And why reunite? Because with the source you are already united—it is a reunion. It is not that you are reaching to the source for the first time; otherwise, from where will you come? You have come from the source. Deep down you are still in the source. Just on the periphery, as if the branches have forgotten about the roots . . . not that they are broken from the roots, because then they cannot live. They have simply forgotten. In their ego, in their height in the sky, with the moon, in their romance, they have completely forgotten that they have roots underground—which nourish them, which sustain them, without which they cannot exist for a single moment. And all this greenery, and all these flowers, and all these fruits, will simply disappear like dreams once they are cut from the root. That's how it happens to man. You move in the branches, farther away from the roots. You come to many flowers. You are enchanted. The world is beautiful all around you. You completely forget about the roots. But it is not that you are uprooted. Forgetfulness is just forgetfulness.

That is the meaning of religion: to reunite, to remember again. This word 'remember' is also beautiful. It means to become the member again, re-member—to become part of the source again, to go to the source and become the member again of it.

Religion is reuniting with your own source. Religion is remembering, becoming again a part of the organic unity that you are. It is nothing to do with the others. The ego is always concerned with the others, this way or that. When you become totally concerned with yourself, ego simply drops. There is no point for it to exist.

Alone you have no ego. Try it! When you are sitting, totally alone, not even thinking of others, is there any ego left? There is no possibility. The ego needs two to exist. Just like a bridge cannot exist if there are not two banks to the river; the bridge needs two to be supported. The ego exists as a bridge between you and the other. So, in fact, the ego is not in you—it is just between you and the other.

This is something to be remembered always: the ego is not in you. It cannot be there. It is always between you and the other —the husband and wife, the friend, the enemy—always the other. So when you go deep inside, there is no ego. In your total loneliness, ego simply drops. That's why ego goes on playing tricks. Even if you start searching and seeking for truth, the ego says, 'Help others'; the ego says, 'Transform others.' And religion is again missed. It becomes a mission.

Religion is not a mission. Missionaries are again on the wrong track. They have again become concerned with the other—now, in the name of religion, in the name of service—but whenever you are concerned with the other, you have left the source. A religious man also helps others, but he is not concerned. It is natural; it is not a mission. It is not something on the mind. He is not seeking and searching to help somebody. It is just by the way. Out of his inner treasures, he simply shares. And he is not to change anybody! He is not after you to mould you in a certain pattern. Because that is the subtlest violence possible in the world —to try to change the other, to mould the other. That means you are cutting and being aggressive. And you don't accept the other as God has created him. You have better proposals and you have better ideas than the Divine himself. You want to improve on the Whole. You are simply stupid.

This is how ego comes in.

I have heard about a small Sunday school. The priest, the missionary, was teaching the boys who had been forced to go to the Sunday school to learn about the Bible, Christ and God. It is just inhuman to force children, but you can force them. That's why so many people later on become irreligious, anti-religious. They are taking revenge. In the beginning you forced religion on them; then they take revenge, they throw it, they move to the other extreme. Christmas was coming near so the priest, the missionary, said to the boys, 'Now, this is your duty: you should bring more boys to the class; and each of you should try to bring at least two boys. This is how you will help the work of Jesus on this earth.'

The boys were not very enthusiastic. They themselves had been forced and they wanted somehow to escape. They looked at each other—nobody was showing any interest. Then suddenly one boy, a new recruit—and new recruits are always dangerous, because they can go too much to the extreme in their enthusiasm —a new boy raised his hand. The missionary was very happy. He said, 'So you are ready to bring two boys to the class.'

The boy said, 'Not exactly. Two are too much, and two are too difficult. I can try only one. I have a young feller in my neighbourhood whom I can lick. And I promise you, sir, that I will do my damndest to bring him.'

This is what missionaries of all religions have been doing all over the world: doing their damndest to force people towards religion.

Religion is not a mission. You need not force anybody towards it. When the urge arises, it arises. It cannot be artificially created. Nobody can create an artificial religious urge. That is impossible. It is just like artificially creating a sexual urge in a small child. Even if a child asks questions about sex, he is not interested in sex. Even if he asks from where babies are coming, you misunderstand him if you think that he is interested in sex. He is simply curious about babies, from where they are coming. He is not interested in sex at all. And don't start teaching him about sex, because he will be simply bored. It will be nonsense to him, because when the urge is not there, when he is not sexually mature, anything you say about sex just goes above his head.

And the same happens with the spiritual urge. It is very similar to the sexual urge. One comes to a maturity, a spiritual maturity, something has ripened within you, and then the search starts. Nobody can enforce it. But all the religions have tried to enforce it, and they have killed the very possibility of the urge.

185

The world is so irreligious because of the missionaries, the priests. The world is so irreligious because you have taught too much religion, without ever thinking whether the urge exists there or not. People are fed up with your teachings. Churches simply bore. And beautiful words like 'God', 'prayer', 'love', 'meditation', have become ugly. The greatest words have become the dirtiest —because of the missionaries. They have been forcing these beautiful words on you. And when something beautiful is forced, it becomes ugly. You can participate in beauty, but you cannot be forced towards it—then it becomes violence.

Religion is not concerned with others. It is concerned with you, absolutely with you. Religion is personal. It is not a social phenomenon. In fact, there cannot be any sociology of religion; there can only be a psychology. Society is a totally different matter; the crowd is a totally different matter—where peripheries meet. Religion is when you are so alone that there is nobody left to be met. In that total, virgin aloneness, the suprememost ecstasy is born. But you have to come to a ripeness.

Remember, ripeness is all. Before it nothing can be done. And you may be thinking that you are ready, or somebody else may be thinking that he is ready; your curiosity may give you a wrong feeling, a notion that you are ready—but readiness only means that you are ready to stake your life; otherwise it is not a readiness.

Religion is higher than life because life is life with others, life is a relationship, and religion is a non-relationship. It is higher than life. It is the capacity to be alone. It is total independence from the other. Unless you are ready to sacrifice life to it, unless you are ready to die completely as you have been up to now, you are not ready. In that readiness, a small message can become so powerful that it can transform you.

Religion is not concerned with others. And, finally, religion is not concerned with scriptures, words. Wise words are there, but for those words you are not the target; they were never addressed to you. Krishna talked to Arjuna; it was a personal dialogue. Jesus talks to his disciples—a small group of disciples, a personal dialogue—he knows everybody; he knows what he is saying; he knows to whom he is saying it. But the Bible becomes dead, the Gita becomes dead.

Religion is not like a broadcast on the radio. You don't know to whom you are talking. In the air you talk. The face of the listener is not there. The center of the listener is not there. There is nobody. It may be, it is possible, that nobody is listening to the broadcast and you are talking in a vacuum. Religion is like a personal letter. You write it to somebody and *only* to somebody; it is meant for somebody. That's why I have never tried to write anything—except letters. Unless you are here, alive centers, receptive, listening, I cannot say anything. It 'is impossible. To whom to say it? It is not a dead word. When there is a listener, the dialogue becomes alive; then it has a significance which no scripture can ever have.

So everybody has to seek alive Masters. You can read the Gita—it is beautiful; you can read the Bible—it is wonderful; but they are pieces of literature—beautiful as literature, poetry, prose, but not as religion. Religion happens only between two persons: one who knows, and one who does not know but is ready to know. Suddenly religion is born. This is the third thing.

These three things you remember, then we can move into this story.

A powerful king, ruler of many domains, was in a position of such magnificence that wise men were his mere employees.

That's possible; you can hire wise men. If you have enough money wise men can be mere employees to you—but you will not learn by that way. He had many wise men. In olden days, every emperor, every great king, had many wise men. But I have never heard that any emperor ever learnt anything from those wise men.

It is said of the great emperor, Akbar, that he had nine wise men in his court. He could afford them. They were called the nine jewels, but I don't see that he ever learnt anything from them. Because learning needs a different relationship: learning needs that the learner should bow down, surrender. How can you surrender to your own servants? it is almost impossible! You can order them, but you cannot surrender.

It is reported, it happened in the life of Akbar, that he called his nine wise men and he was very angry and he said, 'You are here, and people say you are the greatest wise men in the world today, but I have not been able to learn anything from you. What is the matter? You are here, and I remain the same; then what are you doing here?'

A child had come with a wise man; he wanted to see the court. He laughed. The wise men were silent and the child laughed. Akbar said, 'Why are you laughing? It is insulting to the court! Has not your father told you about manners?'

The child said, 'I am laughing because these nine wise men are silent, and I know why they are silent. And I know why you have not been able to be benefited by them.'

Akbar looked at the child's face—very innocent, but very ancient also. Whenever a child is very innocent, you can see the deep ancientness in his eyes—because no child is a child. He has lived, experienced much; he carries all the knowledge from all his experiences in the past. Akbar said, 'Then can you teach me something?'

The child said, 'Yes!'

Akbar said, 'Then teach!'

The child said, 'Then you have to follow me. You come down here where I am sitting, and I will sit on the throne. And then you ask like a disciple, not like a Master.'

And it is said that Akbar understood. Those nine wise men had been absolutely useless. He could not learn, not because they couldn't teach—they could teach—but he was not ready, and he was not receptive, and he was not humble enough.

It is said that he sat down, and the child sat on the throne and he said, 'Now you ask like a disciple, not like an emperor.'

Akbar never asked anything. And it is said that he thanked the child, touched his feet and said, 'There is no need to ask. Just by sitting in a humble attitude near your feet, I have learnt much.'

Humbleness is the basic thing. Even without a wise man, if you are humble, you will learn much. You can learn from the trees and the springs and the clouds and the winds. If you are humble, the whole existence becomes a teacher to you. But if you are not humble, and a Buddha is there, no intimacy happens. A Buddha is around you, but no intimacy happens—you are not humble. You would like to learn, but without bending, without bringing down your ego.

A powerful king, ruler of many domains, was in a position of such magnificence that wise men were his mere employees.

It is easy! You can collect wise men around you—but that is not the point. The real point is not to bring a wise man to your house; the real point is how to go to a wise man, because in the very going you learn. And these wise men could not have been real wise men either, because a wise man will not waste his life in the courts. They may be intellectual, very knowledgeable, great scholars, but not wise. Knowledge and wisdom are totally different.

Just the other day we were talking about the fact that the question of knowledge is very dangerous. If the doctor had told the woman, 'You go on a fast for forty days,' it would have been knowledge. But he told the woman, 'Now there is no possibility of any cure. You drop any idea about fertility and this and that. You are going to die in forty days.' This is wisdom, the difference between knowledge and wisdom.

Knowledge is a dead response. You have learnt something and you go on applying it to everything. Wisdom is an alive response. You look at the situation, and you respond. It is not a reaction; it is a response. When you react, you react out of the past. When you respond, you respond here and now. He looked at the woman, her body—too much fat. He felt the heart of the woman, the pulse. He was a wise man; he created a device. He lied to the woman: 'You are going to die.' And the woman was transformed.

People who go to the courts and to the capitals, and can be purchased, cannot be much of the wise.

It happened in Japan: An emperor became very anxious to know about death and life beyond death. He had all the wise men in his court. He asked them; they said, 'If we knew, we would not have been here. We are just as ignorant as you. You are rich,

189

we are poor—that's the only difference. We don't know. If you really want to know, you will have to move out of the court. You will have to seek and search for the Master. The Master cannot come to you. You will have to go to the Master.'

The emperor tried. He went to all the well-known persons —of course! that's the way one seeks—he went to all the well-known saints, but was not satisfied. Again he came to the court and told his wise men, 'I have been searching all over the country.'

Those people said, 'You are again searching wrongly. You go to the well-known persons—it is difficult to find a Master there. Because in the first place, it is very difficult for a real Master to become well-known, very difficult. It rarely happens. Secondly, a real Master tries to hide himself in many, many ways, so that only real seekers can reach him, and not curious people who just by the way would like to ask something. You have been searching in the wrong places.' And those wise people said, 'We know a man here, in this town, in your capital, but you will have to come to the man.'

He was a beggar and he lived under a bridge with other beggars. The emperor could not believe it, but something was coming out of him, some emanation, something from the beyond, that touched his heart, that changed the beat of his heart—a magnetic force. Without knowing why, without ever knowing what he was doing, for the first time he touched the feet of a man. And then suddenly he himself was shocked at what he had done. He had touched the feet of a beggar! But the beggar said, 'You are accepted.'

This is the way in which one starts learning.

The man was rich:

> A very rich king, ruler of many domains, was in a position of such magnificence that wise men were his mere employees.

Rich people can afford wise men—but those wise men will not be really wise. You cannot purchase wisdom. You can purchase everything in this world, but you cannot purchase wisdom.

It is reported in Mahavir's life that a king came to him, a very famous king—his name was Prasenjit. He came to Mahavir and he said, 'I have everything that this world can offer. I am deeply contented. There is nothing more to achieve. All my ambitions are fulfilled. Only one thing goes on and on in my mind: What is this meditation? What is this *dhyan*? I am ready to purchase it. And whatsoever the cost—you say, and I will give. This is the only thing that has been haunting me: What is this meditation? dhyan? samadhi? Only one thing am I lacking; in my treasuries, only one thing is lacking and that is samadhi, dhyan. You give it to me. I have heard that you have attained it, so you can give it to me! And whatsoever the cost—don't bother about the cost.'

Mahavir said, 'There is no need to come to me, so far away from your capital. In your capital itself there is a very poor man; he may like to sell it. And he has attained. You better go to him.'

Mahavir played a joke. And Mahavir said, 'I don't need to sell it. You go to this man, a very poor man in your capital, and he will be happy.'

Prasenjit returned, immediately went to the man with many bullock-carts loaded with gold coins, diamonds, emeralds, many riches, and just emptied out all the bullock-carts before the house of the poor man. He said, 'Take all these, and if you ask more, I can give more—but where is that dhyan? Give me that!'

The poor man started crying and weeping, and he said, 'I may be poor, but this is impossible. I would like to thank you for all your riches you have brought to me, but the bargain is not possible. Meditation is a state of being—I cannot give it to you. I am ready to give my life if it is needed. I love you, respect you; I am ready to give my life. You can take it right now, you can cut my head. But meditation, samadhi, how can I give it to you?'

Just see: even life can be given, but not dhyan. Dhyan is higher than life. You can sacrifice your life, but you cannot sacrifice samadhi. It is impossible! And life can be taken from you, anybody can kill you—samadhi cannot be taken from you. Nobody can take it, purchase it, steal it, kill it. And unless you attain to samadhi, you have not come to the real treasure. Even life is not a real treasure. That which cannot be taken away from you is real treasure. Even death cannot take it away from you. That is the criterion.

Whatsoever you have, always put it to the criterion: whether death will take it away from you or not. That should become a constant contemplation. You have money—will death separate you from it or not? You have prestige, political power, fame, beauty, physical strength, body, whatsoever you have, put it to the criterion: whether it will be taken by death, whether you will be separated from it, or not. And you will find that, except sama-dhi, everything will be taken by death. That's why Sufis say it is better to die to all these things which will be taken by death finally. Eventually they are going to be taken away. Die to them, and arise in samadhi—because that is the only thing which is deathless.

The king had everything. He had employed many wise men. But he could not have learnt anything. In the first place, the wise men must not have been very wise. In the second place, when you employ a wise man, how can you learn anything from him? You have to become a servant to a wise man; you have to fall at his feet and surrender, only then can you learn, because learning is possible.... Wisdom is just like water flowing downwards. Water goes on moving downwards, finding holes and valleys and lakes, and filling them. Become a lake-like phenomenon; near a wise man, become a valley. Don't try to be the peak of the ego, become a valley, and suddenly you will be filled.

And yet one day he felt himself confused and called his sages to him.

It comes. When you have lived too much in riches, the moment comes. The moment comes when one feels frustrated with all that riches can give. When you live in the palaces, a moment comes when you feel that this is not life. Death starts knocking on the door. Miseries enter. You cannot protect yourself from sadness. And this king, at that time, was in trouble. A neighbouring country was planning to attack. And the neighbouring country was a very great country, more powerful than him. He was afraid—death, defeat, despair of old age. And then he started seeking.

He called his wise men and he said to them:

'I do not know the cause, but something impels me to seek a certain ring, one that will enable me to stabilize my state. I must have such a ring, and this ring must be one which, when I am unhappy it will make me joyful, and at the same time, if I am happy and look upon it I must be made sad.'

He is asking for a key, a key with which he can open two doors: the door of happiness and the door of unhappiness. But he wants one key by which both the doors can be opened. He must have attained to a certain understanding.

When you live a rich life of many experiences, good and bad, you attain to a certain understanding. I always feel that a man who has not lived in many ways—wrong and right, moral and immoral, rich and poor, good and bad—who has not lived in all the opposites, never attains to a very deep understanding of life. He may become a saint, but his saintliness will be a poor saintliness. When a Buddha becomes a saint, his saintliness becomes incomparable, unique. From where does this uniqueness come to Buddha? It comes from his multi-dimensional life. He has lived all, and when you live all, by and by you rise above all. Through living you come to understand that this is useless. It is beautiful to remember again and again Buddha's life.

When he was born, the astrologers said, 'This boy will either become a *chakravartin*—an emperor of the whole world—or he will become a sannyasin. These two are the possibilities.' The two most extreme possibilities? Either the emperor of the world, or a man who has renounced all and has become a beggar on the street —homeless, rootless, a vagabond, a sannyasin. Two extremes.

The father asked, 'How is it so? You talk about two extremes. What is the meaning of it?'

The astrologers said, 'This is always so. Whenever a man is born to become a chakravartin'—'chakravartin' means the emperor of the whole, of the whole earth—'whenever a person is born who is capable of becoming a chakravartin, the other possibility is always there.'

The father still could not understand. He said, 'Tell me in detail.'

The astrologer said, 'We don't know much about the phenomenon of sannyasin, but this much is said in the scriptures: that when a man has everything, then suddenly an awakening dawns into him that everything is useless.'

Only a beggar hankers for the palace; the man in the palace is already finished with the palace. A man who has not known women, beautiful women, always hankers. A man who has known, is already finished. Only knowledge, experience, changes you. So if this man is going to have the whole world, how long can he remain in it? Sooner or later, he will renounce. All the Buddhas were born kings, all the Hindu *avatars* were born kings, all the Jain Teerthankars were born kings—there is something to it; it is not just coincidental. They lived, they indulged, and they indulged so totally in everything that there was no barrier to them. Sooner or later they came to the bottom of the whole phenomenon—there was nothing.

It is just like when you go on peeling an onion—what happens? If you peel one layer, another layer is there, fresher than the first, younger. You peel another, an even more fresh layer is there, more young. You go on. If you don't peel the onion to the very last, you will always think that something must be there still. But if you peel the onion completely, suddenly a moment comes—the last layer is broken and there is nothing in it. The emptiness.

That's what happens to an emperor. He goes on peeling the onion of life; he can afford it. A beggar cannot afford the whole onion—mm?—he remains just on the periphery. If he can peel the first layer, that is too much: 'Then there are other layers!' And he always hopes somewhere inside: 'I have not attained to bliss in this world because I don't have the whole world in my hand. If I had the whole world, who knows?—maybe I would have become blissful, I would have attained to deep contentment.' That haunting desire remains. With an emperor the whole onion is in the hands.

The astrologers said to Buddha's father, 'This is always so. A chakravartin *always* has the alternative of becoming a sannyasin.' And from the other end also it is true—it has not been said there, but I would like to add it to the story—that a sannyasin is always a chakravartin. Whenever there happens a sannyas, that *means* that the man has lived through many, many lives through all the experiences. He is finished. That is the maturity. A chakravartin has the alternative of being a sannyasin. If you *really* become a sannyasin, that shows only one thing: that you have been a chakravartin; not in one life, but in many lives, spread out, you have lived all.

Buddha's father was very worried and he said, 'Then what to do? I have only one son, and he too was born in my old age. I am young no more. And my wife died immediately when Buddha was born so I cannot hope for any more sons, and the whole kingdom will go to ruins. What to do? Suggest something.'

They suggested, and they suggested very knowingly. This is how knowledge fails. They were not wise people. They were great astrologers, they knew the scripture, they knew the word, but they didn't know the spirit. They suggested an ordinary course, such as any man of knowledge would have suggested— but not a man of wisdom. They suggested: 'You do one thing: don't allow this boy to come to face any misery, any pain, any unhappiness. Don't allow him to know that old age comes. Don't allow him to know that people die. And arrange as many beautiful women around him as you can manage. Let him live a life of total indulgence, and *no* frustration. Without frustration, nobody ever becomes a sannyasin.'

This was pure logic, and this was done. There was no difficulty; the father could manage. Three houses were made for Buddha, for three seasons, in different places. He would live in a cold region in the summer; and that way he would change— every four months he would move to another house, great palaces. All the beautiful girls of the kingdom were called; never has a man remained with so many beautiful women together. Buddha lived in indulgence. It is said that even in the garden of Buddha's palace, no flower was allowed to die. Before it started dying, it had to be removed. Never did Buddha see a dry leaf. It had to be removed in the night so that the idea of death would never arise, and he would never come to think about the fact that life is going to end. Because if that thinking came, then he would start thinking of renouncing the life which is going to end.

Buddha knew only the beautiful things, he knew only the dreams, he lived in those dreams—but reality is too much. It penetrates every dream. You cannot avoid reality. Howsoever you manage, even with an emperor father managing everything, you cannot avoid reality. It bumps into you from here and there; you stumble upon it. How can you manage to dream continuously twenty-four hours a day?

One night, Buddha was enjoying; the girls were dancing, there was great music and dance, and he enjoyed. And then he fell asleep. It was midnight and he was tired, and all the girls fell asleep. Suddenly in the middle of the night, he became awake and he looked at the girls—the beauty was not there. Saliva was flowing, somebody's mouth was open and it was looking ugly. Somebody else was in a nightmare and she was crying and weeping. Suddenly he became aware: 'I was thinking all these women were so beautiful—and they have suddenly become ugly?'

In that night, reality penetrated. He kept it to himself.

One day, he was going to participate in a festival. On the way he came to see an old man. He had never seen one before. He came to see a dead body being carried to the burning *ghat*. He had never seen one. He asked his driver, the chariot-driver, 'What is the matter? What has happened to this man? Why has his face become so wrinkled? And why is his back bent? What calamity has fallen upon him?'

The driver said, 'It is not a calamity, sir. It happens to everybody. It is a natural thing. Everybody becomes old and wrinkled.'

The reality penetrated. And then he asked, 'What has happened to this other man? Why are people carrying him on their shoulders?'

The driver said, 'This man is dead, sir. This is the next step after old age.'

Buddha suddenly said, 'Stop the chariot! *Am I also going to die?*'

The driver hesitated. He knew what the father was doing. But he was a very true man, simple and authentic. He said, 'I am not allowed to say, but since you have raised the question I cannot also be a liar to you. This man is dead. And just like this man you will also be dead. Everybody who is born is going to die.'

And then, suddenly, a sannyasin who was following the dead man appeared. Buddha asked, 'And what has happened to this man? Why this orange robe?' He had never seen a sannyasin before. Really, unless you see a dead man, how can you see a sannyasin? It is a logical sequence—old age, death, sannyas.

The story is beautiful—whether it happened or not; that is not the point. But the story is beautiful and true—whether it happened or not, it is true—because after death, encountering death, what else remains but sannyas?

The chariot-driver said, 'This man has understood life; he has understood that life ends in death, and he has renounced.'

Buddha said, 'Turn back to the palace—I have renounced.'

At that moment even the driver couldn't understand what he was saying. By the night, he had left the palace.

When you live life in its totality, you *have to renounce it!* Only those who have not lived rightly, who have not lived at all, or who have lived lukewarm and tepid lives, they cling. Clinging shows an ignorant mind which doesn't understand. Renunciation is simple, it is a natural outgrowth, it is a maturity.

Those astrologers were men of knowledge. They helped Buddha, really, not at all knowingly, to renounce. If it had been asked of me, if Buddha's father, Suddhodan, had asked me, I would not have suggested this—because this is the natural way to renounce the life. I would have suggested: 'Starve this man; don't give him as much food as he needs. Starve him so much that he thinks and dreams about food. Don't allow him to touch a woman, or come near to a woman; keep all the beautiful women at a distance so he hankers and desires; starve him sexually also. And don't make too many palaces; let him live a beggar's life—then he will never renounce.'

That's what has happened to you all. You cannot renounce because you have lived a beggar's life. Only beggars are unable to renounce. Emperors are always ready to renounce. Only emperors can become sannyasins, not beggars. How can a beggar think of renouncing? He has not got anything—how can he renounce? You can renounce only that which you have got. If you don't have, you cannot renounce—what will you renounce?

This king, in a deep crisis, came to understand that happiness and unhappiness are not different. He was wiser than his wise men. That's why he asks for one key which can open both the doors. In fact, happiness and unhappiness are not two things. They are one phenomenon: two faces of the same thing, two aspects. So one key will open both.

Watch—when you are happy, can you say with absolute certainty that no unhappiness exists side by side? Happiness may be in the center, but by the corner is not unhappiness waiting for you? Is not somewhere in your happiness a seed of unhappiness already sprouting? When you are unhappy are you absolutely certain you are simply unhappy? Or is there some possibility gaining strength which will transform unhappiness into happiness?

It is just like in the morning when the sun rises—you cannot see evening coming, but in the morning the evening is hidden. It has already come. With the morning it has entered. When there is a noontide of light, and the sun is at its peak, at its omega point, who thinks about night and darkness? But in that very omega point, the seed of the night is there, growing, waiting for its time. And at the omega point, the sun has already started setting, it is already moving toward the west. In the darkest night, the morning is pregnant; it is there in the womb. And the same is true of all the opposites. When you are in love, the hate is there as a seed. When you are in hate, the love is there as a seed. When you are happy, already you have started to move towards unhappiness. When you are unhappy, just wait a little—the happiness has already knocked or entered the door.

The opposites are together. This is a great understanding. And once this understanding is there, the key is not far away.

'I do not know the cause,' said the king . . .

Nobody knows the cause. You have come to me—do you know the cause? Why have you come to me? Nobody knows the cause. But a deep unconscious desire has brought you towards me. And you will never be the same again, you cannot be. I have become a part of you, a member of you. Even if you forget me completely, you cannot be the same again. I will remain in your forgetfulness.

Do you know the cause why you have come—from so many countries, from so many different corners of the world, to a man who has nothing to give to you, or only nothing to give to you? What is the cause? Why have you come here? You may not be aware right now, because the cause is in the unconscious, but the deeper your meditation goes, by and by you will become aware that it is life that has thrown you towards me—it is life with its miseries; it is life with its frustrations. Of course, there are moments of happiness, but the misery is so much that even those moments of happiness become poisoned by it. You have loved; you have enjoyed a few moments, peak moments; you were ecstatic—but then again you fall back into the valley. You have come to me because you have felt unconsciously that happiness and unhappiness are one, and that if you go on desiring happiness, you will go on becoming unhappy.

> *The king said, 'I do not know the cause, but something impels me to seek a certain ring . . .'*

There is a story behind this story. It is said that Sufis have a ring—a very occult way of saying things—Sufis have a ring, and if you can get that ring, you will go beyond life and death; you will go beyond darkness and light; you will go beyond day and night; you will go beyond misery and happiness—you will go beyond dualities. Sufis have a ring, if you can get hold of that ring. . . . The king must have heard about it, so he said:

> *'I don't know what the cause is, but something impels me to seek a certain ring, one that will enable me to stabilize my state, my being. I must have such a ring, and this ring must be one which, when I am unhappy it will make me joyful . . .'*

He's asking for a secret alchemical formula: 'When I am joyful, it will make me miserable, sad; when I am sad, it will make me joyful, happy.'

What is he asking? He is asking mastery of his moods. And

this is the only mastery! When you are unhappy, you are unhappy. You cannot do anything; you are just a victim. You say, 'I am unhappy. I cannot do anything.' When it comes, it comes—you are unhappy. Sometimes you are happy; nothing you can do about it either—when it comes, it comes. You are not a master.

What is he saying? He is saying, 'I am in search of a secret formula so that I can become master of my moods. And when I want to transform my happiness into sadness, I can. And when I want to change my sadness into ecstatic happiness, I can.' What is he saying? He is saying that he wants to become master of his moods; he wants to create his moods—he doesn't want to be a victim. He wants that whatsoever he wants, he can create it.

And there is a formula. And there exists a ring with a secret message in it, which can transform. And then it is simply wonderful when you can change your moods. You can just put them on and off.

'. . . when I am unhappy it will make me joyful, and at the same time, if I am happy and look upon it I must be made sad.'

With the first you will agree. With the second you will say, 'What is the necessity?' But they both exist together. If you become master of one, you become master of the other also. And there is nothing wrong in being sad if you are the master.

Sadness has a depth to it, which no happiness can ever have. Sadness has a beauty of its own, a very soft beauty—deep, soft. No happiness can have that. Happiness has a shallowness about it, a vulgarity about it. Sadness has a depth, a greater plenitude than any happiness can have. You have not enjoyed because you have not been able to bring your awareness towards it. When a man becomes more and more aware he enjoys everything, even sadness. Then sadness settles around him like evening settling, and everything becomes silent. Even the birds don't sing, even the winds don't blow—everything becomes silent, and everything settles in a deep relaxation.

Sadness is beautiful if you know. If you don't know that even happiness is not beautiful, how can sadness be beautiful?

The king said, 'I want to become a master of my moods,' and

that is why he says, 'to stabilize my state.' If you are not the master of your moods, and they blow on their own, how can you have a stability? How can you have a crystallized being? A mood comes suddenly, and you are unhappy, and everything starts trembling within you. Another mood comes, and you are happy; again there is excitement and everything trembles within you.

Have you observed that a long mood of happiness also *tires* you? Because it is an excitement. You cannot be happy for a long period, otherwise it will be too much for your body, for your mind; for your psychosomatic being it will be too much. You cannot be because it makes you tremble, it is like a fever. People cannot remain happy for ever. They will die; they will have heart attacks, blood pressure, and many things.

It happens that miserable people live longer than happy people, because miserable people are less excited, happy people are more excited. Excitement is a burden on the heart. Successful people have more heart attacks than failures do. In fact, unsuccessful people don't have heart attacks. What is the use of having a heart attack? A heart attack is a medical certificate that you are a successful man. It comes near about forty, between forty and forty-five, because that is the peak of a man's success. Then the heart attack comes, because success brings more and more excitement.

Miserable people, sad people, live longer; on average, they live five to ten years longer than people who are happy, successful. What is the matter? Sad people are more settled; in their gloom they are less in excitement. And if you try to understand both the phenomena deeply, you will find they are interrelated and that each turns into the other. It is like a wheel: sometimes the spoke of happiness is at the top, sometimes it is at the bottom, then the other spoke is at the top. It goes on moving. And you are in the grip of the wheel, as if you are tied to the wheel and you move with the wheel. How can you stabilize yourself?

The king is right. He said, 'So that my state becomes a stabilized state, so that I can become settled within my own being, I would like to have the ring Sufis have been talking about. Where is that ring?'

The wise men consulted one another . . .

That's why I say they were not very wise. Experts consult. Never wise men. 'Experts' means people who are knowledgeable; they consult each other—mm?—because you may not know something, the other may know. But a wise man simply knows! It is not a question to think about. A wise man is not a thinker. He simply knows!—and he responds with his total being. There was not a single wise man—they consulted.

The wise men consulted one another and threw themselves into deep contemplation.

A wise man need not throw himself into deep contemplation. He *exists* in it. He *is* deep contemplation. Only fools contemplate. A wise man never contemplates. He is the contemplation, the very quality. But they were not wise men, they were not wise people.

Finally they came to a decision as to the character of this ring which would suit their king.

I know another version of the story, and I think the other version is better. The other version is that they couldn't come to any conclusion. And that seems right. How can experts come to a conclusion? They can fight, argue. Have you ever known people who are argumentative, philosophers, theologians? Have you ever known them to come to any conclusion? No. Even if you give them a conclusion already concluded, on that conclusion they will fight and move in different directions. That's how it has been happening always.

It happened in this century with Freud—a man of much knowledge, but not a wise man, not wise in the sense a Buddha is wise—a very deep, penetrating thinker. And, by and by, all his disciples—Karl Gustav Jung, Adler, and others—who had come to him thinking that there was a conclusion, that something had been found . . . it simply proved to be a crossroad where they separated. All his disciples went in different directions. And those who remained with him were minor figures; amongst those who remained with him there was not a single genius. All the geniuses departed—argued, fought, departed, and became enemies.

It is impossible for men of knowledge, knowledgeable men, to conclude anything. The other version says they couldn't conclude so they went to a Sufi saint and asked his advice. The Sufi saint had the ring already—wise men always have the ring already. He just took the ring off his finger, gave it to them, and told them, 'Give it to the king. But tell him there is one condition: only when he feels that now it is impossible to tolerate, then he should open the ring. Hidden underneath the stone is the message, but he should not open it just out of curiosity because then he will miss the message. The message is there, but a *right* moment in *your* consciousness is needed to meet it. It is not a dead message that you can open and read. It is written under the stone, but a condition is to be fulfilled: when *everything* is lost, and the mind cannot do anything more, the confusion is total, the agony perfect, and you cannot do anything else, you are absolutely helpless, then only should it be opened—and the message will be there.'

And this is right. I would also like to make this condition, because without this condition it means the message is there and anybody can read it—then the message is not of much value. You have to rise to a certain consciousness; only then can you understand. The understanding is not in the words—the understanding is within you. The words will only trigger the understanding, that's all, but it has to be there to be triggered.

The king followed the message. The country was lost, the enemy became victorious. Many moments came when he was just on the verge of taking off the stone and reading the message, but he found that it was still not total: 'I'm still alive. Even if the kingdom is lost, I can regain it, it can be reconquered.'

He flew out of the kingdom just to save his life. The enemy is following him, he can hear the horses, their sounds coming nearer and nearer. And he goes on running. Friends are lost, his horse dies, then he runs on his feet. The feet have become bloody, cut everywhere. He cannot move even an inch and he has to run continuously. He's hungry, and the enemy is coming nearer and nearer. And then he comes to a cul-de-sac. The road finishes, there is no more road ahead. There is just an abyss. And the enemy is coming closer and closer. He cannot go back; the enemy is there.

He cannot jump. The abyss is so big, he will simply be dead. Now there seems to be no possibility—but he still waits for the condition. He says, 'Still I am alive. Maybe the enemy will move in some other direction. Maybe if I jump into this abyss I will not die. The condition is not yet fulfilled.' And then suddenly he feels the enemy is too close. And when he looks to jump he sees two lions who have by now just come in the abyss, and they are looking at him—hungry, ferocious. Now there is no moment left, and the enemy is coming nearer and nearer and nearer, and his last moments he can count just on the fingers.

Suddenly he takes the ring, opens it, looks behind the stone. There is a message and the message is: 'This, too, will pass.'

Suddenly everything is relaxed—'This, too, will pass.' And, of course, it happens: the enemy has moved in another direction, and he cannot hear their noise so much; they are moving further away. He sits down. He takes a good sleep, rest. And within ten days, he collects his armies, comes back, reconquers the country, is again in his palace. There is great jubilation and celebration. People are going crazy. They are dancing in the streets, there is much colour and light and fireworks. And he is feeling so excited, and so happy, and his heart is beating so fast, that he thinks that he may die because of happiness. Suddenly he remembers the ring, opens it, looks into it. It is written there: 'This, too, will pass.' And he relaxes. And it is said that he attains to the perfect wisdom through this message: 'This, too, will pass.'

Whenever a mood comes to you, of anger, hatred, passion, sex, misery, sadness, happiness, *even* while meditating, a moment of bliss, always remember: This, too, will pass. Let it become a constant mindfulness: This, too, will pass.

And what will happen to you if you can remember it continuously? Then happiness will not be happiness—just a phase, a cloud that comes and goes. *It is not you!* It comes and passes. *It is not your being.* It is something accidental. It is something on the periphery. You are the witness.

When you remember: 'This, too, will pass. This, too, will pass. This, too, will pass'—suddenly, you are separate from it. It comes to you, but it is not you. It goes away, you are left behind

—intact, untouched. Misery comes; let it come. Just remember, it too will pass. Happiness comes; remember, it too will pass. And, by and by, a distance is created between the moods and you. You are no longer identified with them. You have become a witness. You just look at them, a spectator. You are no more concerned, you have become indifferent.

A silence descends on you—silence which is not created by you, silence which is not a forced stillness; a silence which suddenly descends from unknown sources, from the Divine, from the Whole. And then you are crystallized. Then nothing shakes your foundations. Then nothing makes you tremble. Nothing!—happiness, unhappiness. And then you know that they are both the same. If the face is of happiness, the back is of unhappiness. If the face is of unhappiness, the back is of happiness. They are the same. When happiness comes towards you, it looks like happiness; when it goes away from you, look at the back—it is unhappiness.

The more distance, the more awareness. The more awareness, the more distance. You become settled. You become a Buddha under the Bodhi Tree.

But this will not happen to you until you die as you are. This is a resurrection, the birth of the absolutely new. The old has to give way. Your old attitudes, concepts, philosophies, ideologies, your old identity, the old ego, they have to give way for the new. The new is always there, but there is no space in you for it to come. The guest has come, but the host is not ready. Give space! Become more spacious within you. Create room, emptiness.

And this message is wonderful. This is a master-key. Remember it.

> The ring which they devised was one upon which was inscribed the legend:
>
> 'THIS, TOO, WILL PASS.'

Let it become a constant remembrance. Let it become so deeply continuous, that even in sleep you know: This, too, will pass. Even in dreams you know: This, too, will pass. Let it become like breathing, continuously there, a presence. And that presence will transform you. It is a master-key; it can open the secretmost door into your own being, and from there, via there, into the very being of existence.

18 April 1975

IX
Almost Dead with Thirst

Shibli was asked: 'Who guided you in the Path?'

Shibli said: 'A dog. One day I saw him, almost dead with thirst, standing by the water's edge. Every time he looked at his reflection in the water he was frightened and withdrew, because he thought it was another dog.

'Finally, such was his necessity, he cast away fear and leapt into the water; at which the reflection disappeared.

'The dog found that the obstacle, which was himself, the barrier between him and what he sought, melted away.

'In this same way, my own obstacle vanished when I knew that it was what I took to be my own self. And my Way was first shown to me by the behaviour of—a dog.'

I LOOK into you ... and I don't see any other barrier than yourself. You are standing in your own way. And unless you understand it, nothing is possible towards inner growth.

If somebody else was the barrier, you could have dodged him, you could have bypassed him. If somebody else was the barrier, you could have escaped. But *you* are the barrier. You cannot dodge—who will dodge whom? You cannot bypass—who will bypass whom? You cannot escape, because wherever you will go *you* will be there.

Your barrier is you, and it will follow you like a shadow.

This has to be understood as deeply as possible. How does this barrier arise? What is the mechanism of the ego which becomes the barrier? A hard crust around you—and you cannot fly into the sky, you cannot open into the world of love and prayer. This shell of the ego, how is it born? If you can understand the birth of the ego, you will know the secret of how to dissolve it. The very understanding of the arising of the ego becomes the freedom.

The ego is born—not that you know yourself—the ego is born through reflections. You see your reflection in the eyes of others, in the faces, in their words, and you go on accumulating those reflections. Not knowing who you are, you have to find an identity.

A child is born—he does not know who he is. But he has to

know who he is, otherwise it will be impossible to live in the world. And he cannot become a Buddha immediately. He does not even know the problem. He has not entered into the world yet. He will really enter into the world when he starts feeling who he is.

That's why you cannot remember many things of your childhood. If you go backwards, you will be able to remember up to the age of three, four. Beyond that you will not be able to penetrate. What is the matter? Was not memory functioning? Were not there any experiences, imprints on the mind, impressions? They were there! In fact, a young child of three years or two years of age is more impressionable than he ever will be. And millions of experiences are happening to the child. But why is the memory not there? Because the ego is still not ripe. Who will carry the memory? What will be the nucleus of the memory? The child has not yet identified who he is. No identification has come up yet.

How will he get the ego? He looks into the eyes of the mother. The eyes are happy, smiling. He gathers the impression, 'I must be beautiful, I must be lovely, valuable, precious. Whenever the mother comes near, she becomes so happy. She comes and kisses me.' The child is gathering impressions. The father comes and the father goes crazy—throws the child into the air, plays with the child . . . and the child is watching. The father becomes the mirror. The mother becomes the mirror. Neighbours come—and, by and by, he's accumulating. He is filing into the mind who he is.

That's why, if a child has been brought up without a mother, he will always be lacking something in his identity. And he will not be able to love himself, because the basic impression of somebody loving is not there. He will be in certain ways always shaky; he will not be sure. The mother gives the surety and the certainty— that you are loved, that you are precious, that you make people happy, you are valuable. And as the child moves, neighbours, friends, school-teachers, millions of impressions, millions of mirrors are all around. And he goes on gathering.

Of course, very soon, he starts filing impressions in divisions. Those who love him, he cherishes. Those who hate him, he does not like. So, many impressions which are not good for the ego, he goes on throwing them in the basement of the mind, in the unconscious. Somebody hits him; somebody says, 'You are ugly'; the teacher says, 'You are stupid'—these impressions he goes on throwing in the unconscious. A division has started.

The conscious is that which you cherish and love—your beautiful image. And in the unconscious you go on throwing the ugly image. Division has entered into the mind. This is the beginning of schizophrenia. If it goes to the very extreme, you will become split into two personalities. Normally, also, you are not one; you are two.

When you are angry, the suppressed personality takes possession. Watch somebody who is getting into anger: the face changes, the eyes change, the behaviour. Suddenly, he is not the same person. It is as if something foreign has entered. He is possessed. And he will do things he himself could not imagine that he can do. He can commit a murder in rage and anger—and he will not be able to understand how it happened. Many murderers in the courts say that they never did it. And they are not lying. In fact, they never did it. Somebody else, a faraway personality, with which they are not identified, possessed them.

See a person who has fallen in love—suddenly a transfiguration happens. His eyes are no more the same; a new light shines through the eyes. His face is no more the same; a softness has entered. He is more flowing. Suddenly, out of darkness a morning is born. Deep down inside him, birds are singing, and flowers are opening.

In love, a man is totally different. In anger, you cannot make these two persons meet. They are separate personalities. In anger, your identity comes up which you have suppressed in the unconscious; in love, your identity which you always cherish.

This split is the cause of all the miseries that happen to humanity, and all the mental agonies that happen to the human mind. Unless this split disappears, you will never be whole. And unless this split disappears, you will never be able to know who you *are*. The conscious is *as* false as the unconscious, because both are just reflections gathered from others. You have not encountered yourself directly, but via the others. There are some mirrors in which you look beautiful. There are some mirrors in which you look ugly. There are some mirrors in which you look divine. There are some mirrors in which you look just animal.

This has been my observation, that whatsoever your identity, whatsoever your ego, deep down there is confusion—because the other condemned part is always there. In your foundations it is always there, and you are always shaky and confused. If somebody really asks you 'Who are you?' the answer is not there. If nobody asks, you know who you are. But if somebody asks, persists, 'Who are you?' you don't know.

St. Augustine has said, 'I know, when nobody asks, what time is. But if somebody asks what time is, I don't know.'

And exactly the same is the case with the ego. If nobody asks, you know. If somebody asks, suddenly the certainty is gone.

That's why it is polite not to ask anybody, 'Who are you?'— because the certainty is just on the surface. How can you be certain just by gathering reflections? And reflections from many sources—they are antagonistic, contradictory, confusing. You are a chaos. Your ego is just a trick to hide the chaos, just a blanket word in which you can go on hiding everything. You are a madness within.

This is the first thing to be understood: that nobody can know himself through mirrors—because mirrors will interpret. In fact, a mirror never shows who you are. A mirror simply says how *he* reacts to you. The mother smiles: it is not that she is saying something about you; she is saying something about herself. She is happy; she has become a mother. And every mother smiles— even to the ugliest child the mother smiles. A very ordinary child, but the mother always thinks that he is going to be a Napoleon, or Alexander, or a Buddha. The mother is not saying something about you. She is happy in being a mother. She is saying something about herself. And if the child smiles, the mother is also gathering ego. If the child smiles, the mother feels very good— she thinks the child is smiling at her.

Everybody is in the same boat. The child is not smiling at the mother; he is not saying anything about the mother. Every child smiles at the mother because she is the source of food and love.

And this is just diplomacy that the child should smile, because that's how he gets more love, more nourishment. Within a few days, the child becomes a politician. He knows when to smile and when not to. He starts giving punishment, prizes. If he is not feeling good about the mother, he will not smile, he will not look at her. She will have to persuade him.

The child is showing something about himself, not about the mother. The mother is showing something about herself, not about the child. When you go to the mirror, the mirror is saying something about itself, not about you. If it is a good mirror from Belgium, it shows something about itself, that 'I am from Belgium.' And if it is Indian-made, it shows that 'I am made in India'— nothing about you. If your face looks beautiful, that shows only that the mirror has been made in a beautiful way. It reflects, it reacts!

This has to be understood—particularly for the seeker, this is one of the basic things—that everybody else around you, *all* the mirrors, reflect. They are their reactions. They are not saying anything about you. How can they say? You yourself don't know yourself—how can they know? Impossible! They do not know themselves—how can they know you?

Ego is the accumulation of impressions, shadows, reflections. And with this ego you live, you live in a hell. Unless you drop this ego, the possibility for heaven will always remain closed.

And don't try to drop it—because right now, the dropper will be the same: the ego. And then you will gain a subtle ego, that 'I am dropping the ego. I have dropped the ego.' And again you will look around to see how people are feeling and they will say, 'We have never seen such a humble man!' And you will collect the reflection that you are the most egoless person, that you are so beautiful, so humble, so simple, you don't have any ego. And you go on collecting.

You cannot drop it, you can only understand.

And there is no need to drop, because there is nothing to drop!—just shadows. You have to understand how you have accumulated your self-identity, how you have gathered your self-image. And this self-image is confusing because you have gathered it from many sources—divergent, diametrically opposite—so you are always a crowd, you don't have a unity. These impressions can't have unity.

If you had lived with one man and you had never come across another man, your ego would have been absolutely certain —but that too is difficult, because one man is not one man either. One moment he is something, another moment something else. In the morning the mother was smiling, and by the afternoon she is angry and hitting you. If you had lived with one man of one single mood, then your ego would have been one. But you have lived with many many people, with millions of moods—all impressions are there. Your ego is a crowd. It is not a crystallization, it is not a center; it has no center. It is just a crowd, a mob.

You cannot drop it. You can simply look and watch and understand. Once you understand, suddenly you feel it is dropped. *You never drop it!* When you understand, it is there no more. It is just like darkness: you bring a candle, and the darkness is not there. You bring understanding, there is light, and the ego disappears, the shadows have gone. And when the ego disappears, for the first time you become a unitary being. Your unconscious and conscious simply lose their boundaries. There are not any boundaries in fact.

And Freud is absolutely wrong, because he thinks the unconscious and conscious have some substantial boundaries. They have none. It is only because of the ego. The accepted part of the ego has become the conscious because you accept it; it can come to the surface. The rejected part of the ego, because you reject it, you throw it away—where will it go?—it falls deeper in you. There is no darkness: you are just standing with your back towards the rejected part.

Once you understand that the ego is just a crowd of multi-million impressions—and the rejected and the accepted are of the same quality, because both are false—to understand that the ego is false and a crowd, suddenly the crowd disappears and the falsity drops. In a single moment, the boundaries between the conscious and the unconscious are dissolved. A merger, a flood-like merger happens.

And your unconscious is very big, nine times bigger than your conscious. So unless you are joined with the unconscious, your life will be very, very fragmentary, superficial. You will live only a part; you will not be able to live the whole. You will do everything, but it will be done only by the part. The whole will never be in it.

And to me, to be whole in anything is to be meditative: to be whole in anything. Meditation is not something apart from life. Meditation is just a quality of being whole and total in something. You can fetch water from the well and it can become meditation— if you are totally in it. When you are drawing water out of the well, you are totally in it. Just the movement of drawing exists. You fill the pots. You carry the water. Just the movements. Nobody else separate, divided. It is meditation.

Lin-chi was asked when he became Enlightened, 'Now, since you have become Enlightened, what do you do?'

He said, 'I chop the wood. I carry the water from the well.' Only this much he said. And at that moment he was chopping wood. He said, 'Everything is perfect and beautiful. I chop the wood and I carry the water from the well and everything is perfect.'

If you become total in *anything,* I say—walking, listening, talking—if you become total, it is meditation. Otherwise, you can go on chanting mantras with part of your mind, and the other part goes on on its own. The crowd goes on. One member of the crowd goes on chanting, 'Ram, Ram, Ram.' Another part of the crowd goes on with its own work. Some part is in the market, some is in the house, some has moved to the future, some is in the past, some is chasing a woman, some is reading the Koran and the Gita, and some part is chanting, 'Ram, Ram, Ram.' You are a crowd. And this crowdedness can never become meditative.

So the dropping of the ego, not by you—dropping of the ego, *not by you* but by your understanding—dropping of the ego... it drops itself. Suddenly you are flooded. Your unconscious rushes into your conscious. You become one. Now whatsoever you do, you are totally in it. And this is the ecstasy—no past, no future; just in the moment here and now; totally in it and of it.

Only in that state do you for the first time become aware of

who *you* are. Before that, all identities are false. You have to come
to yourself directly. It is going to be an encounter face to face
with yourself, with your own reality. No other mirror is needed—
because mirrors can show only the form. They can never show the
formless that you are. Mirrors can only show that which can be
seen by others. Mirrors can never show that which cannot be
seen by others but only by you.

When you stand before a mirror, what happens? That which
is reflected in the mirror is just the periphery of you. Your center
cannot be reflected in a mirror—just the periphery, the form.
When you look in the mirror, it is not *you* who is reflected in the
mirror, because you are not the seen but the seer. You are not
that which is reflected in the mirror; you are that who is looking
at the reflection, who is watching the reflection.

You are always the seer, and the seer cannot be reduced to
the seen. You are subjectivity, and you can never become an
object. You are irreducible. . .so how to encounter oneself?

One has to move withinwards. One has to drop all the
mirrors—the mirrors of the eyes; friendly eyes, inimical eyes, indifferent eyes, all sorts of mirrors one has to drop. One has,
really, to close one's eyes and move withinwards, and to see that
which cannot be seen—to meet the seer. It happens.

It is very absurd. It is illogical, but it happens. How can you
see the seer? Logically, it is impossible. But it happens—because
life does not bother about logic. Life is more than logic. It
happens! It can happen to you, but you have to move from the
reflective, the mirror-like world that surrounds you.

This story about the Master Shibli is very beautiful. Shibli
is one of the very famous Masters. I would like to tell you
something about Shibli.

The first time Shibli's name became known was the time
when Mansoor Al Hillaj was being murdered. Shibli was a
companion, a friend to Al Hillaj. Many people have been murdered in the past by so-called religious people. Jesus was murdered . . .
but there has been never such a murder as happened with Al
Hillaj. It is the most horrible. Jesus was simply crucified, but Al
Hillaj was not simply crucified. He was crucified and first his legs

were cut—and he was alive—then his hands were cut. He was really tortured. Then his tongue was cut, then his eyes were taken out—and he was alive. And then his neck was cut. He was cut in pieces.

The first time we hear about Shibli is at that moment. One hundred thousand people had gathered to throw stones at Mansoor, to ridicule him. And what crime had Mansoor committed? What sin had he committed? He had not committed any sin; he had not committed any crime. The only crime was this, that he had said, 'Anal Hak.' It means 'I am the Truth, I am God.' Had he been in India, people would have worshipped him for centuries. All the seers of the Upanishads declare this, 'Aham Brahmasmi—I am Brahma, the Supreme Self.' Anal Hak is nothing but a translation of Aham Brahmasmi. But Mohammedans could not tolerate it.

All the three religions which have been born in the West are very intolerant. Jews—very intolerant; that's why they crucified Jesus. Mohammedans—very intolerant, almost blind. Christians, always talking about tolerance, but it is just a talk—not tolerant at all. Even in their tolerance there is deep intolerance. And all these three religions have been murderous, violent, aggressive. Their only argument is violence, as if you can convince somebody by killing him.

Mansoor is one of the greatest Sufis. No other man is comparable to him in the Sufi tradition. He was killed. People were throwing stones at him. Shibli was standing in the crowd. Mansoor was laughing and enjoying. When his feet were cut, he took the blood in his hands and he spread the blood on both his hands. Just like Mohammedans do with water when they go into the mosque for prayer: cleansing of the hands with water—wazu. And somebody asked from the crowd, 'What are you doing, Mansoor?'

Mansoor said, 'How can you do wazu with water? How can you cleanse yourself with water?—because crime you commit with your blood, sin you commit with your blood, so how can you purify yourself with water? Only blood can be the purification. I am purifying my hands. I am getting ready for prayer.'

Somebody laughed and said, 'You are a fool! You are getting ready for a prayer? or you are getting ready to be murdered?'

Mansoor laughed and said, 'That is what prayer is—to die. You are helping me for my final prayer, the last. And nothing better can be done by this body; this body cannot be used in a better way—on the altar of the Divine you are sacrificing me. That will be my last prayer in the world.'

When they started cutting his hands he said, 'Wait a minute! Let me pray, because when hands are no more there it will be difficult.' So he looked at the sky, prayed to the God and said, 'Forgive these people, because they don't know what they are doing.' And he said to God, 'You cannot deceive me, you great deceiver! I can see you in everybody present here. You are trying to deceive me? you have come as the murderer? as the enemy? But you cannot deceive me, I tell you. In whatsoever form you come, I will recognize you—because I have recognized you within myself. Now there is no possibility of deception.'

People are throwing stones and mud in ridicule, and Shibli is standing there. Mansoor is laughing and smiling. Suddenly he started crying and weeping, because Shibli had thrown a rose at Mansoor. Stones—he was laughing. A rose—and he started weeping and crying. Somebody asked, 'What is the matter? With stones you laugh—have you gone mad? And Shibli has thrown only a rose-flower. Why are you crying and weeping?'

Mansoor said, 'People who are throwing stones don't know what they are doing, but this Shibli has to know. For *him* it will be difficult to get forgiveness from the God.'

Shibli was a great scholar. He knew all the scriptures. He was a man of knowledge. Mansoor said, 'Others will be forgiven because they are acting in ignorance; they cannot help it. Whatsoever they are doing, it's okay. In their blindness that's all they can do. More is not expected; more cannot be expected. But with Shibli—a man who knows! a man of knowledge—it will be difficult for him to get forgiveness. That's why I weep and cry for him. He is the only person who is committing a sin here. He knows! That's why.'

This is something to be understood. You cannot commit a sin when you are ignorant. How can you commit a sin when you are ignorant? The responsibility is not on you. But when you know, the responsibility is there. Knowledge is the greatest responsibility. Knowledge makes you responsible. And this statement of Mansoor's changed Shibli completely. He became a totally different man. He threw the Koran, the scriptures, and he said, 'They could not make me understand even this: that all knowledge is useless. Now I will seek the right knowledge.' And later on when he was asked to comment about the statement of Mansoor: 'What was the matter? Why *did* you throw the flower?' Shibli said, 'I was standing in the crowd and I was afraid of the crowd—if I don't throw anything, people may think that I belong to Mansoor's group. The crowd may feel that I am also his companion and friend. They may get violent towards me. I could not throw stones, because I knew Mansoor was innocent. But I could not gather the courage also *not* to throw anything. That's why I threw the flower—just a compromise. And Mansoor was right that he wept: he wept at my fear, my cowardice. He wept because my whole knowledge, all that I had gathered in my whole life, was futile—I was compromising with the crowd.'

All scholars compromise with the crowd. All pundits compromise with the crowd. That's why you have never heard of any pundit being crucified by the crowd. They are the followers of the crowd; they always compromise. And their compromise is this: when they go to the Buddha, or to Mansoor, they bow down to them, and they bow down to the crowd also. They are cunning people, very cunning.

But Shibli changed completely. He understood. The feeling of Mansoor for him, the crying of Mansoor for him, became a transformation. And then later on Shibli became a Master in his own right. It took at least twelve years for him, of wandering like a vagabond, a beggar. And people would ask him, 'Why are you wandering? What are you repenting for?'—because he would continuously beat his chest and cry and weep. In the mosque when he entered, he would cry and weep such that the whole village would gather. It was so heart-rending, such deep anguish, that people would ask, 'What are you doing? What sin have you committed?'

221

And he would say, 'I have murdered Mansoor. Nobody else was responsible there, but I could have understood. And I threw a flower at that man. I compromised with the crowd. I was a coward. I could have saved him, but I missed the moment. That's why I am repenting.'

His whole life he repented. Repentance can become a very, very deep phenomenon in you if you understand the responsibility. Then even a small thing, if it becomes a repentance—not just verbal, not just on the surface; if it goes deep to your roots, if you repent from the roots; if your whole being shakes and trembles and cries, and tears come out; not only out of your eyes, but out of every cell of your body, then repentance can become a transfiguration. That is the meaning of Jesus when he again and again says, 'Repent!'

Jesus' Master, John the Baptist, has nothing much to say. His whole message was just this: 'Repent!—because the Kingdom of God is near at hand. It is just coming—you repent before it comes!' Repentance—not just mental, but total—cleanses, purifies. Nothing else can purify you that way. It is a fire. It burns all rubbish in you.

Mansoor's weeping haunted Shibli continuously his whole life. Waking or asleep, the tears of Mansoor haunted him continuously. And that became a transformation. This is what a Master, only a great Master, can do—Mansoor did it. Even while dying, he transformed a man like Shibli. Even while dying, he used his death also to transform this man. A Master goes on, while alive or dying, or even when already dead, he goes on using every opportunity to transform people.

Now this small story:

Shibli was asked: 'Who guided you in the Path?'
Shibli said: 'A dog. One day I saw him, almost dead with thirst, standing by the water's edge. Every time he looked at his reflection in the water he was frightened and withdrew, because he thought it was another dog.

'Finally, such was his necessity, he cast away fear and leapt into the water; at which the self-reflection disappeared.

'The dog found that the obstacle, which was himself, the barrier between him and what he sought, melted away.

'In this same way my own obstacle vanished when I knew that it was what I took to be my own self. And my Way was first shown to me by the behaviour of—a dog.'

A man who is ready to learn can learn from anywhere. A man who is not ready to learn cannot learn even from a Buddha. It depends on you. A dog can become a god if you are ready to learn. Even a god will not look like a god if you are not ready to learn. It depends. Finally it depends on you. To be ready to learn means to be open to all possibilities. With no prejudice. Watching, with no preconcepts. Otherwise, who will watch a dog? You would not have been even aware; you would have passed by, and you would have missed the opportunity which made Shibli a changed man, which became the guide.

You have been missing opportunities every day. Every moment the guidance is there. The Divine goes on calling you, from different quarters, but you don't listen. In fact, you think you already know. That is the trouble. If an ill man thinks that he is already healthy, why should he listen to any doctor? And then there is no possibility of his illness being treated. The very possibility of treatment is closed. If you know that you already know, you will not be able to know. First recognize that you don't know, then suddenly, from everywhere, things start happening.

'Who guided you on the Path?' somebody asked Shibli.

He could never have imagined that he would say: 'A dog. One day I saw him, almost dead with thirst, standing by the water's edge.'

That is where you all are standing: at the water's edge, almost dead with thirst. But something withholds you. You are not jumping. Something keeps you. What is that? Some sort of fear. Because the bank is known, familiar, and to jump into the river is to move into the unknown.

The known is always dead like a bank, and the unknown is always fluid, flowing like a river. The fear: cling to the familiar. The fear always says, 'Cling to the familiar, to the known.' Then fear makes you move in a circle, because only a circular path can be familiar. You move in the same rut again and again. Everything is known.

People come to me in deep misery, but they are not ready to even leave their misery—because even misery looks familiar. At least, they think, their own. They are not ready to surrender even their misery.

Why can't you surrender your misery? Familiar, habitual; you have lived with it so long that now you will feel lonely without it. This I always feel. And if you cling to misery, how is bliss possible? Both cannot live together. The bliss cannot enter you. It can enter only if misery leaves from this door; then the bliss enters from another door—immediately it enters and fills you.

Nature abhors a vacuum. God also. But you are already filled, and you cling to your misery as if it is a treasure. What have you got? Can't you renounce your misery? Have you not lived enough with it? Has it not already crippled you too much? For what are you waiting?

You are in the same situation.

Says Shibli, 'One day I saw him almost dead with thirst...' Dead with thirst! And the water just in front!'...standing by the water's edge, but every time he looked at his reflection in the water he was frightened and withdrew...' The fear of the unknown and the fear of the reflection. He saw himself reflected in the water and he thought there was another dog. He was seeing himself. There was nobody else.

This is a very, very pregnant sentence. Let me say to you that you are alone in your world. There is nobody else. And all else that you are seeing is your own reflections. You have never moved out of yourself. And, in fact, there is nobody else but you—in your world. All is reflections. And because of those reflections, you are closed in, caved in.

When you meet a person, do you really meet the person he is, or do you simply meet the reflection of your own self in him? Have you ever met anybody?—or just your own reflections, your own interpretations? When you meet a person, you immediately start interpreting the person. You start creating an image about him. That image is yours. The person is not important —just your image. The person goes far away. More and more the image becomes clear; the person is forgotten. And then you live with this image. When you talk to the person, you talk to *your* image of the person, not to the person really.

You meet a man or a woman, you fall in love—do you think you are falling in love with the other? Impossible. You are falling in love with an image that you have created around the other. And the other is also falling in love with an image that he or she has created around you. Whenever two persons fall in love, at least four persons are there; more are possible, less not. And then there is trouble, because you never fall in love with the person—you fall with your own image. And he is not there to fulfill your image. Sooner or later, the reality comes in. A conflict arises between your dream and the real, between your image and the real person who is there, absolutely unknown. And then there is a clash.

Every love affair shatters on the rocks—every love affair. And the deeper the love, the more intense the feeling, the sooner it shatters on the rocks. Why does it happen? It has to happen— because two persons falling in love with their own images, how can they be together? Those images will always be in between them. And those images will be false.

A real person is totally different. He's not your image. And he is not there to fulfill your expectations. Neither are you there to fulfill anybody's expectations. A real person is real. He has his own destiny. You have your own destiny. If you can walk together hand in hand for a few moments on the path, so far so good— beautiful. But you cannot expect that 'You do this—you don't do that.' Once you start expecting, you are bringing your image in: love is almost dead; now it is going to be a dead thing.

Look at husbands and wives. You cannot see why they look so dead and bored—with each other. They simply tolerate. They somehow simply drag. The mystery is lost. The dance is no more in the step. They don't look into each other's eyes any more. Those eyes are no longer lakes in which you can go on and on and on for an eternal journey. They take each other's hands—dead nothing flows. They embrace and they kiss and they make love, but just manoeuvres, things like yoga postures; dead, controlling, doing. But the flow is no more there, the ecstasy is no more there. It is no longer a happening. They don't come out of it refreshed, rejuvenated, reborn. They go into it dead, and they come out deadlier, deader than before. The whole thing becomes rotten. Why does this happen?

This happens because you are always creating a reflection of your own self in the other. You are creating an illusion. And then you are in love, and then you are in hate, then you find friends and then you find enemies, and they are all your reflections.

There is an old Hindu story: A great king made a palace. The palace walls were covered with mirrors, millions of mirrors. To enter into that palace was beautiful. You could see your faces in millions of mirrors all around you; millions of you all around. You could have taken a candle—and millions of candles; and a small candle would be reflected from millions of mirrors, and the whole palace would be filled with light, by a small candle.

One night it happened that by accident a dog entered. He looked around. He was so scared, scared to death—millions of dogs! He was so scared that he completely forgot the door he had come in from. Of course, millions of dogs all around—death was certain. He started barking—millions of dogs started barking. He became aggressive—millions of dogs became aggressive. He crashed with the walls. By the morning he was found dead. And there was nobody except the dog himself.

And this is the whole situation in this world. You bark, you fight, you fall in love, you make friends and enemies, and every person is functioning like a mirror to you. It *has* to be so! Unless you awake, and unless you realize who you are, you will continue seeing in the mirrors of others your own reflection—making love to your own reflection, fighting with your own reflection. The ego is absolutely masturbatory. It is a masturbation—doing everything to yourself through your own reflections.

The dog was almost dead with thirst, but even that was not enough. The fear. I see into your eyes, I see into your heart— dead with thirst. But that thirst still doesn't seem to be enough—

so that you can take the jump, so that you can drop the fear, so that you can choose the unknown. The thirst is there, but doesn't seem to be enough. Fear seems to be more important, more significant, more heavy on you.

Many of you reach to the point in the meditations when the river is flowing and you can jump. But then fear arises. It looks like death. Meditation *is* like death. Fear arises. The thirst is there, but it seems not to be enough. If you are really thirsty, then you will take the jump whatsoever the cost. And a Master is needed to make you more and more thirsty, more and more aware of your thirst—because that is the only way. The more thirsty you become, a fire arises in your heart, and you are burning with thirst. Only then can you drop the fear and take the jump—when the thirst is more than the fear.

Somebody asked Buddha, 'You say Truth cannot be taught. Then why do you teach? And you say that nobody can force anybody towards Enlightenment, but then why do you work so hard with people?'

Buddha is reported to have said, 'Truth cannot be taught, but thirst can be taught. Or, at least, you can be made aware of your thirst—which is already there, but you are suppressing it.' Because of the fear you go on suppressing the thirst.

You go *on* suppressing that which is continuously there. A deep discontent with all that is around you. A divine discontent. A thirst.

> '. . . standing by the water's edge. Every time he looked at his reflection in the water he was frightened and withdrew, because he thought it was another dog.
> 'Finally, such was his necessity. . .'

Remember these words. I cannot do anything unless the moment comes for you when you can feel such is your necessity that you have to take the jump, that you have to explode into the unknown, that you have to step into it.

> 'Finally, such was his necessity, he cast away fear and leapt into the water; at which the reflection disappeared. . .'

because when you jump into the water, the mirrorlike river is no more mirrorlike. The reflection disappeared. The dog was no more there. And Shibli must have been watching, sitting by the bank, looking at this dog—his fear, his continuous effort to go and then withdrawing again and again and again. He must have watched very keenly for what was going to happen. And then the dog jumped. The reflection disappeared.

'The dog found that the obstacle . . .' was not outside, it was he himself. The dog was not there in the water. The dog in the water was not preventing him, as he was thinking before. It was he himself '. . . which was himself, the barrier between him and what he sought, melted away.'

He was himself the barrier between his thirst and the water, his hunger and the satiety, his discontent and the contentment, his search and the goal, his seeking and the sought. There was nobody else, just his reflection in the water.

And that is the case, absolutely the case, with you all, with everybody. Nobody is hindering you. Something of the sort of your own reflection between you and your destiny, between you as the seed and you as the flower—there is nobody else hindering, creating any obstacle. So don't go on throwing responsibility on others. That is a way of consoling oneself. Drop consoling yourself. Drop all self-pity. Look deep in the mirror. And everybody is a mirror around you. Look deep—you will find your own reflection everywhere.

'In this same way, my own obstacle vanished when I knew that it was what I took to be my own self. And my Way was first shown to me by the behaviour of—a dog.'

The Way is shown to you from millions of directions. People have become Enlightened through watching a dog, through watching a cat. People have become Enlightened through watching a dead leaf falling from the tree. People have become Enlightened through every sort of situation. But one thing is absolutely necessary, and that is watching. Dog, cat, the tree, the river—irrelevant. People become Enlightened through watching.

So whatsoever the situation, you watch. And watch without

any prejudice. And watch without the past. Watch without any thinking on your part. Don't interpret. Watch! If your eyes are clear, if your perception is clear, and you watch silently, every situation leads towards the Divine. And this is how it should be! Every situation, every moment of life, leads toward the Divine.

Somebody asked Rinzai, a Zen Master, 'What is the way to know the Ultimate?'

Rinzai had gone for a morning walk with his staff in his hand. He raised his staff in front of the eyes of the questioner, and said, 'Watch this staff! If you can watch this, there is no need to go anywhere else.'

The man must have found it a little puzzling. He looked here and there and he said, 'But how can one attain to Enlightenment just by watching a stick?'

Rinzai said, 'It is not a question of what you watch. The question is that you watch. Right now it happened that the staff was in my hand, that's all.'

Anything, if you watch, will give you the clue. Watching is the only method. Call it awareness, call it observation, call it witnessing—but watch. Live life with a watchful eye. And everything, the smallest, leads to the greatest. Everything leads to God.

You have heard the saying that 'Every road leads to Rome.' It may not be true—but every path leads to God.

Wherever you are, become watchful, and your face is immediately turned toward the Divine. Through watching, the quality of your inner consciousness changes. Be watchful!

Jesus goes on saying to his disciples, 'Be watchful!' But as it happens, disciples are almost deaf. When it was the last night, and Jesus was going to be crucified the next day, that night he said, 'Now I will do my last prayer, and you all watch. Be alert! Don't fall asleep!'

After an hour, Jesus came back from the tree where he was praying—all the disciples were fast asleep, snoring. He woke them and said, 'What are you doing? I had told you: be watchful, alert!—and you have fallen asleep.'

They said, 'We were tired. And we tried, but the sleep took over.'

Jesus said, 'Now be more watchful—because this is the last night! I will no more be with you again.' And again after half an hour he came back, and they were fast asleep.

What was he saying? He was giving them the key word: 'Be watchful.' And what else can a Master give when he is departing? In this word, 'Be watchful,' all the scriptures exist in their essence.

Thrice Jesus came again. There are only two things infinite I say: the compassion of a Master and the stupidity of the disciple. Infinite, two things. Thrice he came and he said, 'Again you are asleep?' And that night would have become Enlightenment for all those disciples, because Jesus was at his pinnacle—the very peak. And he was praying: in that moment of Jesus' prayer the whole atmosphere in that Garden of Gethsemane was *charged*. If those disciples had been watchful, immediate sudden Enlightenment would have been possible. But they were fast asleep.

To you also, I say, be watchful!—because I will not be here for long. A little while more. You can miss and you can find excuses. Be watchful! Be alert!

Jesus always used to tell a story, that a master went for a journey. And he told his servants, 'Be watchful twenty-four hours a day, because any moment I can come back. And if I find you asleep, I will throw you out. So keep alert! Somebody *must* be alert and aware. You can divide the time by shifts, but I must find a few servants alert and aware whenever I come.'

But the servants thought, 'The journey is very long, and it will take almost years, so no need to worry about it right now. After a year we will be watchful. For this whole year we can enjoy and indulge and sleep well. And we are free—the master is gone.'

And when the master came. . . . He came after three years, but when for one year completely you sleep and indulge and become lazy, then it is not easy. Then they started postponing: 'He has not come yet, and no message has come. Who knows whether he is alive or dead? And we have not heard anything at all.' They forgot completely. When the master came, they had not only forgotten that the master existed, they had not only forgotten that they had to be alert, they had completely forgotten that they were servants. They had become the masters by that time.

230

This is what has happened to every mind, to every consciousness.

And remember: God can knock at your door any moment. If you are not watchful, you will miss. He can knock from a dog. He can knock from a flower. A bird takes wing—and He can knock there. He can use any opportunity to knock at your door.

Remain alert so that when the Guest comes He does not find you asleep; when He knocks at your door, you are ready and you have prepared the house for the Guest—and your heart is ready to receive.

Be watchful. Through being watchful, by and by, the ego will die, because ego is created by a non-watchful mind, an unalert mind. Through watching, witnessing, the ego dies. And nothing is possible until you die.

19 April 1975

X
A Rose is a Rose is a Rose...

A disciple came to Maruf Karkhi and said:

'I have been talking to people about you. Jews claim that you are a Jew; Christians revere you as one of their own saints; Muslims insist that you are the greatest of all Muslims.'

Maruf answered:

'This is what humanity says in Baghdad. When I was in Jerusalem, Jews said that I was a Christian, Muslims that I was a Jew, and Christians that I was a Muslim.'

'What must we think of you then?' said the man.

Maruf said:

'Some do not understand me, and revere me. Others do not either, so they revile me. That is what I have come to say. You should think of me as one who has said this.'

A RELIGIOUS man is always misunderstood. If he is not misunderstood, he will not be a religious man.

Humanity lives in a non-religious attitude towards life—sectarian, but not religious. So a religious man is a stranger. And whatsoever you say about him will be wrong, because *you* are wrong. And remember: whatsoever you say about him—I am not saying that if you say something in his favour, that will be right, no; whether you are in favour of him, or against him, it makes no difference—whatsoever you say will be wrong about him until you yourself have become a religious consciousness.

Before that, your reverence is false, your condemnation is false. You may think of him as a sage, and you have misunderstood. You may think of him as a sinner, and again you have misunderstood.

So the first thing to remember is: unless *you* are right, whatsoever you do, say, be, is going to be wrong. And a religious man is such a tremendous phenomenon, such a strange phenomenon, that you have no language to talk about him. All your words are futile in concern with him. Your whole language is useless, meaningless, because a religious man *is* religious because he has gone beyond the dualities, and the whole of language exists *within* dualities.

If you say he is good you are wrong, because he is bad also.

If you say he is bad you are wrong again, because he is good also. And now the trouble arises, because you cannot conceive how a good man can be bad also. You can comprehend only a part of the whole, because the other part is by necessity the opposite. It *has* to be so.

A religious man is a miniature God. Just like God, he is paradoxical and contradictory. Just like God, he is summer and winter, day and night, life and death. Just like God, he is divine and devil both. Then the mind staggers.

The mind is very efficient if you are working in polarities. If you say yes, the mind can understand. If you say no, the mind can understand. But if you say yes and no both, then it goes beyond mind. Unless you have gone beyond mind, you cannot have the feeling of what a religious consciousness is.

I was born a Jain. Now religion has nothing to do with your birth. You cannot be born in a religion. Just on the contrary: religion has to be born in you. I was born a Jain—just a coincidence. I could as well have been born a Christian or a Jew. An irrelevant fact—because by your birth religion cannot be given to you. It is not a gift. It is not a heritage. My father is a Jain, my mother is a Jain—they cannot give Jainism to me. I can inherit their wealth, I can inherit their prestige, I can inherit the family name—but I cannot inherit religion. Religion cannot be a gift, a heritage. It is not a thing. It is something one has to seek for himself. Nobody else can give it to you.

So whatsoever is given by the birth is a sect, not a religion. Hinduism, Christianity, Mohammedanism, Jainism, Buddhism, are sects, not religions. Religion is one. Sects are many, because sects are the forms, dead fossilized forms. Sects are like footprints: somebody one day walked there, but he is no more there—just footprints left on the sand, on the sand of time. A Buddha walks, footprints are left, and you go on worshipping those footprints for centuries. There is nobody there now. Just a form in the sand. Nothing else.

Sects are forms in the mind, just like footprints. Yes, somebody was there one day, but he is no more there. And you go on worshipping those forms. You are born into those forms. You are conditioned into those forms, indoctrinated. You become a sectarian.

And don't think that you have become religious, otherwise you will miss. For religion to be there, you have to seek it on your own. It is a personal growth, a personal encounter with reality —face to face, immediate and direct. It has nothing to do with tradition, nothing to do with the past. You have to grow into it. You have to allow it to grow into you.

Religion is a revolution, not a conformity. It is not a conviction intellectually attained. It is a conversion of your total being. How can you be born in a religion? Of course, you can be born in an ideology. You can learn a theology, words about God, theories about God, dogmas and doctrines, but to know about God is not to know God. The word 'God' is not God. And all the theologies together are nothing compared to a single moment of encounter with the Divine—because then for the first time, the spark, your inner light starts. You start rising in a different dimension.

Religion is a personal search. It is not part of society.

I was born a Jain. Of course, they tried to force me to be a Jain. Fortunately, they failed. It is one of the misfortunes that they succeed in many cases. They failed and they have been angry against me. So if you ask the Jains, only rarely will you find a Jain here and there who will say that I am a Jain; otherwise they will say that I am the enemy of Jainism, and I am destroying their ideology, and I am corrupting their sources. And both are right in a way.

Those who say that I am against Jainism, they are right in a way—because I am against Jainism as they understand it. I *am* against, because that is not religion at all. A dead fossil—of course, one of the most ancient. Jainism seems to be the most ancient religion in the world, even older than Hinduism. Because even in the Vedas, in the Rig-Veda, Jain Teerthankaras are mentioned, and mentioned with deep reverence. That shows Jain Teerthankaras are older than the Rig-Veda, the first Hindu scripture, the oldest in the world. And when a scripture talks about a Master like the first Teerthankara of the Jains, Rishabh, the Vedas talk with so much reverence that it is almost certain that he was not a contemporary. He must have been dead for at least one thousand years; only then can you talk with such reverence. About contemporaries nobody talks with such reverence. Followers can talk, but Hindus are not followers of Jains—antagonistic religions. At least one thousand years must have passed, and the man must have become a legend.

Jains are very old. Now historians are working on the ruins and findings in Harappa and Mohenjodaro. And they say that there is every possibility that Harappa and Mohenjodaro were Jain civilizations. Before Aryans came to India, India was a Jain country—there is every possibility. A very ancient religion, and of course, very much dead. The older a religion, the more dead. Everything fossilized. You cannot find a more dead person than a Jain monk. He goes on cutting his life; it is a slow suicide. And the more dead he is, the more he is worshipped—because death itself seems to be like a renunciation. If he is a little alive, then Jains become afraid of him. Older religions crucify their followers, they murder them.

The older the religion, the greater the weight. Like a Himalaya on the heart of a small man—burdened, crushing, you cannot move. And traditions go on gathering. They are like snowballs: they go on gathering weight, they become fatter and fatter. Dead, but still they go on gaining weight. They become monstrous, and then they kill the spirit. They always remain true to the word—and the more true to the word, the more poisonous to the spirit.

If you ask the Jains only a few will say, 'Yes, this man is a real Jain.' Many will say, 'This man is against us, the greatest enemy.' And both are right in a way—and both are wrong in a deeper way. I am a Jain. If you look at Mahavir, I am a Jain. Mahavir is a religious man, not because he is born in a religion. He searched. He enquired. He encountered reality. He threw all dogmas. He threw all civilization. Even clothes he threw away, because they, too, are a part of the civilization and the culture; and they, too, carry the society with you. He remained naked. For twelve years he completely stopped talking, because if you go on

238

talking, you use the language of the society, and that language carries the germs of the society.

Whenever you talk, immediately you become a part of a society. A silent man is not part of any society. He may be part of nature, but he's not part of society. In fact, language is the only thing that makes you human and part of human society and the human world. When you drop language, suddenly you drop out of human society and civilization. You become part of the trees, rocks, the sky.

For twelve years Mahavir would not use any language, remained completely silent. This man I love, because this is a religious man. And he started speaking only when silence was total within him. And he spoke not out of scriptures, he spoke out of himself. He spoke out of his silence. And whenever a word is born out of deep silence, it is alive, throbbing with life. And those who hear it directly, they are most fortunate—because soon it will die. Everything born dies.

A word is born. It is alive for a few moments. It throbs around you. If you can listen to it, it will enter into your being, it will become part of your being. If you don't listen to it, if you take notes, and you think that you will try to understand it back home, it will be already dead. Then you will understand something which was not said at all. You have already made a private scripture.

Mahavir spoke out of his inner silence. His words are the most wonderful ever spoken. I love that man. He is the most anti-social man you can find, and anti-traditional. The other twenty-three Teerthankaras, twenty-three Masters of the Jains, they were all clothed. This man became nude. Tradition has it that Jains in those days tried to deny this man. They said, 'What is he doing? Our other Teerthankaras have never been nude, and why is he moving nude?' They did everything to deny this man, and because of that denial Jainism has been divided into two parts from that very day. They have two sects: those who followed Mahavir in his nudity, very few people, they are called Digambaras—people who believe in nudity. The other older sect, who tried to avoid this Mahavir, who tried to deny this Mahavir, they are the

Swetambaras. They believe in white clothes; their monks are white-robed. And the conflict has continued.

If some Jain says, 'Yes, this man Rajneesh is a Jain,' he is right. I love Mahavir—a rare flowering, a rare fragrance, very rare and unique. But the others are also right when they say, 'This man is not a Jain but against them, the enemy.' They are also right—because I am against tradition, against all rituals and forms, against scriptures, against the past. I am all for religion, and all against sects. They are also right.

If you ask Hindus, Hindus will say, 'This man is Jain, and trying to sabotage Hinduism from within; because no Jain has ever talked about the Gita, and no Jain has ever commented on the Upanishads. This man is trying to sabotage Hinduism from within.' This is what the Shankaracharya of Puri says about me: 'Beware of this man! He is not a Hindu.' And he is right in a sense. In the sense that *he* is Hindu, I am not. But in the sense he is Hindu, Hinduism is worthless.

I am Hindu in the sense Patanjali is Hindu, Badrayan is Hindu, Kapil and Kanad are Hindu. The really religious people, they never belong to the establishment. They cannot. It is possible that the establishment may follow them; and some day around them an establishment may be created. That is possible. But they are never part of any establishment—either of others or their own. They cannot exist in the establishment. They are free! Freedom can never be a part of any establishment. And whenever the establishment becomes too much, the freedom dies. Then the bird cannot be on the wing; the wings are cut. The bird has been encaged then, in a golden cage—beautifully decorated, very costly, precious, but *now the cage is more important*, not the bird. And, by and by, people will forget the bird completely, because the bird will die and they will go on worshipping the cage, and they will go on making it more and more decorative, and temples will arise around it, and a great tradition, establishment, and nobody will bother: 'Where is the bird?' A dead corpse in a golden cage.

I am Hindu, if you believe in Hinduism as a bird on the wing, as the Upanishads are Hindu; but I am not a Hindu in the sense the Shankaracharya of Puri is Hindu—a dead bird in a golden cage.

If you ask Mohammedans, they will say I have no right to talk on Sufis or on the Koran. Once in a town I was talking about Sufis, and the *maulvi* of the town approached me and he said, 'You have no right. You are *not* a Mohammedan, you don't know Arabic. How can you talk on the Sufis and on the Koran?'

I said, 'The Koran has nothing to do with Arabic. It has something to do with the heart, not with the language.'

The Koran has nothing to do with the language. It has something to do with silence, not language. The Koran has something to do with the reality, not with the symbols. And I am not a Mohammedan if you think that I am a follower of Mohammed—no, I am not. I am nobody's follower. But I am a Mohammedan, just like Mohammed is a Mohammedan; just as Jesus is a Christian, I am a Christian—but like Mohammed and Jesus. Was Mohammed a Mohammedan? How can he be? Because Mohammedanism never existed before. Was Jesus a Christian? Christianity never existed before. How can he be a Christian? If Jesus is a Christian, I am a Christian. If Mohammed is a Mohammedan, then I am a Mohammedan. But otherwise, I am not a Mohammedan and not a Christian.

A religious man does not belong to any sect. In fact, all sects belong to the religious man. But this is how the formal mind goes. He thinks in terms of ideology, language, ritual, and he misses the whole point: that religion has nothing to do with these things.

Then what is religion?

Religion is an oceanic feeling where *you* are lost and only the existence remains. It is a death and a resurrection. You die as you are, and you are resurrected totally new. Something absolutely new arises out of the death of the old. On the grave of the old something sprouts and becomes a new flower.

Religion is an inner revolution, an inner mutation. It is not in the temples, not in the mosques, not in the churches. Don't look for religion there! If you look there you will waste your time. Look for religion inwards. And the further inwards you move, the deeper you will find the ego there—which is the barrier. Drop that barrier and suddenly you are religious. There is only one thing which is not religious and that is the ego. And that can never be religious. And sects never kill it; on the contrary, they strengthen it.

Through rituals, temples, ideologies, the ego is strengthened. You go to the church and you feel that you have become religious. A subtle pride arises in you. You don't become humble; on the contrary, you become more egoistic. You do a certain ritual and you feel gratified—and you start condemning those who are not doing the ritual. You think those are the sinners and they are going to be thrown into the fire of hell; and your heaven is secured—just by doing certain rituals? Whom do you think that you are deceiving?

A man sits for one hour turning the beads, and he is thinking his heaven is secured, and others who are not doing this stupid thing, they are going to hell. And you go to the mosque, and you kneel down, and you say foolish things to the Divine: 'You are great'—is there any doubt about it? Why are you saying it?—'I'm a sinner, and you are compassion.' What are you doing? buttressing? Do you think God has an ego-like thing?—so that you can say who you are, 'You are very great and we are very small. And you are compassion and we are sinners. Forgive us!' Whom do you think you are deceiving?

The ego is playing the game. You think God is also an ego which can be buttressed? God is not a person at all, so you are talking to yourself. There is nobody else to listen to it; only the walls, the dead walls of the mosque or the temple, or a stone statue. Nobody is listening.

In fact, you are doing something mad. Just go into the madhouses and see people talking to somebody who is not there. Even those mad people are not so mad, because that somebody may be somewhere. They may not be here; a madman may be talking to his wife who is not here in the madhouse, but somewhere maybe—but your God is nowhere. Your madness is deeper, greater—dangerous.

How can you talk with existence? With existence you have to be silent. All talking should stop. You are not to say something. On the contrary, a prayer is a listening. *You have to listen to existence, not to say something.* If you speak, who will listen? If you talk and you are too much involved in the words, then who will listen? And every moment there is a message.

Every moment, from everywhere, there is a message for you. It is written all over. The whole existence is the scripture of the Divine. The message is everywhere. On every leaf is the signature. But who will see? Your eyes and your mind are filled with yourself. Rubbish you have, but you go on rotating that rubbish in the mind. Drop it all!

This is something to understand, because a prayer can be Christian, a prayer can be Hindu, a prayer can be Jewish—then they are sectarian prayers and *not* prayers at all. A real prayer cannot be Christian, Hindu, or Bauddha. A real prayer is just a silence, a waiting. How can you say silence is Hindu? How can you say silence is Christian? Can silence be Christian or Hindu? Silence is simply silence!—neither Hindu nor Mohammedan. When two persons are absolutely silent, can you say who is Hindu and who is Mohammedan? In silence sects disappear. In silence societies disappear. In silence civilizations disappear. In silence, you disappear. Only silence is—you are not there. If you are there, then silence cannot be because you will do something or other, you will think something or other, you will go on chattering inside.

When you are not, society is not, sects are not; no words, no prayer; you are not reciting the Koran, not reciting the Veda; not doing a TM meditation, 'Ram, Ram, Ram'—all foolish. When you are simply silent, a meeting happens, a merger happens —you dissolve! Just as ice melts, and the boundaries dissolve, and then you cannot find where the ice has gone . . . it has become one with the sea.

The sun rises, ice melts, becomes water. Silence arises, the mind, the ice-like, frozen mind, starts melting, the ego dissolves. Suddenly there is ocean and you are not.

This is the moment of religion. Religion is born in you.

Nobody is born in religion. Religion 'borns' in you. You have to become a mother, a womb, for religion to become impregnated in you, to grow in you. You have to give the birth. You *cannot* be born in religion. You have to give birth to religion. And then it is beautiful. Then it is something from the unknown. Then it is not concerned with man.

That is the meaning of Jesus' virgin birth. The whole meaning is simply this: that a man like Jesus is not born out of man. *Religious* consciousness is not born out of man. It is born out of the unknown. Mary, Jesus' mother, is virgin; no man has corrupted her. This is a symbolic thing. It is not that Jesus is born out of a virgin biologically. Then you miss the metaphor; the beautiful story becomes an ugly doctrine. Then you miss the poetry. And then for centuries Christians have been arguing, and trying to prove somehow that Jesus is born, really, from a virgin mother. How can theologicians be so stupid? It is a wonder! And they go on trying and proving, and very intellectual people, argumentative —but blind.

And whenever you miss the poetry and try to create an argument out of it, you destroy religion. You are not a help. You put people *off* religion. Then the whole of Christianity becomes absurd —because of some absurdity in the foundation. And these are poetic truths. And poetic truths are not logical truths. Logical truths are nothing, they are ordinary facts. Poetic truths are extraordinary facts, so extraordinary in their quality that you cannot make an argument out of them. Argument is too narrow. They need much space. Only a poetic symbology can give that space.

This is beautiful poetry. I also say Jesus is born out of a virgin mother—because there is no other way. Because religious consciousness is uncorrupted by man, untouched.

Religious consciousness means you have dropped all that is man-made: doctrines, dogmas, churches, words, language, prayers, forms, rituals—all that is man-made you have dropped. Then in that silence, God Himself becomes part of you. You become pregnant with the God. You carry the pregnancy. It grows every day. And the more it grows, the more alive it becomes, the more you start feeling that now you have something more valuable than your life.

A mother is always ready to die for the child. If there is a crisis and only one can be saved, either the child or the mother, the mother is always ready—the child should survive. She is ready to die.

There is another parable I would like to tell you. It is said that whenever a Buddha is born, the mother dies immediately. That, too, has created problems for Buddhists, because they say if Mary is alive and has not died and Jesus is born, Jesus cannot be a Buddha—because whenever an Enlightened man is born, the mother dies! Buddha's mother died. Then Mahavir cannot be a Buddha and Krishna cannot be a Buddha, because the first thing is missing. This is how beautiful symbols become ugly. It is beautiful! I don't know whether Buddha's mother died or not. That is irrelevant. Whether she lived or died, that is not the point. But the point is: whenever religious consciousness is born in you, when you are pregnant with Buddhahood, when you are pregnant with Enlightenment, and you carry Enlightenment as a child within you, *you will die,* because both cannot live.

And this is the whole message of this series of talks: Until you die, nothing is possible. The mother *must* die for the child to be born, because both cannot exist—because *you* are the mother and *you* are the child. You are not two. When you become Enlightened, the old *must* die *immediately.* If you cling to the old, then you will cripple your Enlightenment. If you cling to the old, you will suffocate the child. If you cling *too* much, the child will be dead before the child is born.

Always remember: Religion is poetry, not logic. It is not even philosophy—it is art. And art is not an argument. Art doesn't bother about argument. Art can seduce you without argument, then why bother about argument? Art is so powerful, it can seduce you without any argument. Argument is needed on the lower realms where the thing itself is not so powerful to convince you —then argument is needed. When the thing in itself is so powerful, so hypnotic, so transforming, that you are suddenly absorbed into it, there is no need to convince you.

I never try to convince you. If you are convinced, good. If you are not convinced, good. But I am not trying to convince you of anything, because conviction is a very ordinary thing. If through argument you are convinced, you will never become religious.

You may become philosophical, you may carry a dogma in your head, but you will never become religious.

Religion is like love. You fall in it—for no reason at all. You cannot prove; proof is not needed. Proof is needed only when you are thinking of a marriage. Argument is needed only when you are thinking of an arranged marriage—then you think about the family, and the parents of the girl, and the money, and the dowry, and the future possibilities, political relationships, and everything you think about. But when you fall in love, you fall in love—it happens so suddenly, there is no time gap.

And it is the same with religion. You fall in love with a man who is religious. You cannot prove it. And if somebody argues with you against it, it is very easy to prove something against it; it is almost impossible to prove anything for it. That's why it is a trust, a faith, a deep blindness. But in that deep blindness, for the first time your inner eye starts functioning. The deep blindness from the outside becomes a deep insight from within.

Now try to understand this story.

> *A disciple came to Maruf Karkhi and said:*
>
> *'I have been talking to people about you. Jews claim that you are a Jew; Christians revere you as one of their own saints; Muslims insist that you are the greatest of all Muslims.'*
>
> *Maruf answered:*
>
> *'This is what humanity says in Baghdad. When I was in Jerusalem, Jews said that I was a Christian, Muslims that I was a Jew, and Christians that I was a Muslim.'*
>
> *'What must we think of you then?' said the man.*
>
> *Maruf said:*
>
> *'Some do not understand me, and revere me. Others do not either, so they revile me. That is what I have come to say. You should think of me as one who has said this.'*

Now: A disciple came to Maruf Karkhi and said. . . Maruf Karkhi is one of the Sufi Masters, and it is said that hundreds of people became Enlightened through him. He developed many new devices; and he was really a religious man, not belonging to any orthodoxy, not belonging to any convention, not belonging to any

246

tradition; homeless, without any roots; floating like a white cloud
—absolute freedom in his being.

A *disciple came*. . . The disciple cannot be really a disciple;
he must have been a student. In English translations there is
trouble, because in English you don't make much distinction
between a disciple and a student; you don't make much distinction
between a Master and a teacher. But in the East, a *vast* distinction,
difference, exists between these two terminologies.

A teacher can have students, cannot have disciples. A teacher
teaches. Of course, a teacher can teach only that which can be
taught. Religion cannot be taught. Things about religion can be
taught. Mm?—that is what theology is: things about God. But
God Himself cannot be taught. Concepts about God, theories—
whether this is right or that. And there are millions of theories.

Man has been inventing so many theories about God that
God is completely lost in theories. He has almost become non-
substantial. When you utter the word 'God' no substance is felt
in it. It looks like an air-bubble, carrying nothing but hot air
within. When you say 'God', no bells ring in the heart. When you
say 'God', it falls flat. It does not carry much significance. The
so-called religious thinkers have killed the word completely. They
have destroyed the beauty of it. The moment you utter the word
'God', you put many off. The word carries much violence, ugliness, strife, narrowness—of so-called religious people. It has no
poetry now.

A teacher can teach you everything about God. You can
become a doctor living with a teacher, a doctor of divinity—a
D.D. It is simply unbelievable that things like this exist on earth
—people who carry a degree of doctorate about Divinity. God is
not a theory. It is an experience. You cannot be taught about It.

Says Lao Tzu, The Old Boy . . . the word 'Lao Tzu' means
The Old Boy. Another parable: It is said Lao Tzu was born old—
when he was eighty-four years of age. For eighty-four years he
lived in the womb of the mother. When he was born, he was
already absolutely ancient—all his hair white, wrinkled. What is
the meaning? The meaning is that whenever religious consciousness is born, it is always ancient: new and ancient, both. Hence,

Lao Tzu's name: The Old Boy. Lao Tzu means The Old Boy—
old, yet young.

Says Lao Tzu: 'Truth cannot be said. And all that can be
said will not be true.'

A teacher is one who teaches truth which cannot be taught.
He teaches *about* truth. He goes round and round. He beats around
the bush. He never hits the center. And a student is one who
is enquiring *about* God, not desiring God; who has come to know,
not to be; whose search is intellectual, not total. A student is
trying to gather more knowledge; he wants to become more
knowledgeable. He wants to accumulate much information.

It is said about one of the students of Maruf . . . he became
very famous, the student; he became so famous that people started
coming to him and asking him things, even when Maruf was alive.
Even sometimes it would happen that Maruf was sitting there with
the student, and people would come not to Maruf but to the student
and ask him things. He became so efficient in the scripture, he
crammed all the scriptures, and he was perfect like a computer.

One day somebody came and he asked a question about some
passage in the scripture, and the student recited the whole scripture, then recited all the commentaries that had been made about
the scripture—within minutes, all that was there in the scriptures,
he brought it down. And he argued this way and that and tried
to prove a conclusion. Maruf was sitting and listening. The man
was astounded—so much knowledge. He said to Maruf, 'You are
fortunate to have such disciples. This boy is a rare gem! So much
knowledge: I have never come across such a brilliant mind, such
a genius. What do you say about him?'

Maruf said, 'I am always worried. I am worried because he
reads too much. And I am worried that he has no time to know;
his whole time is going in reading. And I am always worried as to
when he will know—he has no time.'

A student is concerned not about knowing, he is concerned
about knowledge. A teacher attracts students. A Master attracts
disciples. A disciple is not a student. He has not come to know
about God. He has come to become God, to be God. He has not
come for more information, he has come for *more being*. Let me

repeat: a disciple asks how to gain more being, and a student asks how to gain more knowledge. He has come to the Master to *be*. And that is a totally different enquiry. The dimension is altogether different. Not only different, it is diametrically opposite. A student go to the west, and a disciple goes to the east. It is said that east and west never meet—I don't know. They must meet somewhere because the earth is round. But one thing I know: a student and a disciple never meet. They cannot. Unless a student drops being a student, he cannot become a disciple.

It is said about Maruf that whenever a person would come ... and thousands were coming to him from distant corners of the world. Maruf became an institution, a university—of being, of course, not of knowledge. Whenever a student, or a disciple or a seeker would come to him, the first question Maruf used to ask was this: 'Do you want to learn, or unlearn? Do you want to be a student or a disciple?' This was always his first question, because that would decide everything.

This man who reached Maruf must have been a student. He could not have been a disciple because a disciple is one who has already attained to a trust. A student is seeking. A disciple has come to a conclusion in his being that 'This is my Master.' Hence, he is the disciple. 'This is my Master! I have come to the man I was seeking. This is my shelter, my refuge.' Suddenly the disciple is born! A disciple is born out of this trust. He does not enquire about such things this man is enquiring about. He has fallen in love. He has attained to faith. He has surrendered. A student is not surrendered. He will learn, watch, observe, see, and if he's convinced ... and remember, *if* he is convinced; that is, the conclusion will come out of his head.

Just the other day I was reading a very, very ridiculous thing said by an Indian guru who has become famous in the West, Sri Chinmoy. He teaches in the UN in Geneva. I was always wondering what he is doing there, and just the other day I came to read a statement he has made. Somebody asked him, 'How to judge and how to find the Master?'

He said, 'Use your brain.'

Now I know why he is in the UN—because politicians,

stupid people, are there. 'Use your brain!' And, the thing becomes more and more ridiculous because then he says, 'Keep one hundred marks in your mind to be given, then watch whether the Master is honest, sincere, true to his word, his morality, his behaviour—everything you watch, and go on giving the marks inside the mind. If the Master gets thirty marks, he is not for you; you leave. If the Master gets near about eighty to ninety marks, then he is your Master.'

This is ridiculous. You will find a teacher, you cannot find a Master—if you use your brain. Then finally *you* remain the decisive factor; *you* decide. Do you know what honesty is? First give marks to yourself! Use your brain! Do you know what honesty is? Do you know what morality is? Are you certain of what is good? and what is bad? Do you know what is evil and what is not evil? First give marks to yourself—use your brain. If you get thirty marks, drop yourself completely. You are useless! And if you can get eighty or ninety percent, then you don't need a Master. You are already a Master—you go and seek disciples.

To use the brain is simply unbelievable! A Master is not a commodity in the market. A Master, by his very *being*, is an unbelievable thing. You cannot use the brain. A Master, by his very being, is mysterious. Opposites *meet* in him. Dichotomies *merge* in him. Dualisms—he comprehends all of them.

You can find a teacher if you use the brain; then you will be a student. If you use your heart, you can find a Master—and then only can you become a disciple. A disciple is in love! And love is always total, not eighty percent, ninety percent. Love is total. Either it is or it is not. Always total. If it is not, then, too, total. And there is no compromise in it. Percentage is not possible; percentage is the way of the brain. Totality is the way of the heart.

This man must have been a student. So, let me say:

> A student *came to Maruf Karkhi and said: 'I have been talking to people about you.'*

Must have been using the brain. Must have been a student of Sri Chinmoy. '*I have been talking to people about you.*' You have to encounter a Master *directly*—face to face, eyes to eyes, heart to heart. What nonsense to talk about the Master to other people to know who this man is!

Many of you do the same here also. They move around. They talk to people about me. Why not come directly to me? Why waste your time with people? And this is the foolishness of the human mind, that you never know the person you are talking to about me—you *trust* that person, and you cannot trust me. If you are really a brain-oriented person, then talk about that man to other people, and about those other people to other people. Because first you have to decide about that man, whether he is sincere, believable: 'Whatosever he says about the Master, can we take it to be true?'

You ask A about me—why not ask about A to B first? And then about B to C? Then you will be in an infinite regress. And if A says something wrong about me, you take it. Now it will always be a part of you. Or if A says something good about me, you take it and that will be a part of you. And that will decide the whole thing. And you never ask about this A, who this A is!

Why go in rounds and circles?—there is no end to it. There is only one way to come to the Master: face to face, eyes to eyes, heart to heart! And don't ask anybody else because then you will carry a prejudice either for or against. And that prejudice will always be in between the Master and you, that will become the barrier. You will always be seeking whether that prejudice is right or wrong. It will colour your mind. And any foolish man can prejudice your mind. You are so unaware that *any* man—the taxi-driver who brings you to the ashram—he can corrupt your mind. You can ask about me... and many of you must have asked taxi-drivers—because the mind goes on seeking information, what others are saying: 'and they must be knowing.' You must ask the neighbours here: 'they must be knowing.' And they are the last people in the world to know about me. *Neighbours*—they cannot know.

Jesus has two sayings. One saying is: Love your enemies just as you love yourself. And second: Love your neighbours just as you love yourself. It seems enemies and the neighbours are the same people.

This man must have been an ordinary enquirer. He said:

'I have been talking to people about you. Jews claim that you are a Jew; Christians revere you as one of their own saints; Muslims insist that you are the greatest of all Muslims.'

He must have met the disciples, the people who had fallen in love with the Master. Maruf lived near Baghdad. Baghdad became a capital of religious consciousness when Maruf was alive. This man must have met the disciples, those who had already fallen in love.

If the disciple is a Jew, he will say, 'My Master is the *most* perfect Jew possible.' I have many Jews here and they know that I am the most perfect Jew. Once you are in love, whatsoever is beautiful, great to you, you project on the Master. I have amongst my disciples almost all sorts of people, belonging to all sorts of religions—Jews, Hindus, Mohammedans, Christians, Jains, Buddhists. If a Buddhist comes to me and falls in love with me, he will think that I am the most essential Buddhist. And he will find everything to convince him that this is true.

Maruf answered: 'This is what humanity says in Baghdad.'

That means: 'My disciples, my people, my community people. You should have been in Jerusalem. This is what humanity says in Baghdad—that is, my community people, my people.'

'When I was in Jerusalem, Jews said that I was a Christian, Muslims that I was a Jew, and Christians that I was a Muslim.'

Enemies. And for a religious man to find enemies, the best places are Jerusalem, Quaba, Kashi. These are the best places to find enemies, because these are the sectarian strongholds—Kashi for Hindus, Jerusalem for Jews, Quaba for Muslims. These are the sectarian strongholds, fortresses, where the fossilized religion is protected and saved; where the dead body is continuously decorated, painted, for believers—to deceive them that the body is not dead; where religion is continuously modified to suit new situations so that there is no need to drop it; where dead continuity is continued. There is the problem.

If you want to find people antagonistic to a religious man, go to these sacred places, holy places. In fact, they are the unholiest in the world; they have to be—because the dead corpse of religion stinks. Can you find a more dirty place in the world than Kashi? Everything stinks of dead religion. But if you are a believer, then you don't listen to your senses, you don't listen to your own consciousness. You go on seeing things which are not there. You go on projecting things which are not there.

Said Maruf, 'This is what humanity says in Baghdad. When I was in Jerusalem just the opposite was the case. Everybody was saying that I don't belong to them, I am the enemy. Jews thought I was a Muslim, the enemy. Muslims thought I was a Jew, the enemy. Christians thought I was a Muslim, the enemy. And in all these three religions, nobody, *nobody* was ready even to accept me in their fold.'

Religious persons cannot be accepted in any fold. They can be accepted only in the loving heart, but in no organization. They cannot be accepted because organizations have no hearts. A religious man cannot be absorbed in any establishment; only a personal feeling, a loving heart, can become a shrine for him.

The man must have been puzzled now, because he had come to enquire who he was. Perhaps the man was a Muslim and he wanted to be convinced that this Maruf was a Muslim so that he could follow him. The man may have been a Jew and wanted to be convinced that this Maruf was a Jew so that he could follow him.

You follow yourself. You never follow any Master.

If you are here because I say things which you already know are right, then you are not with me. Then I am only voicing your own mind. If you are here because you see in me a Jain, because you are a Jain . . . and when I talk about Mahavir I can immediately count how many Jains are there. Their eyes simply change. Their backbones become straight. They look very intense. Now for the first time they are alert, otherwise they were falling asleep. If I talk about Jews, I can count immediately how many Jews are there. And if I cannot decide who you are, then only are you with me.

Because if you *are* a Jew, and you listen to me, and you feel that whatsoever I am saying is what Jewish religion is, then you remain a Jew. I am just a support for your convictions, just an outside support. I have not entered you. You have not allowed me to enter in you.

Many people come to me and they say, 'Whatsoever you said was beautiful, because this is what I have believed my whole life. And you said it better than I can say.' So that's all. He's finished with me, and I am finished with him. There has been no meeting. He has heard his own voice in my voice. He has interpreted his own mind. And he remains a believer in his own ego. He has not dropped even a bit of his old luggage. Rather, on the contrary, now he is more convinced of the old luggage and he will carry it with more strength and with more conviction.

No! Remember this: I am not here to make you a Jew, or a Hindu, or a Christian—no. I am here only to make you a religious man.

The man must have been puzzled.

'*What must we think of you then?*' *said the man.* 'You have puzzled me. You confuse me.'

All religious people are, in a way, confusing. They create a chaos in you—because first you have to be uprooted. First you have to be demolished. No religious person is interested in renovating you, because howsoever renovated, you will remain the old, the dead thing; modified, of course, but not fresh and young. A religious person is interested in demolishing you completely, in pulling you down to the very roots, and then, in helping you to arise again.

Until you die, nothing is possible. A Master is a death on the one hand, resurrection on the other. A Master is a crucifixion, a cross. As you are, you die. And as you should be is born.

The man was puzzled.

'*What must we think of you then?*' *said the man.*
Maruf said: '*Some do not understand me. . .* '

Listen to these words. Very significant.

A ROSE IS A ROSE IS A ROSE...

'Some do not understand me, and revere me.'

They do not understand, *hence* they revere. People are really foolish. If they don't understand a thing they start revering it, because they think there must be something very mysterious: 'When I cannot understand—I, such an intelligent and genius man—when I cannot understand, there must be something very, very deep and mysterious.' And many people exploit such attitudes. Many people.

If you read Hegel's books, you will find that is what he is doing. He goes on trying to make everything as difficult as possible. It is *not* difficult! It is a good exercise to study Hegel, a German philosopher, in his own day thought to be the greatest. But as time passes, he comes again and again lower and lower and lower—because as you understand him his mystery is lost. And nothing is there. Just verbiage. If he can say a thing in a single word, he will use a hundred pages. If he can say a thing in one sentence, he will go on and on, round and round, into pages. You will not be able... He writes long sentences, sometimes one sentence in one page—you will not be capable of remembering the beginning of the sentence when you reach to the end. You will have to read it again and again. And he mystifies.

There are many people, mystifiers, exploiting the human stupidity of believing that whatsoever you cannot understand must be something superb, of the sublime, of the unknown, of the mysterious. These people are exploiters.

Just the reverse is the case with people who are *really* wise. They speak in short sentences. Their sentences are not complicated. They are simple. Whatsoever they say can be understood by anybody who is normally intelligent. They don't mystify. Whatsoever they teach is very, very simple—simple as life is simple; simple as existence is simple, rivers and mountains are simple, birds and trees are simple.

Wise men are simple. But the more you understand them—and to understand them is simple—but the more you understand them, the deeper you penetrate in their simplicity, the more you find new dimensions of mysteries opening. Their words are simple, but what they want to indicate is mysterious. Their indication is simple, but the indicated is mysterious.

Look at my finger—a simple thing!—and I indicate with my finger towards the moon. The moon is mysterious, not the finger. The finger is a very simple phenomenon; nothing to say about it. Words are like fingers. And they point, they finger, indicate, towards the mysterious.

'Some do not understand me, and revere me.'

And you have revered many people, and you have revered many doctrines, just because you cannot understand them.

There are many followers of Gurdjieff; because they cannot understand him, they follow him. Gurdjieff is not like Hegel, he is not mystifying, but he has something else to do. He does not want unwanted people to come near him, so he writes in such a way that unless you are very patient you will not be able to penetrate into him. He is not difficult. He is simple. But the methodology is such that he puts you off. You cannot read more than a few pages. I have not come across a single person yet who has read his *All and Everything* completely. People have gone through it, but. . . . And he knew it, that this is going to be so. He writes in a tedious style. He *bores* you. And this is a very considered method. He puts you off.

When for the first time the book *All and Everything* was published, the pages were not cut. Only the introductory pages, a hundred pages were cut, and the other pages were not cut. And there was a note on the book saying that if you can read the hundred pages, then open the others; otherwise return the book back to the shop and take your money back. First try with the hundred pages, and if you are still interested, then open the other pages, cut them. Otherwise, don't destroy the book. And many books were returned back. Many were not returned; that doesn't mean that people read them. They were just curious. They thought, 'Maybe it is a trick and only in the introductory pages he is boring. Inside he may not be.' But if you cut, then you cannot return the book.

But I have not come across a single person who has read the

whole book thoroughly. People skip. Then they miss—because here and there he hides the diamonds, and everything else is just a camouflage. Here and there, in the bushes of words, he hides the diamonds. Those diamonds can be sorted out and can be written on a postcard. And that book is one thousand pages!

Many people follow Gurdjieff because they cannot understand. Suddenly, when you cannot understand, you feel there is some mystery. It is not so. Truth is very simple. Everybody has the capacity to understand it. Truth is as simple as anything can be. You have to be just silent, understanding, ready, and it is revealed to you.

> *Maruf said: 'Some do not understand me, hence their reverence. And others do not either, so they revile me.'*

Then there are the people who if they cannot understand— they cannot believe that there can exist anything which *they* cannot understand—then they revile. It is against their egos. But remember: both are the egoistic viewpoints.

One ego thinks, 'I am so understanding. If I cannot understand, then there must be something mysterious.' Another ego says, 'If I cannot understand, then there cannot be anything at all. This man is simply deceptive. There is nothing. *If there were anything*, then how come I cannot understand it? A genius like me will understand everything.' Both are egoistic standpoints. And one has to drop out of them both—only then can you understand a Master.

One has to drop out of both. Don't revere a thing because you don't understand. Don't revile it because you don't understand. In fact, don't refer the thing to your ego, don't bring it in the context of your ego. That is useless! Just listen to the thing. If you cannot understand, try to understand—meditate more, contemplate more, become more silent. Come to it again and again from different standpoints. And finally come to it with no standpoint at all. You will understand. And the mystery will be revealed. If you cannot understand, don't start reviling it—because you are not the last word in understanding. You are not the last capacity of understanding. You are not the omega of understanding. You are just a beginner on the first rung of the ladder. And the ladder is vast and big.

Millions of things are waiting for you to be. You are just at the door. You have not even entered the shrine. Maybe just on the steps, or maybe just on the path. Not even come up to the steps. Not even at the door.

Don't bring your ego in either way. You are not the deciding factor as to whether it is mysterious or nothing. You listen. The more you listen to a man who has attained, the more and more you will understand. And the more you understand, the more it will become mysterious. The mystery of life is not something which can be solved or which is *ever* solved. It has to be lived! It is not a problem to be solved. It has to be *lived*.

The more you know, the less you feel you know. The more you know, the more you feel the unknown surrounds you from everywhere. And in the final moment of knowing, all knowledge drops. You know nothing. That final moment of knowing is like *vast* ignorance, a vast dark night. But only out of that dark night is the morning born. Out of this vast ignorance a light arises— which is knowing, which is understanding; which Buddha calls *praggya*, *sambodhi*; what Patanjali calls Samadhi, the Enlightenment.

> *Maruf said: 'Some do not understand me, and revere me. Others do not either, so they revile me. That is what I have come to say. You should think of me as one who has said this.'*

The man was asking to label Maruf somehow—whether he is a Jew, or a Mohammedan, or a Christian. Once labelled, you think you have understood. Labelling is a trick. You label a certain thing and you feel you have understood.

I show you a flower, an outlandish flower you have never seen before, and immediately you ask, 'What is the name?' Why are you so anxious to know the name? How is the name going to help you? X, Y, Z, whatsoever the name may be, how is it going to help you? If I say X, you think now you know it. You have labelled it. Now you can show to your child that this is X flower. You have become a knower. What have you known about the flower? Just the word X? I could have called it Y, or Z. They would have been as relevant as X. How do you know it?

I was reading Gertrude Stein's book. When she said in a poem, 'A rose is a rose is a rose,' it became world-famous. She goes on that way with many things. She does not define. She does not say anything—'A rose is a rose is a rose.' Nothing is defined; nothing is said really.

Somebody asked, 'Why have you said this? We *all* know a rose is a rose is a rose. It makes no sense. It adds nothing to our knowledge.'

Stein said, 'Because poets have been talking about roses for millennia—millions of poetries about roses, everybody has read them and sung them, and everybody has repeated—the word "rose" has lost its rosiness. It doesn't say anything any more. That's why I had to repeat, "A rose is a rose is a rose"—so that you are awakened out of your sleep, so that you are shaken a little: "What is this woman saying? the absurdity of it!—a rose is a rose is a rose." You *may* listen. Otherwise, rose—who listens? Everybody knows.' And she said, 'Repeating this I have brought the redness to the rose again.'

Words can't say much. And if you think that just knowing the names and labels, you have known, you will miss everything.

Try to avoid words. Don't try to label. You *immediately* label! Labelling is such a great disease. It is an obsession. You see a man, you say 'beautiful'. You see a woman and you say 'ugly'. Why in such a hurry? Wait! The woman has many faces. Even the ugliest woman sometimes has a beautiful face no beautiful woman can compete with. Ugliest—I have seen the ugliest woman in a certain posture, in a certain mood, in a certain climate, so beautiful that your Miss Universe will look a little pale before her. And I have seen the *most* beautiful woman ugly in certain moods. Wait! Don't label! Otherwise your label will not allow you to see the reality. Even beautiful women, in anger, in jealousy, in possessiveness, become so ugly. And their ugliness is deeper than the ordinary ugliness of a body. Their ugliness is spiritual and inner, and it comes all over their body like a rash. When a woman is jealous and possessive, she may be beautiful on the surface, but something emanates around her—poisonous, snake-like. She's ugly. You touch her in that moment and you will feel that you have touched a reptile, not a woman. Poisonous. Fumes coming out of her of poison.

Don't label. Reality doesn't believe in labels. Reality goes on moving and changing. It is flux, a river. You cannot step twice in the same river—not even once. It is moving all the time.

Don't categorize. And you have pigeon-holes in the mind. Immediately something is there, you put it in a pigeon-hole, and finished! And you think you know! This man is good, and that man is bad. Have you not ever observed bad becoming good, good becoming bad? Have you not seen an honest thief? Have you not seen a very, very sincere criminal? Have you never seen a sinner, but holy? Categories don't belong to life. They belong to the mind. Categories are your games. Don't categorize.

And this man had come to ask Maruf, 'How to categorize you? Where to put you?' Maruf is an alive man. If he was dead he would have said, 'I am a Mohammedan, of course, a humble Muslim, a Sufi,' but he is not a dead man. He won't allow categorization. He is alive, utterly alive.

He says, 'You remember me by only this. Nothing else. *That is what I have come to say. You should think of me as one who has said this.* Just this much you remember, that those who don't understand me, they revere me; and those who don't understand me, they revile me. In Jerusalem, Jews think I am a Christian and Muslims that I am a Jew. And in Baghdad, where people are in love with me, in my community, Jews think I am the most perfect Jew, Christians that I am a reborn Christ, and Muslims that I am the last word in being a Muslim.

'More I will not say. This much I say to you. And if you want to know how to remember me, you can only do this: *You should think of me as one who has said this.*'

He remains uncategorized, unlabelled. He does not give any clue. Rather, he becomes more mysterious. The man may have come with something, some prejudice, some idea, about this Master, Maruf. He has demolished his mind completely. He has cut through all his prejudices. He has left him in the vacuum.

That's what a Master does—leaves you in emptiness. But that is the most beautiful gift that can be given to you—nothingness, emptiness, vacuum.

In that vacuum arises all. In that nothingness arises all. In that emptiness the Absolute is born. But until you die, that's not possible.

You are here—let me be your death and resurrection.

20 April 1975

information

For information on coming to the ashram, or on Bhagwan's books, meditation music, or lecture cassette tapes, contact: Geetam Ashram, P.O. Box 576, Highway 18, Lucerne Valley, California 92356, Phone: (714) 248-6163 or your nearest Rajneesh Center, or write to the source: Shree Rajneesh Ashram, 17 Koregaon Park, Poona, India 411 001, Phone: 364783.

rajneesh meditation centers in the United States

KRISHNA, 1714 Southern, Fairbanks, Alaska 99701

BATOHI, c/o Esalen Institute, Big Sur, California 93920; Phone (408) 667-2335

DEEKSHANT, 624 Seabright, Santa Cruz, California 95062

GEETAM, Box 576, Highway 18, Lucerne Valley, California 92356

MADHU, 3326 Dwight Way, Berkeley, California 94704

PARAS, 4301 24th St., San Francisco, California 94114, Phone (415) 285-2122

YOGA INSTITUTE, 3910 El Cajon Blvd., San Diego, California 92115

SATYARTHA, 8933 National Blvd., Los Angeles, California 90034

SATVEDA, 6671 Sunset Boulevard, Hollywood, California 90028

DEVADIP, 2350 S. Dahlia, Denver, Colorado 80222

SARAHA, P.O. Box 431, Lahaine, Maui, Hawaii 96761

DHYANATARU, 375 A Huron Ave., Cambridge, Massachusetts 02138

CHETANA, P.O. Box 34, Woodstock, New York 12498

SATGIT, 415 Central Park West, New York, NY 10025

HRIDAYA, Route 4, Box 146a, Burnsville, North Carolina 28714

PREMSAGAR, P.O. Box 2862, Chapel Hill, North Carolina 27514

TRIMURTI, 326 N.W. 30th St., Corvallis, Oregon 97330

SHANTIDUTA, 3747 Harper St., Houston, Texas 77005

SARVAM, 6412 Luzon Ave., Washington, D.C. 20012

DEVA DEEP, 1430 Longfellow St. N.W., Washington, D.C. 20011

NIRALA, 8907 Fauntleroy Way S.W., Seattle, Washington 98116

books by bhagwan rajneesh

Published by Harper & Row

I Am the Gate (talks on initiation and discipleship)

Meditation: The Art of Ecstasy (talks on meditation techniques)

The Mustard Seed (talks on the sayings of Jesus)

The Book of Secrets, Vols. I, II, and III (talks on Tantric techniques)

The Psychology of the Esoteric (talks on esoteric teachings)

Published by Dutton

Only One Sky (talks on Tilopa's Song of Mahamudra)